T5-BAG-934

REAL VOICES

Also by Philip Davis

MEMORY AND WRITING
THE EXPERIENCE OF READING
IN MIND OF JOHNSON
EXPERIMENTAL ESSAYS ON BERNARD MALAMUD
SUDDEN SHAKESPEARE

Real Voices

On Reading

Edited by Philip Davis

PR
21
,R42
1997

St. Martin's Press
New York

REAL VOICES
Selection and editorial matter copyright © 1997 by Philip Davis
Text copyright © 1997 by Macmillan Press Ltd, with the following
exceptions:
'Critic'/'Reader' copyright © 1997 by George Steiner
'Two Essays at Human Assemblies, copyright © 1997 by the Estate of
Joseph Brodsky
'Trances' copyright © 1997 by Les Murray
'Green Glass Beads' copyright © 1997 by Doris Lessing

All rights reserved. No part of this book may be used or reproduced
in any manner whatsoever without written permission except in the
case of brief quotations embodied in critical articles or reviews.
For information, address:

St. Martin's Press, Scholarly and Reference Division,
175 Fifth Avenue, New York, N.Y. 10010

First published in the United States of America in 1997

This book is printed on paper suitable for recycling and
made from fully managed and sustained forest sources.

Printed in Great Britain

ISBN 0–312–16475–0

Library of Congress Cataloging-in-Publication Data
Real voices : on reading / edited by Philip Davis.
p.   cm.
Includes bibliographical references and index.
ISBN 0–312–16475–0
1. English literature—History and criticism—Theory, etc.
2. American literature—History and criticism—Theory, etc.
3. Reader-response criticism.   4. Books and reading.   I. Davis,
Philip (Philip Maurice)
PR21.R42   1996
820.9—dc20   96–9726
                                                        CIP

AJL 8788

INDIANA
PURDUE
LIBRARY
WITHDRAWN

AUG 1 1 1997

FORT WAYNE

For Brian Nellist

'. . . Visionary power
Attends upon the motions of the winds,
Embodied in the mystery of words:
There, darkness makes abode, and all the host
Of shadowy things do work their changes there,
As in a mansion like their proper home.
Even forms and substances are circumfused
By that transparent veil with light divine . . .'

Wordsworth, *The Prelude* (1805)
Book V ('Books'), 619–26

Contents

The Novel

Acknowledgements

Thanks are due to the publishers of parts or earlier versions of the following essays:

George Steiner's 'Critic'/'Reader' was first published in 1979 in *New Literary History*, and reprinted in *George Steiner: a Reader* (Penguin, 1984).

'So Little Do We Know of What Goes On When We Read', by George Craig, is a revised version of *'Reading: Who is Doing What to Whom?'* first published in *The Modern English Novel*, edited by Gabriel Josipovici (London: Open Books, 1976).

The essays by Joseph Brodsky reprinted here by permission of his estate are also to appear in his most recent collection, *Grief and Reason* (Penguin).

Parts of 'Trances', by Les Murray, are adapted from 'Embodiment and Incarnation' and 'Poems and Poesies' in *The Paperbark Tree* (London: Minerva, 1993), and the poem 'Life Cycle of Ideas' appeared in *Oxford Quarterly Review*, vol. 1, no. 1, and is reproduced by permission of the publishers.

An earlier version of 'Poetry's Subject', by Douglas Oliver, appeared in *PN Review*, vol. 105, 1995; it was originally given as the Judith E. Wilson Annual Lecture on Poetry in the University of Cambridge, 1995.

The arguments set out in Raymond Tallis's 'Theorrhoea Contra Realism' have been presented in more detail in *Not Saussure: a Critique of Post-Saussurean Literary Theory* 2nd edition (London: Macmillan, 1995), and in *In Defence of Realism* (London: Edward Arnold, 1988; 2nd edition London: Ferrington, 1995).

'Green Glass Beads' by Doris Lessing appears by kind permission of Jonathan Clowes Ltd.

Notes on the Contributors

John Bayley was Warton Professor of English Literature at the University of Oxford, 1974–92. His critical works include *The Romantic Survival* (1956), *The Characters of Love* (1961), *Tolstoy and the Novel* (1966), *Pushkin* (1971), *The Uses of Division* (1976), *An Essay on Hardy* (1978), *Shakespeare and Tragedy* (1981), *The Short Story: Henry James to Elizabeth Bowen* (1988), *Housman's Poems* (1992). He has published three novels, *In Another Country* (1954), *Alice* (1994) and *The Queer Captain* (1995).

Josie Billington is a Lecturer in English at Chester College of Higher Education. She has recently completed her PhD thesis on Mrs Gaskell and Tolstoy.

Joseph Brodsky, awarded the Nobel Prize for Literature in 1987, was Poet Laureate of the United States in 1991. Sentenced to hard labour in northern Russia in 1964, he became an involuntary exile in 1972 and was Professor of Literature at Mt Holyoke College from 1981. His most recent volumes of poetry were *To Urania* (1988), *Watermark* (1992) and *Selected Works* (1993). He also published a volume of selected essays, *Less Than One* (1988), and *Marbles*, a play (1990). Joseph Brodsky died in January 1996.

George Craig is Reader in French in the School of European Studies, University of Sussex. He has written on Mallarmé, Proust, Beckett and Duras.

Philip Davis is Reader, English Department, University of Liverpool. His publications include *Memory and Writing* (1983), *In Mind of Johnson* (1989), *The Experience of Reading* (1992), *Experimental Essays on the Novels of Bernard Malamud* (1995) and *Sudden Shakespeare* (1996). He has also edited *Selected Writings of John Ruskin* (1995).

Michael Irwin is Professor of English at the University of Kent. Most of his academic work is about fiction, including a book on Fielding and *Picturing: Description and Illusion in the Nineteenth-Century Novel*. He has published two novels, *Working Orders* and

Striker, and translated numerous opera liberetti, mostly for Kent Opera.

Hester Jones is a Lecturer in English Literature at the University of Liverpool. She was an undergraduate, research student and Research Fellow at Trinity College, Cambridge. She is writing a book about treatments of friendship in seventeenth and eighteenth century literature.

Gabriel Josipovici was born in France in 1940 of Russo-Italian, Romano-Levantine parents. He lived in Egypt from 1945 to 1956, when he came to this country. He read English at St Edmund Hall, Oxford, graduating in 1961, and since 1963 has been a member of the School of European Studies at the University of Sussex. He is now (part-time) Professor of English there. He has published over a dozen novels and collections of short stories, among which are *Contre-Jour* and *Moo Pak*; half a dozen critical books, among which are *The World and the Book* and *The Book of God: A Response to the Bible*; and numerous plays and radio plays, two of which *AG* and *Mr Vee*, were the BBC entries for the Italia Prize. *Touch: An Essay* appears in 1996, and in the academic year 1996–7 he will be Lord Weidenfeld Professor of Comparative European Literature at Oxford.

Doris Lessing has published 20 novels, including *The Golden Notebook* (1962), *Briefing for a Descent into Hell* (1971), *Memoirs of a Survivor* (1975), the five-novel sequences *Children of Violence* (1952–69) and *Canopus in Argos* (1979–83), *The Diaries of Jane Somers* (1984), *The Good Terrorist* (1985) and *The Fifth Child* (1988). Her latest novel is *Love, Again*. There are ten collections of short stories, the latest of which is *London Observed* (1992), drama and poetry, as well as works of non-fiction including *A Small Personal Voice* (1974), *Prisons We Choose to Live Inside* (1986), *The Wind Blows Away Our Words* (1987), *African Laughter* (1992) and the first volume of her autobiography, *Under My Skin* (1994).

Les Murray lives on the north coast farm in New South Wales of his childhood. His volumes of poetry include *The Vernacular Republic: Poems 1961–81*, *Poems against Economics* (1976), *The Daylight Moon* (1987), *Dog Fox Field* (1990), *Collected Poems* (1991) and *Translations from the Natural World* (1993). *The Boys Who Stole the Funeral* (1980) is a verse novel, while *The Paperbark Tree* (1992) is a volume of selected prose.

Douglas Oliver's most recent book is a long poem-satire on the politics of urban America, *Penniless Politics* (1991; 1994). A selection of poetry and prose, *Three Variations on the Theme of Harm* (1990) includes his satire on modern Britain, *The Infant and the Pearl*. Many of the poems in a just-finished prose/poetry book on Africa, post-GATT, have been appearing in national reviews in Britain, the US and France. His prosodic research is in *Poetry and Narrative in Performance* (1989). He lives permanently in Paris with his wife, the New York poet Alice Notley.

George Steiner, Extraordinary Fellow, Churchill College, Cambridge since 1969, Weidenfeld Professor of Comparative Literature, University of Oxford 1994–5 and Professor of English and Comparative Literature, University of Geneva 1974–94, has published *Tolstoy or Dostoevsky* (1958), *The Death of Tragedy* (1960), *Language and Silence* (1967), *Extraterritorial* (1971), *In Bluebeard's Castle* (1971), *On Difficulty* (1978), *Antigones* (1984), *Real Presences* (1989), *No Passion Spent* (1996). His fictional writings include *Anno Domini* (1964), *The Portage to San Cristobal of A.H.* (1981), *Proofs and Three Parables* (1992) and *The Deep of the Sea* (1996).

Raymond Tallis is Professor of Geriatric Medicine at the University of Manchester and a consultant physician in Health Care of the Elderly in Salford. Apart from his medical publications, his published works include *The Explicit Animal* (1991), *The Pursuit of Mind*, co-edited with Howard Robinson (1991), *In Defence of Realism*, (1988), *Not Saussure*, 2nd edn (1995) and *Newton's Sleep, Two Cultures and Two Kingdoms* (1995). *Enemies of Consciousness* appears in 1996. He has published short stories and several volumes of verse, most recently *Fathers and Sons* in 1993.

Introduction: Not on the Run

PHILIP DAVIS

'It saddens me,' complained a recent anonymous contributor to the *Times Higher Education Supplement*, 'to see so little principled and vociferous resistance to the theorists on the part of lecturers who have had a more conventional scholarly training. Academics of wide learning and genuine critical insight are on the run.'

It was originally proposed to me, by a colleague, that we should produce a collection of essays which, so far from being on the run, should be seen as Fighting Back Against Theory. Indeed, that was to be the working title. This is not that collection.

But not because the lecturer who wrote to the *THES* could be dismissed as pointing to something that was simply not happening. All too anonymous, I am afraid, he or she wrote:

> My first and second years learn their lessons early: post-structuralism and radical feminist criticism are what the tutors want and what they will reward. Liberalism and humanism are outmoded, defunct, hopelessly passé and misconceived. So my students produce unintelligible essays crammed with blasé anti-humanist rhetoric, tortuously unconvincing interpretations, and puritanical moralising posing as political insight. Texts are blithely reduced to thinly-veiled expressions of false-consciousness, or routinely shown to subvert their own (lamentably wrong-headed) ideological structures ...
>
> Lecturers see it as their job to disabuse students of their political misconceptions and bring them into line with their own dogma ... Students assume they can apply their 'critical concepts' to whatever literary text they are ostensibly discussing. Most importantly, they will have read even less of the literary canon than their forebears, though this will not prevent them from carelessly dismissing whole literary traditions such as the realist novel with one swipe of the pen.

Speaking merely for myself, and whatever may be the exaggerations in the above, I accept the fundamental charge as obvious: that there is less real reading going on now, both inside and outside

universities and, indeed, in our so-called 'culture' as a whole. Less
not only in terms of quantity, but in terms of sheer quality of
specific, caring attention. It is just such serious mental attention,
and not merely the predetermined application of critical concepts,
that makes reading what I would call real: meditated, looking out,
unmuddied of spirit, alert without cant or fashion, troubled and
delighted, open to thought and feeling, to discovery and memory.
It is the sort of reading George Steiner and George Craig describe in
the opening essays and which, later, Hester Jones and Josie Billington bring to poetry and to the novel.

And yet, with statements like the one from the *THES*, the quarrel
between so-called 'traditionalists' and 'theorists' begins all over
again on easily predictable lines. The very terms of the opposition
create between the two over-emphatically embattled sides the
sheer unreality of mutually self-weakening positions. Not to want
to be sucked into that ugly and reductive model of controversy is
not merely liberal cowardice.

I wanted something both more permanent and less reactive than
just 'fighting back'. Consequently I simply wrote to a number of
people I respected, asking them to write something which showed
– in any way they chose and in mind of any audience that seemed
to them reachable – what reading meant to them. I am not saying
that my choices were neutral ones – they were in line with the
intuitions implicit in my sense of respect. But there was no 'we',
no party line, no set vocabulary. I wrote to potential contributors to
say that I was looking for them to write essays that offered a
personal vision of a human vocation in literature, showing what
individuals may stand for as individuals – even if (or precisely
because) current thinking often denies the possible existence of
any such creature. I wanted people who had in them a *voice*,
by means of which to narrow the gap between writers and
readers, as well as between readers inside and readers outside the
university.

Many of the authors of the essays in this volume are themselves,
first and foremost, writers: poets and novelists. And, significantly,
most of the academics here, as is shown in the Notes on the Contributors, are also committed to the writing of fiction and poetry in
ways that have personal connection with their teaching and their
criticism. A great critic, says Wilbur Sanders, thinking in particular
of Samuel Johnson, is simply a great writer, thinking about books;
and so it is with good critics too:

Criticism is just another variety of literature – literature about books seen as part of a thinking person's life. One is interested in a critic for the same reasons one is interested in a novelist or an essayist – Who is this man? this woman? What do they make of the world? How rich is their experience of it? How deeply pondered are their conclusions?

'Who Owns Literature?', *Universitites Quarterly*, vol.40, no.3, p.237.

And: How do they *help* us, in the understanding of the book and of what it represents, in the pursuit of thinking about living?

I went for people who, I believed, had something passionate to say that was real to them. *Pour encourager les autres.* Among the contributors as a whole, I simply trusted that a certain common spirit would emerge, unthreatened by personal and particular differences and even enhanced by them: the common spirit of personal commitment.

The reader will find plenty of different emphases and even disagreements in this collection of essays, containing as it does both young and old, male and female, poets and novelists, right and left, believers and secularists, realists and modernists – the varied and overlapping proportions between them all emerging finally through human circumstance rather than conscious editorial design. But the differences are, I believe, the product of neither the weak liberalism of mere variety nor the abrasive reactiveness of crude controversy. Most of the disagreements offer a reader access to the arena of serious thought in which difference of emphasis represents the serious weighing of individual choices. Michael Irwin and Gabriel Josipovici, for example, write very different novels; George Steiner and Raymond Tallis finally think differently about the relation of theory and theology. You may not agree with a particular accent, personal viewpoint or tone of thought, but it should offer you entry into the general realm of consideration which that individual must seek to represent in his or her own particular way.

'The poetic experience', says Les Murray, 'is not of course confined to verse.' And the literary experience is not confined to literature. On the contrary, as Wilbur Sanders, one of my own past teachers, again puts it, with all the directness of freedom:

The quality of human life is more important than what is said about it, and the justification of literature must lie, if anywhere, in the way it serves that life, not in its own self-enclosed activity. It's the mark of a great writer, often, to see this very starkly – finding the cloud-capped towers and gorgeous palaces he can so easily conjure up, trifling and ineffectual; feeling that he may as well break his staff and drown his book, for all the difference it makes to the real world. The fictionality of art oppresses him, until writing can come to seem an activity unworthy of a grown man or woman. 'Life is short,' Tolstoy wrote to an importunate publisher in 1859, 'and to waste it in my adult years writing . . . stories . . . makes me feel ashamed.' It's the mainspring of Tolstoy's greatness that he doesn't care about literature. Only by not caring about it was he freed to put into literature the life-content that made it *worth* caring about.'

'Who Owns Literature?', p. 226.

People go to particular books because there are places, or even mere tiny moments, in them which give particular readers an opening onto what seems the very life of life. 'Emotion in ordinary life cannot fuse perfectly with thought,' argues Douglas Oliver in *Poetry and Narrative in Performance* (Macmillan 1989): conceptualization comes too late, conscious thinking can never get into the speed of the emotional dynamic. But Poetry, in its sheer instants of being, says Oliver, 'discovers a way to unify the time-scales of emotion, concept, and verbal music'. Or again, as Les Murray says of the poetic experience in 'Embodiment and Incarnation' in *The Paperbark Tree*: 'We can have it repeatedly, and each time timelessly, but we can't have it steadily. We are as it were not yet permitted to live there.' The essays in this book at times seem to me to make it possible to live 'there', or to live out of the resonance from there, a little bit more, a little while longer. That is one of the emphatically unironic purposes of thinking and writing about reading.

This book is written in search of all serious readers, inside and outside universities; lecturers, teachers, researchers or undergraduates; writers and would-be writers; readers in tube stations and at home, young and old; graduates who wish they had done more in their undergraduate days or retained links with their interests then; people who have never had or perhaps never wanted the opportunity to study literature formally. The book employs the different voices of its writers in order to find echoes in a wide variety of different readers, however and wherever it can reach them. Raymond Tallis is first of all a medical man. Joseph Brodsky came from

Russia to write in America, Les Murray writes from his farm in Australia, Douglas Oliver out of France. But if indeed amidst all these voices *Real Voices* makes one statement, it is probably this one, from the poem 'The Trances': that the thing still 'goes on'. The real thing, in literature and through literature, goes on – despite the varying obstacles of discouragement, failure, loneliness or unbelief.

Most of the essays in this volume were written for the purpose: where they are not entirely new, they have been revised accordingly. The most lightly revised are the speeches given by Joseph Brodsky, who died as *Real Voices* was going to press. In saddened memory of him too, 'it goes on'.

The editor of *Real Voices: On Reading* can claim no definitive, summarizing or final word as to its contents. One privilege alone I allow myself. In every school, university or organization in general there is, says Doris Lessing, always one person who is *the* one, quietly, implicitly, even secretly – 'the teachers . . . how valuable they are, and how unvalued, except by their pupils who may cherish thoughts of them all their lives.' Gabriel Josipovici writes of Hugo Dyson, and many students will long remember John Bayley. In my own place, in Liverpool, Brian Nellist has been the one, all his teaching life. To him, sheerly as a representative of all the others elsewhere, this book is dedicated.

Part One
Reading

1

'Critic'/'Reader'

GEORGE STEINER

I

Some distinctions between *critic* and *reader* may be worth testing on the understanding that, for purposes of focus, these two terms are being used with fictive stringency, that they are being hypostatized.

It may be that the reciprocal relations of the 'critic' and of the 'reader' to the text are not only different but, in certain respects, antithetical. The critic is an epistemologist. This is to say that the distances between himself and the text are of themselves fertile and problematical. In so far as these distances are made explicit and subject to investigation, they generate intermediate texts, or what are currently known as 'metatexts'. The separation between the critic and 'his' text – in what sense is it 'his'? – is reflexive. It makes sensible, it dramatizes its own inhibitory or translational status. 'Inhibition' and 'translation' are the cardinal and kindred categories of the critic's distancing. There are obstacles and opacities to be overcome or to be sharply delineated in the space between himself and the text. There are, conversely, translations to be made of his texts into analogous or parodistic modes of statement (used neutrally, 'parodistic' is a legitimate notion, comprising as it does the whole range of critical restatements and interpretative parallels from punitive dismissal to mimetic enchantment). Inhibition and translation are cognate because it is the obstacle 'in front of' the text which compels circumvention and transfer ('translation'), which prevents the critic's total, exhaustive restatement and repetition of the original text. Such tautologous repetition, on the other hand, is one of the cardinal instances of 'reading'.

The critic argues his distance from and towards the text. To 'criticize' means to perceive at a distance, at the order of remove most appropriate to clarity, to *placement* (F.R. Leavis's term), to communicable intelligibility. The motion of criticism is one of 'stepping back from' in exactly the sense in which one steps back from a painting on a wall in order to perceive it better. But the good critic makes the motion conscious to himself and to his public. He details his recessional steps so as to make the resultant distance, the elucidative measure, the prescriptive perspective – distance entails 'angle' of vision – explicit, responsible and, therefore, open to argument. It is this activation of distance between critic and object (the 'text' from which he is stepping back and which may, of course, be a painting, a musical composition, a piece of architecture) that makes all serious criticism epistemological. Criticism demands that we ask of and with it: 'How does perception traverse the chosen distance?' 'How was this particular distance chosen?' Examples of what is meant here are so ready as to trivialize the implicit issue. But for the sake of initial argument, consider the contrastive topographies, the contrastive mappings and measurements of a historicist nineteenth-century critic on the one hand, and of a New Critic – whose sight-lines are those of the synchronic close-up, of Mallarmé's *distance abolie* – on the other.

Because it purposes adequation to its object and clarity, because the distance established when the critic 'steps back' invites analysis, apologia and didactic transmission to others – there are, since antiquity, received methodologies and 'schools' of criticism, manuals of the art, journals in which it is exercised – criticism is simultaneously epistemological and legislative. The point is a central one, and the uses of *critique* in the Kantian idiom make it succinctly. We have said that the critic steps back from the object of perception in order to 'get closer to it' (focus, clarity, intelligibility are factors of direct access, of nearness to the relevant phenomenon). He establishes and argues distance in order to penetrate. He widens or narrows the aperture of vision so as to obtain a lucid grasp. This motion – we step back to come nearer, we narrow our eyes to see more fully – entails judgement. Why should this be? *Because action* (the critic's motion) *is not, cannot be indifferent.*

The point I am putting forward is not the suspect commonplace whereby there are supposed to be no value-free, no rigorously neutral perceptions – 'suspect' because it is, at least, arguable that one's perception of the correct solution of an equation is not, except in some quasi-mystical sense, a value judgement. No, what is meant here is something different. The critic is an activist of apprehension. His demarcation, his 'pacing' of the elucidative distance between himself and the 'text-object' is operative, instrumental, functional. Operation, instrumentality or function are not, cannot be indifferent. Indifference does not act. Whether 'disinterestedness' does act is one of the questions ahead. The dynamic distancing of the critic is explicitly intentional. All critics in action are intentionalists whose *modus operandi* performs, emphatically, Husserl's model of cognition ('to perceive' at all is 'to intend'). The critic 'grasps'. He experiences and articulates a *prise de conscience*. His perception is *ein Vernehmen* ('an interpretative taking'). Etymologies are only naively demonstrative; but in these three banal instances, the radical of acquisition, of seizure, is obvious and illuminating. No grasp is indifferent; it assesses the worth of its object.

This allows a first rephrasing of our initial antinomy: if critics are Husserlians, 'readers' are Heideggerians (but it is just this which needs to be shown).

It hardly needs saying that refusal, negative intentionality, rebuke, even ridicule are valuations in the full sense. The critic who turns away, who 'overlooks' a given object, is exercising judgement. He empties, he chooses to make inert the potentially vitalized space between perception and perceived. The history of criticism is replete with lifeless, atrophied spaces, even as museums are stocked with 'invisible' pictures. Each invisibility comports an accident or a history of negation. It takes positive inaction to establish, let alone sustain, a vacuum, a zone of unseeing. This inaction also is legislative. Whence a provisional truism: *criticism is ordering sight.* The act of critical viewing takes place in, it delimits and externalizes for argument, an intentional distance from the object. The good critic is one whose stepping back, whose 'making of space', is accountable. The good critic establishes his focal distance in a way which we too can measure, whose angles of incidence we can calibrate. His distance is one which we in turn can pace for ourselves. The underlying scheme of accountable motion is, very likely, geometrical, just as Husserl's scheme of the intentionality and intentional logic of cognition is geometrical. But when we say 'ordering sight', when we say 'placement', when we say *critique*, we say 'judgement'. We very nearly say, having for such assertion a mass of epistemological authority, that all clear seeing is judgement, that every perceptive motion is legislative – because it is act and motion. Can this truism be faulted or, at least, qualified in non-trivial ways? Are there orders of insight which do not 'grasp'?

To ask this is to suggest a second way of starting this paper, of testing its conjecture of difference.

Ordering sight ('criticism') objectifies. To make this plain may help to remove the spurious problem of 'critical objectivity'. There never has been, there never can be, any *objective criticism* in the proper sense of the term simply because, as we have seen, indifference, non-intentionality, cannot be a property of action. To adduce the patent relativity and instability of 'taste', to cite the historicity of every aesthetic ranking, is a boringly self-evident move. What needs to be understood is the rationale, the integral structure of the arbitrariness of all acts of criticism. No two distancings can be perfectly identical: a photograph can be reproduced, a facsimile can be made of an original; but the particular photographic act – the 'taking' of the picture – cannot be tautologically repeated. A given critical gymnastic – the style of 'the stepping back' from the given object – can methodize itself. It can seek to transmit its practice through didactic exemplification. We saw that there are schools and manuals of criticism. But no critical *reprise*, however scholastic, however servile – e.g. neo-Aristotelianism in the declining Renaissance, the *feuilleton* assembly lines after Sainte-Beuve, the mimes of Parisian semiotics today – is homologous with, is equivalent to the distancing which it seeks to perpetuate. Each and every act of criticism is an intentional specification. It is teleological in respect of the particular case – 'this painting', 'that piece of music', 'this text'. And the category of the teleological, of that which is focused by an act of choosing volition, cannot be 'objective'. It cannot be impartial or take a stance outside itself.

Ecstasy, the capacity or need to stand 'outside oneself', is a theological potential. It may be that the contrast between the teleological and the theological is a third way of phrasing the cut between 'critic' and 'reader'.

Active apprehension and the valuation, the normative placement of the object apprehended which it entails, have no claim to the status of independent facticity. Critical findings are historical facts. They may be psychological facts, though the notion of 'psychological' remains obscure and probably unsatisfactory in this context (as I.A. Richards came to admit). What is certain is that no critical judgement has 'factuality' in any logical, let alone experimentally verifiable, sense. The quest for a verifiable or falsifiable factuality in critical propositions has been a compendious chapter in the history of the art: in Aristotle, in Kant, in Taine, in the earlier Richards. But it remains a chapter of fertile error, of borrowed metaphors. No critical ruling can be refuted. Action knows reaction and counteraction, not refutation. Preference is undecidable. Balzac's suggestion that Mrs Radcliffe was an abler novelist than Stendhal, Tolstoy's considered conclusion that the major tragedies of Shakespeare are 'beneath criticism', the closely argued verdict of a generation of art critics in reference to Rosa Bonheur's superiority to Cézanne – these are not 'eccentricities' or 'lapses'. There can be no eccentricities where there is no stable centre, no 'lapse' where there is no axiomatic paradigm from which to fall. On the contrary: such prescriptive viewings are typological; they are highly instructive, in so far as they make salient the essence of arbitrariness and of free will in every act of ordering vision.

At the risk of repetition: there can be no grammatical, no logical, no statistical cancellation or falsification of the assertion that Shakespeare was a mediocre playwright or Mozart a third-rate composer. Formally and substantively, these are perfectly coherent, intelligible 'positionings' (*prises de position*) towards the relevant object. The fact – and are we always quite certain that it is a general fact? – that these particular postures are chosen or maintained by very few is of no importance. Epistemological spaces are not subject to the ballot. Time, moreover, shifts the statistical balance – essentially irrelevant as that balance may be – between the idiosyncratic and the commonplace. It is the fatality of today's avant-garde to house within itself tomorrow's postcards and art-school plaster casts. In turn, the prognostication that there will be a date at which the 'general consensus' will judge Mozart to have been a third-rate composer is strictly unfalsifiable. But it is a prognostication without inherent interest. It says nothing of the critical act that has judged otherwise. Equally vacant are the demonstrable statements that painters, authors, musicians once held to be mindless charlatans are, now, sanctified (Van Gogh, Joyce, Wagner). Such data belong to the history of criticism. But the critical act, the deed of ordering sight and the space of intentional legislation which it generates, have no history. They are synchronic. Aristotle's placement of Euripides as 'the most tragic' is fully available and instrumental today. This is to say that implicit distancing, the focus chosen – in this example, it is a focus directed preferentially at the density of relative pathos among the three principal tragedians – can be adopted, can be 'paced out' at present. By the same token, Matthew Arnold on Keats or T.S. Eliot on Baudelaire will be functional tomorrow. Vision has historical, social, local (perhaps even physiological) context; but there is a precise sense in which it does not date. It can be rebuked, countermanded, censored, ridiculed, labelled as statistically null. But it cannot be superseded. To declare that Hanslick was 'wrong' about Wagner, whatever 'wrong' may signify in such an assertion, is not to supersede his finding.

Does this wilful, always singular format of the critical act mean that every sighting is equally worthwhile? Are some valuations more authoritative than others? Or is irrefutability – one cannot conceivably prove that Balzac was mistaken in regard to Stendhal or that abstract art may not be a confidence trick – evidence that all judgement is inherently anarchic? I have never seen a convincing answer to this possibility. The answers given are purely contingent. They tell us what constitutes a 'good critic'. But 'range', 'style', innovative commitment, influence, etc. are merely attributes or *post hoc* ornaments. They are not primaries. They have no probative force. They are opinions on opinion. Perhaps the hoary dilemma can be rephrased.

The useful critic does two things. First, he makes the tenor of his arbitrariness transparent. The angle of his ordering vision is clearly manifest. There are as many rational, arguable spaces as there are geometries. The critic may adopt a posture whose configuration – the word *figura* allows the right overlap between gesture and symbolic code – is mainly moralistic. He can step back from the object and ask: Of what benefit is it to man and society? Is it finally educative? Is it life-enhancing in its implicit or explicit proposals? (*Mutatis mutandis*, Platonism, Tolstoy's position, or that of Leavis exemplify this aesthetic, or more properly speaking, 'anti-aesthetic'.) The critic may function at distances and perspectives which are historicist, biographical in the old sense, psychoanalytic in the new, Marxist, or formalist. His mapping may be largely rhetorical (in a genuinely inventive vein, this would be something like Kenneth Burke's 'space' of ordering sight). He can be – more often than not, he is – eclectic and variable in his adjustments of focus and aperture. 'Critical impresionism' is no less rigorous than 'engagement' or 'determinism' (i.e. Sainte-Beuve is no less rigorous a critic than Lukács or Derrida, if we attach to 'rigorous' any clear connotations of proof or refutability). His is merely a different stylization of the critical exercise, a different 'choreography' and, therefore, distancing between points. But whatever his stance of intentionality, the useful critic offers this stance for identification. He must render unmistakable its partiality (in *parti pris* we again find the key notion of 'seizure'). *Partiality*, in this context, has two main meanings. Every geometry, every argued space of perception, is only one of a set of alternatives which may be formally unbounded (it may well be the case that *anything* can be said of *anything*). It is therefore, incomplete, 'partial'. Secondly, however catholic the critic's temper, however embracing the largess of his receptivities, his every act of ordering sight is, can only be, 'partial' in the sense of being biased. It stems from one particular angle. As there is no such thing as indifferent action, so there is no such thing as impartial ('objective') criticism. Only immobility is unbiased. But in good criticism, bias is made visible, is made lucid to itself.

The honest critic does a second thing: he ranks (criticism is *ordering* sight). In the arbitrariness which is the epistemological condition of his *métier*, he includes the concept of 'arbiter', of *arbitrage* between values. The intentionality of his vision, the act of assuming a stance in front of one object rather than another, is by definition preferential and discriminatory. Whether explicitly, in the magisterial vein, or implicitly, via the functional trope of an 'epiphany' (the object reveals and imposes itself upon the viewer), the critic's placement is hierarchical. Euripedes, rules Aristotle, 'is the most tragic'; it follows necessarily that Aeschylus and Sophocles were less so. 'Dante and Shakespeare divide western literature between them, there is no third', says T.S. Eliot. His verdict is diacritical; it relegates all other poets to a more slender status. The semantics of criticism are inescapably comparative. To perceive normatively is to compare. It is to assay contrastively, a praxis evident in the Arnoldian term *touchstone*.

Thus it is mere cant to profess that a critic ought not to enter the *bourse*, that he ought not to provide market quotations, leaving such concerns to the 'reviewer'. The critic, however eminent, however theoretic in bias, assigns and ascribes valuations every time he views and designates. He may do so with a complexity of motives and with a heuristic care far beyond those of ephemeral marking or fashion. He may, in other words, be an august broker rather than a harried jobber on the floor of the exchange (though the line is always fluid; where, for instance, would we draw it in the works of Hazlitt or of Edmund Wilson?). But no less than the reviewer, the critic is a marker. He marks down – in the 1930s and 1940s the term

was 'he dislodges' – Milton, and marks up Donne. He 'rates' Hölderlin above, say, Mörike; he underwrites new issues, such as the
modernist movement, as being more productive, as offering a
higher yield to attention and sensibility than the late Romantics or
Georgians. The instruments of criticism, teaches Coleridge, are
'speculative instruments'. Critical scrutiny values and compares. In
'speculation' inhere perception as well as the forward gamble of
conjecture.

And because his 'job of work' (R.P. Blackmur's humbling phrase)
is always derivative, because it is often punitive and facile as compared to that of the artist, the good critic is one who will run
speculative risks. He will declare his interests and lay himself open
to loss. This loss can take various forms: the contempt of the artist
whom he is criticizing, the indifference of the market to the values
which he proposes, the ridicule or oblivion which later history will
visit on his judgements. This declaration of interest and speculative
commitment produces a listing (a series of 'quotations' in a sense
familiar to both the *bourse* and the life of letters). It produces 'the
great tradition', 'the hundred best books', 'the modern masters'. In
this ineluctable context vulgarity can be compensated for, and then
only in part, by the critic's nerve, by his readiness to invest even
more in a sinking share if such investment represents his lucid
conviction. The 'classic' in literature is the 'blue chip', 'the gilt-
edge', that has long been prized as such by the market. No real
critic can or will seek to escape the crassness and fallibilities of
choice.

The critic's listing establishes a 'syllabus'. The teleology of a
syllabus is economic. It instructs us, even by virtue of omission, on
what texts we should expend time and the resources of feeling, and
what other texts would constitute waste. The notorious footnote in
F.R. Leavis's *The Great Tradition*, cautioning the reader that among
all of Dickens's novels only *Hard Times* repays adult interest, is a
graphic example of this 'economy of syllabus'. So are the reading
lists handed out to generations of undergraduates, lists on which
particular chapters are often cited with the manifest inference that
the remainder of the book does not merit investment. The apologia
for a syllabus is one of purgation: vital space is cleansed and con-
served for the 'enduring', for the 'authentic', for the 'classical'.
Dead or noxious matter is set aside. Too many canvases, canvases
hung too close, inhibit ordering sight. A museum is an ocular
syllabus, hence its crowded basements or rummage rooms. The

critic selects and 'prices' so as to narrow our options towards excellence, so as to minimize waste motion.

The 'reader' does not aim at a syllabus, but at a 'canon'. This is a fourth stab at articulating the polarity which my argument is testing. 'Canon', of course, remains to be defined.

I have said that ordering sight 'objectifies'. I have tried to show that such objectification in criticism has nothing to do with the phantasm of 'objectivity' – which would be pure stasis, a zero point. What then is meant by 'objectification', by the assertion that it is of the nature of criticism to see that which it sees as an object? It means simply that the *telos*, the thing aimed at by the act of ordering perception, is a datum, a *donné*. It is 'out there', at a distance, at an angle, in a perspective which criticism determines with a view to intelligibility and estimate. This 'givenness' of the object or text as it presents itself for circumspection, elucidation and judgement, this 'out-thereness', is a definitional platitude. How can there be sight if there is not something 'out there' to be seen, to be stopped, as it were, in front of? But if it is a platitude, it is one of considerable epistemological and ethical consequence.

The fundamental postulate of the critical act is one of realism. The critic cannot operate in a solipsistic, in a rigorously Fichtean, scheme. He cannot collapse subject and object. Were he to do so, there would be no distance at which, 'across which', to exercise ordering sight. Glued to the canvas, the eye would be blind. One can go further: the critical postulate is one of materialism (and it is just this which underlies the discomforts of Platonism when attempting to deal with poetry and the arts). The painting, the piece of music, the text have a material status. They are significant substances. In respect of material artifacts in the 'naive' sense – pictures on wood or canvas, statues hewn of stone or cast in bronze – the primal materialism or substantiality has never been problematic. The art critic finds no handicap in including in the coordinates of evaluative reflex such dimensions as pigments, fabric, texture and so on. It is, moreover, only this epistemological materialism which validates the whole concept, so compelling in western sentiment and in the art market, of some radical difference between the original and even the most faithful of copies or reproductions. Contrastively, we shall see that in the epistemology of 'reading', the copy, the act of copying, may prove to be equivalent to that of creation.

In the case of a language object (a text), the postulate of materiality may seem elusive. And, certainly, the analogies so often drawn between literature on the one hand and painting or sculpture on the other are insipid or inexact. It is only in esoteric or historically decidable instances that the literal substance of the text – epigraphy, watermark, impression – has any immediate critical bearing. Critical grasp does not consider whether its object is quarto or folio size, and the valuation of a text is indifferent as to its first edition or the most mechanical of reproductions. Nevertheless, the language object is an object, a datum 'out there'. This means that the cardinal qualifiers of objective existence do apply to it. The verbal material has been 'produced'; it is, properly, a fabrication. It can, indeed it must, be located in immanence.

The 'reader' is answerable to the possibility of 'transcendence' rather than of immanence. This is, possibly, a fifth way of stating the disjunction which this essay aims at.

The immanent character of the objects of criticism can be categorized variously. The customary rubric is historical. The text was produced, encoded and made public by this or that author in this or that place and time. It embodies – *embodiment* signifying at this point, and provisionally, not a synonym for but rather a contrary to *incarnation* – a particular selection from the totality of the linguistic raw material and constraints available to the given author. Recent emphasis by Marxist, sociological or semiotic critics on the economic structures of all 'textuality' – texts are manufactured, they compete for attention in the market, they are objects of merchandising, consumption and accumulation – only dramatizes an obvious constant. So does the modish notion of *écriture*. However exalted by intent of style and address, a text is indeed an artifact, a 'piece' of language materially cognate with any other piece of language. Thus, when the structuralist-semiotic critic tells us that the poem is part of a seamless continuum with each and every semantic, scriptive act – the bill of lading, the piece of advertisement copy, the most mundane of notations – all of which are, like itself, *écriture*, he is only rephrasing (and trivializing) the postulate of materialism implicit in perceptual objectivization.

He reiterates this same postulate, this time more cogently, when he reminds us that ordering sight (criticism) can be understood as a branch of a more general 'theory of information'. When matter matters, it informs. Hence the critic's legitimate interest in 'how the thing is put together', in the anatomy of its composition and history of its manufacture. The art critic seeks to bring to light the initial sketch, the parts of the canvas painted over in successive manipulations. The literary critic and the critic-musicologist ponder drafts and cancellations. The inherent commitment is that made to temporal, historical substance (to immanence). The postulate is that of the objective reality of compositional process. The critic is a 'geneticist' (where it may be that the 'reader' is an 'ontologist'. This would be a sixth antinomy). In a way which tends to go unnoticed, this compositional perspective is also an assumption of contingency. The art object, the piece of music, the text 'out there', with its historical genesis, might not have been; or it might have been altogether otherwise. It 'happens to be' – which does not mean, to be sure, that its phenomenal emergence in this or that location, at this or that date, in one or another milieu, ought not to be investigated and, so far as is possible, explained. But there is not in the production of artifacts, as the objectivization of the critic's ordering sight perceives them, any formal or substantive imperative of inevitability. There is, even at the 'sublime' reach, a realization of occasion, an occasionality in the strict sense of the term.

So far, I have tried to make arguable and, in consequence, nontrivial, two main propositions. The critic functions at a certain distance. The determination (and honest explication) of this distance, the space in and through which his purposive action is executed, are the integral facts of his ordering, legislative sight. Secondly, I have said that he is distant from and 'distant to' an object, a substance which he finds and situates 'out there'. He focuses on, he sights and appraises 'something' which is a particular, contingent presence. In this classical scenario, there is no fusion betwen perceiver and perceived. The critic after Aristotle is a realist in just that formally elusive but pragmatically unwavering sense in which Kant is a realist when he states in the *Critique of Pure Reason* (sec. 3): 'Our exposition establishes the *reality*, that is, the objective validity, of space in respect of whatever can be represented to us outwardly as object.' Common sense is the working hypothesis, the underwriter of cognitive distance. It authorizes the conviction that the painting will not disappear when the viewer turns away from it, that there is a run-of the-mill sense in which its existence, if not its cultural status, is independent of notice.

We have seen that there are many and diverse ways in which the critic can assume his stance, and that these ways generate many and diverse 'spaces' or conventions of vision (even as there are many geometries in which the 'same' objects can be diversely situated and described). But whereas, in the case of alternative geometric mappings, such location and description remain formally neutral and, as topology teaches us, interchangeable, the intentionality of the critic's vision, the purposiveness of his act, entail very different relations to the object. The point is an obvious one, but needs to be made carefully. Different critical postures (methodologies, analytical presuppositions, metavocabularies) pertain to practice, to 'how ordering sight' is initiated and performed. Relations, as they are realized within and across the chosen distance, pertain to motive, to 'why it is' that the critic does his essentially derivative, parasitic 'job of work'. Modern physics tells us that we cannot separate the concept of a 'space' from that which takes place in it. And there is a strong sense in which the 'how' and the 'why' of the act of criticism are also conjoined. Nevertheless, the objectivization that comes of the realistic epistemology of criticism is a more general, a more diffuse category than motive. And it is only if we look more closely at motive that we can define more exactly in what way art or literature becomes an object not only 'of' but 'for' criticism.

Patently, there can be as many sorts of motivation as there are critics. There are, however, compendious and usefully vague chapter headings under which the different purposive relations enacted by critical practice can be registered. These would, roughly and readily, include political relations, exemplary-didactic relations, relations whose motor force is primarily philosophically investigative, relations which I would call 'dramatically reproductive', ceremonially propagandistic relations, relations of irony or chastisement. Given the summary scope of this discussion, these and kindred types of critical relation, of the intentionality of different ways of seeing, can only be stenographed – and the citation of names is an unavoidable shorthand.

'Political' is too loose a tag altogether; but one would take it as enveloping those orderings and assessments of the critical object according to its positive or disabling agency in a larger public scheme. Plato would posit this scheme to be the state; for Tolstoy it would be the enforcement of personal and communal altruism; in Lukács's model the scheme is 'history'; in that of Sartre, the realization of 'freedom'. But note that there is, within certain flexible limits, independence as between method and motive: a Platonic purpose can be generated by a New Critical exegesis; 'structuralism' can be either of the 'right' or of the 'left'; Sartre modulates from a historicist to a largely psychoanalytical angle of decipherment. The 'exemplary-didactic' relation overlaps at numerous points with the 'political'; but it shows a more pronounced 'scholastic' edge. I have in mind the Aristotelian programme for the induction and transmission to the audience of states of cognitive and emotive poise (a 'politics of feeling'); Schiller's doctrine of the aesthetic as the principal vehicle of the nurture of civic sensibility; Matthew Arnold's view of high literature as a 'criticism of life' from whose radiant ambience and energies a society acquires moral and executive style.

By 'investigative' in the philosophical vein, one would understand the modes of criticism whose purpose is the explication of an art object or text in terms of its specific nature, operant substance and phenomenal status. Here the proceedings of the critic belong fairly to the more general class of aesthetics. To divorce the critical motive from the philosophical-thereotic one in, say, Kant, Croce, Walter Benjamin or Burke would be to urge an empty nomenclature. What I mean by 'dramatically reproductive' relations in criticism are those in which the critic's delineation and judgement of the object are achieved by a kind of mimesis, performative encapsulation or parallel presentment of that object. The critic's own text is a 'retelling of the thing' with an evaluative appendage. It is the 'summary +' of the plot, the description of the painting or the verbal equivocation – taking this word in its worrying sense – of the piece of music. (When Schumann, on the contrary, offered an explicative critique of a composition by replaying it *in toto* he was, I think, exemplifying the cardinal distinction between 'critic' and 'reader'.) In dramatically reproductive criticism, illustration, quotation are of the essence. The critic quotes strategically so as to make his point, so as to achieve persuasive economy. His critique is a summation towards judicial ends; quotations are the exhibits it offers in evidence. If philosophical criticism is a branch of aesthetics, performative or mimetic criticism is one of the multiple forms of applied rhetoric. At a guess, one would say that this form comprises nine-tenths of the craft. It stretches from the iceberg mass of daily reviewing – the 'art critic', 'the book critic', 'the music critic' in the media – all the way to such undoubted pinnacles of judicial re-enactment and summation as Samuel Johnson's discourse on Shakespeare or T.S. Eliot's on Dante. But it may be that Eliot on Dante is inspired criticism, whereas Mandelstam on Dante is 'reading'.

Very often this almost ubiquitous order of criticism will have praise as its motive. The aim of the act of ordering sight is to advance the fortunes, to strengthen the impact of a given piece of work or movement. In its hectoring innocence, the communist term *agitprop* strikes the appropriate note. It would characterize Zola's polemics on behalf of Manet, Ezra Pound for modernism, G. Wilson Knight in propagation of Byron's moral fineness. Each of these viewers is, in the given case, a virtuoso of celebration. The contrastive category is that of a critical distancing calculated ('motivated') to diminish, to strip bare, even to eradicate the object – i.e. to bring about its removal from the syllabus, from the public gallery to the basement. This is Apollo's musical critique of Marsyas, Pope's vivisection of Grub Street and his editorial competitors such as Theobald, or Leavis in pursuit of Auden. Though antithetical in purpose, festive advocacy and chastisement are both a part of the general class of 'presentational' or performative critical practice.

Even a thumbnail sketch of these different orders of critical motive raises an obvious question: Can anything useful be said of a phenomenology so various that it includes Aristotle's *Poetics*, Hegel's lessons on the philosophy of art, Baudelaire on Wagner and I.A. Richards on Coleridge at one end, and the pandemonium of daily academic-journalistic market quotations at the other? The inchoate plurality is undeniable. But so, I believe, is the presence of certain 'primals' and constants. These derive from the epistemology of objectivization.

Distancing objectifies; or to use a term which is in vogue but which is accurate: it *reifies* (*es verdinglicht*). The object of the critical act, be the motives for this act diagnostic or mimetic, laudatory or punitive, is seen as and thus made a 'thing'. Criticism resorts perpetually to the notion of 'living art', of 'vitality', of the 'life-force' in music or poetry. It has, since the *Poetics*, made of the 'organic' both an explicative criterion and an ideal. But these invocations of vitalism are instrumental fictions. For purposes of ordering perception, of placement and verdict, the critical object is reified. One does not anatomize and label living tissue; or, note again the demonstration by Schumann of the antithesis between a musicological presentation, however instinct with approval and analytic authority on the one hand, and the replaying of the piece on the other. Secondly, we have seen that the distance between critic and object is activated by motive. Now whatever the order of intention, the relation established is, in the first place, derivative. The critic, whether he comes to dissect or to mime, to praise or to negate, relates to 'that which is there before him' – in which self-evident proposition 'before' carries both its locative and its temporal meanings. The object existed in time before the critic came upon it, even if this precedence is only one of a few hours as in the case of the journalist-reviewer. Therefore, the ground of being, the *raison d'être* of even the most formidable and far-reaching of critical arguments is the precedent status of the art object or text. The Sophoclean versions of Oedipus are prior to the *Poetics*; the *Lyrical Ballads* come before the brilliancies of Coleridge's 'practical criticism' in which so much of the modern technique of vision is rooted; Marvell's poems long antedate T.S. Eliot's insights. All criticism is posterior, and this sequent status is not only temporal but existential. The work of art, the text, the musical composition exists not only prior to the ordering sight of the critic; it can exist without it. No critic is, either formally or in fact, the cause of that which he perceives and relates to.

This existential posteriority, this dependence of the perceptual and normative act on the prior and autonomous nature of the object, signifies that all criticism is, ontologically, *parasitic*. The Platonic paradigm makes graphic the degree of derivation. The carpenter imitates the Idea of the table. The painter mimes this mimesis whose literal form he can neither execute nor judge properly. The critic of the painting expatiates at fourth hand on the mimicry of a shadow. But even in any less caustic model of the orders of executive action and perception, the dependent, ancillary, occasional – because 'occasioned from outside' – nature of all critical vision and utterance is manifest. *The critic is not the maker.* That such a platitude requires emphasis and may even take on polemic resonance is a symptom of the absurdities and reversals of value prominent in today's academy and in the current condition of letters. Sainte-Beuve was morosely right in saying that no one was raising statues to critics; but he may have been a bad prophet.

The reification of the object of criticism and the *necessarily* (not accidentally, not remediably) parasitic nature of the critic's response to this object, determine a fundamental instability in the whole enterprise. Simultaneously criticism judges (even where adjudication is one of hyperbolic acclaim) and knows itself to be a secondhand, an epiphenomenal act. From this asymmetry comes the absolutely central fact that all criticism is, in a certain sense, 'adversative to' its object. This needs to be spelled out clearly. Even where its programme is one of epiphany, of disclosure through placement and praise, even where it seems itself to be the devoted outrider and herald to the work of art, criticism stands not only 'outside' and 'after' its cause: it stands 'against' it. It is, to use Kenneth Burke's pivotal designation, a *counter-statement* to it.

And precisely because it knows itself to be simultaneously magisterial and parasitic, prescriptive and dependent, normative and occasional, criticism harbours inside itself strong solicitations to autonomy. The more lucid it is about its own existential secondhandedness, the more unavoidably will criticism be under pressure of the impulse towards integral status. Implicit in all criticism, not by virtue of historical accident or culpable vanity, but as an ineluctable condition of its being, is the instinct for autonomy. Consciously or not, criticism labours to transcend relation. Criticism contains, at its methodological and intentional core, the potentiality, paradoxical, even absurd in regard to logic, of existing 'beyond' its object. It experiences a constant temptation to make of its object not the necessary and sufficient cause of its own existence, but a mere starting point and receding suggestion. Thus it exhibits a precise drive towards usurpation: it would work away from its own existential derivativeness and take on the ontological primacy of its cause.

This is the aetiology and underlying explanation of the present-day character and hypertrophy of criticism, particularly in reference to literature. The current scene is little short of ludicrous. In the academy and the media, the critic has a prepotent, monumentalized station. Critical methodologies, with spurious claims to theoretical profundity and performative rigour, are multiplied and offered to secondary and tertiary investigation (there are critics of criticism, journals of 'dia-' and 'meta-' criticism in which critics dispute the merits of each other's jargon; there are university qualifications in criticism). In a mode of narcissist terrorism, criticism now proposes to 'deconstruct' and to 'disseminate' the text, to make of the text the labile, ultimately contingent source of its own prepotent display. Such display is sustained by the construction of metalanguages of autistic violence and obscurity. The resultant terror and mist envelop the text object to the point of deliberate effacement. The act of criticism has 'ingested' its object (Ben Jonson's term for parasitic consumption) and now stands autonomous. There are, indeed, specific historical and sociological grounds for this cancerous and inflationary condition. There are local, temporal reasons why criticism today occupies a status unequalled since the Alexandrian scholiasts and grammatologists (there being in both periods a concomitant enfeeblement of literature). But the potentiality of this inversion of values as between the critic and the prior object is implicit in *all* criticism. It has been there from the start. The implication is a necessary and dynamic entailment of the fact that criticism is competitive with the object of its ordering sight, that the critic is not, as the cliché would have it, a failed artist, but a 'counterstater' and rival to the work.

Undoubtedly, moreover, it is the case that a fair amount of criticism takes on autonomy by force of expression. The relevant sections in Coleridge's *Biographia Literaria* are 'literature' in a sense not drastically removed from that which we attach to the poetry they analyse and judge. Criticism can outlast its object by virtue of material hazard: many of the paintings and statues viewed and judged by Vasari have now disappeared. Or criticism may do so because the stature of the critic is, pragmatically, greater than that of the author. Who but the specialist now reads the minor poets about whom Samuel Johnson found memorable points to make? But such supersedures should be accidental, involuntary, arising from factors outside the critic's purpose and control. 'Planned supersession' – the critic's determination to fix his voraciousness on minor or enfeebled objects such as an inferior Balzac novella, the rhapsodies of a Lautréamont, a *kitsch* film – is a methodologically and ethically vitiated turn. Subconsciously, perhaps, it seeks compensation, even vengeance for its own parasitism on the object which is, eternally, its precedent and cause of being. Such vengeance can be effective. We are surrounded, currently, by minor or spurious texts which criticism has exploitatively aggrandized, and by major art and texts which criticism has diminished or obscured. We direct students to T.S. Eliot's criticism on Dante; we do not direct them to reading the *Commedia divina*. 'Criticism' and 'reading' grow apart.

Now, unquestionably, parasitism is necessary to life. The bird pecking clean the hide and wounds of the rhinoceros is performing a delicate, vital piece of work. The critic *is* necessary to the life of art and letters. But it is because he is, in significant respects, of an identical species with his host, with his carrier and *raison d'être*, that this symbiosis breeds ambivalence and usurpation. The solicitation to betrayal, through an act of sight which 'screens' instead of elucidating, through narcissim of theory and idiom, through masked or outright misprision (the critic can bear false witness *and* be hanging judge in a tribunal of his own devising), is always present. It is of the essence of the critical relation. It is, probably, for this reason that great criticism relates to its cause in an intimacy of peculiar sadness.

II

Roughly half a dozen contrastive pairings have come up in relation to the initial polarization: 'critic' as against 'reader'. They include the dissociation between an epistemological and an ontological base (a Husserlian bias on the one hand, a Heideggerian one on the other). We saw that there may be a significant difference between the establishment of a 'syllabus' and the acceptance of a 'canon', between objectivizations of the text whose presuppositions are realistic-immanent, and those which draw on a category of transcendence. The teleological motion of criticism, its purposive economies, may differ from the theological tenor of the guarantor or 'third party' implicated in the act of 'reading'. Operative in and through these contrarieties is the intimation of an essential distinction between the judicial authority of the critic, his normative placement of the text or art object at and from an argued distance, and the 'dynamic passivity' or sufferance of the 'reader' who is, where 'reading' achieves its plenitude, the 'one being read'.

These suggestions concerning the 'reader' are admittedly vague and portentous. It is easy to say something about criticism worth looking at and/or disagreeing with. It is difficult to say anything useful about 'reading' in the sense in which this paper seeks to articulate the term. Criticism is discursive and breeds discourse. 'Reading' yields no primary impulse towards self-communication. The 'reader' who discourses is, in a certain manner, in breach of privilege. The surest testimonials we have to major acts of reading tend to be oblique; they tend to be tangential in exactly the sense in which Walter Benjamin, himself a master reader, argues that great translation is tangential to the vulgate meaning of the original. Reading is done rather than spoken about (one of the very few convincing narrations of the act of reading, of *une lecture bien faite et*

plénière, that I know of, is to be found in Péguy's *Dialogue de l'his-
toire et de l'âme païenne*, another in Nadezhda Mandelstam's
memoirs; but both of these are narrations, not analyses, not
attempts at methodological abstraction 'from outside'). The
antinomies, the play of irreconcilable difference, no less than
the mystery of interrelation, lie between Narcissus and Echo.
Again, this is to invoke the metaphoric. Nevertheless, the diacritical
'cuts' I have listed may, in part at least, be worth arguing more
closely.

To the 'reader', in which designation I include whosoever's apprehension of a text, of art, of music, of formed motion is not, is not
primarily, that of the critic's legislative sighting, the 'otherness' met
with is not 'a thing out there', is not, first and foremost, an 'object',
Now it is perfectly true that criticism also has queried, imaged,
metaphorized the 'non-objective' phenomenological status of the
poem, the painting, the piece of music. Criticism too will often
ascribe to the matter of its speculative and judicial concerns a
singular epistemological nature, a kind of 'third realm' in Popper's
suggestive terminology. Certain schools of criticism have been
more than willing to grant that 'great art' has, by virtue of its
inspirational genesis, unrepeatability, formal inexhaustibility and
energies of impact, a substantive mode other than that of, say,
natural or manufactured objects. But for the critic this extra-territ-
oriality remains a preliminary concession to be made in respect of
aesthetic and psychological unknowns ('unknowns', as it were, yet
to be discovered). It is a concession which does not inhibit the
exercise of delineation and of judgement.

The 'reader', by contrast, inhabits the provisional – in which
manifold term he recognizes as relevant the notions of 'gift', of 'that
which serves vision', and of that which 'nourishes' indispensably.
He situates himself within, rather than traversing it with conventional concession and logical embarrassment, the supposition that
the text, the work of art, the musical composition are *data* not in the
'scientific' or realistically objectivized sense, but in the primary and
archaic signification of 'that which is given to us'. That they are not
'objects' even in a special 'aesthetic' category, but 'presences', 'pres-
entments' whose existential 'thereness' (Heidegger's word) relates
less to the organic, as it does in Aristotelian and Romantic poetics
and theories of art, than it does to the 'transubstantiational'. The
adjective, as well as the concept aimed at, is almost hopelessly
pompous and awkward. But the evidence whereby meaning and

experience can be attached to them is not negligible. What is implicit is the notion and expression of 'real presence'. The reader proceeds *as if* the text was the housing of forces and meanings, of meanings of meaning, whose lodging within the executive verbal form was one of 'incarnation'. He reads *as if* – a conditionality which defines the 'provisional' temper of his pursuit – the singular presence of the life of meaning in the text and work of art was 'a real presence' irreducible to analytic summation and resistant to judgement in the sense in which the critic can and must judge. But a presentness, a presence of what?

There are different 'as ifs', different modes of provisionality, as there are different configurations and styles of focus in criticism. Authority for the intimation of a 'real presence' can be sought from the Platonic or Romantic trope of 'mantic inspiration'. The art object is *not* an object in any normal sense because it springs out of a mystery of alien ingress, out of the the *daimon*'s rush into the momentary vacancy of man's reason and identity. *Poiesis*, the poet's, the singer's inventions, are imperatives from without. The products of true art have in them the live vestiges of transcendent intrusion. A variant on this trope is that of the sacramental as it obtains in the reading and exegesis of 'revealed' texts (where 'revelation' can, but need not be, transmitted by dictation as it is in the paradigmatic account of the rhapsode in Plato's *Ion*). The relevant presumption is that of an inherence, however esoteric, however eroded or possibly falsified by human transcription, of a 'spirit' in, 'behind', the letter. It is just this presumption which underwrites the concept of the 'iconic', the belief that the icon is not so much a representation of the sacred person or scene as it is the immediate manifestation, the epiphany of that person or scene. In other words, the latter are 'really present' to the beholder not by virtue of a voluntary imaginative concession or transposition on the beholder's part, but because *they* have taken dwelling in the icon. A third model of 'inherence' is that provided by the application of an absolute philosophic ontology to aesthetics. It is that which justifies Heidegger's ascription of a total *Dasein*, of a total 'presentness of being', to the worn pair of boots in the Van Gogh painting. As Heidegger urges, the 'real presence' of these boots on or 'within' the canvas is of an order and intensity, of a phenomenological necessity, denied not only to this or that actual pair of boots but denied as well to the most rigorous chemical-functional analysis of 'what it is that boots are made of and for' (a complete reversal of the

Platonic scheme of third-hand mimesis and of the naive realism operative in 'criticism').

The enabling models which authorize a reader to assign iconic status to his text vary. But singly or together, they allow him to grasp concretely and to organize his experience of the text in accord with a class of assertions made by writers and artists themselves (assertions to which the 'critic' can only concede a rhetorical validity). In this class, I would include Michelangelo's witness: 'Se il mio rozzo martello i duri sassi forme d'uman aspetto or questo or quello, dal ministro, ch'l guida iscorge e tiello, prendendo il moto va con gli altrui passi.' ('When my rough hammer transforms hard stone to this or that figure of human shape, it moves solely by the volition of Him who guides it; it follows solely in His path.') Or Tolstoy's testimony to Katkov that Anna Karenina 'had broken away from him', that the imagined persona had taken on autonomous will and being (*va con gli altrui passi*) outside of, indeed against, the novelist's design and understanding. Or one might include the arcadian arrogance of Picasso's: 'I never seek, I only find.' In each of these and innumerable analogous cases, the apprehension undergone by the 'begetter' and the reader is of a kind which entails perception and invites terror (both are active in 'to apprehend').

The ascription, even where it remains only a provisional constant, of 'real presence' to the text, means that the reader's engagement with the text is not 'objectifying', that it cannot be a relationship of reification, of competition and, by logical extension, of supersedure. The reader opens himself to the autonomous being of the text. The dialectic of encounter and of vulnerability (the text can bring drastic hurt) is one in which the ontological core of the text, its presentness of inward being, both reveals and makes itself hidden. This pulsing motion is a familiar one. As we come to know the text, the painting, the piece of music better, as we become more at home in its idiom, there is always more which seems to elude us. Echo draws us inward with a deepening intimation of understanding as yet unfulfilled. Phrased in this way, the observation is routinely psychological. But when the true source of this apparently contradictory pulse of disclosure and concealment is assigned to the text, to the work of art, the presumption is one of 'real presence'. In the iconic text, as this text 'comes upon' the reader, there is both 'sense' and 'force' (*Sinn* and *Kraft* are the two cardinal markers in Frege's theory of meaning, serving to suggest how it is that the sentence carries significations and immediately comprehensible directions much beyond those manifest in the individual, interchangeable word). Such essential excess of meaning characterizes the order of texts or art forms with which the reader engages. All serious aesthetics aims to elucidate what can be termed, to borrow a Marxist econometric vocabulary, the phenomenon of 'surplus value', of the 'forces' in and beyond 'sense' generated by art.

Where the act of reading is sufficiently apprehensive of the ontological pulse in the text, of the concomitant motion of radiance and withdrawal, it will register both the purity and the irreducibility of the pertinent 'force'. *Purity* in this context means essential disinterestedness. The *raison d'être* of the painting or poem or musical composition being only being, I say 'essential' because, of course, the notion invoked here is, again, a more or less fictive absolute. Even the highest art can involve impurities of motive, such as didacticism, social occasion, public or private record, and so on. But where there is the 'presentness' which I have been implying, these mundanities of motive and performance will not, finally, determine the status and force of the work. Often, in fact, this autonomous force in the work will come to refute the voluntary programme, the temporal meaning with which the artist invested his material. Though he proceeds from an altogether different orientation, Marx seized on precisely this internal dialectic when he noted that the effects, the agencies of survival, in Balzac's novels were the ideological negation of those which the writer had purposed.

'Irreducibility' signifies 'non-paraphrasability', the untranslatability of an iconic presence into any other form without loss and estrangement (where 'sense' can be preserved, 'force' cannot). As lived by the true reader, the text is irreducible to, inexhaustible by, even the most penetratively diagnostic, explicative of visions – be they linguistic, grammatological, semiotic, historicist, sociological, 'deconstructive' or what you will. The text can be restated, as Schumann restates the piece of music. There is, in consequence, a sense in which much of 'reading' is reiteration; but the reader's repetition (his 'asking again') is not the critic's quotation. It aims not at illustrative excision from but at complete re-entry into the text. Whether such re-entry can ever be wholly achieved, whether facsimile is ever total, is a dilemma which long exercised scribes and ministrants. The evident reason for the irreducibility of the iconic is that that which declares and conceals itself in the text or canvas or musical structure is of the order of being rather than of meaning, or, more accurately, that it has force incarnate in but also in excess of sense. It 'is' before it 'means', and the meaning(s) we derive from it are a function of its disinterested autonomy of existence – an existence which does not address itself to any particular beholder but must be met with by him (the Angel was not looking for Jacob). It is this immediate infolding of meaning into force of being which makes of music the most 'iconic', the most 'really present' essent known to man. It follows that music is also that which most absolutely resists paraphrase or translation. But infolding and resistance of this kind characterize all living texts and art.

To summarize: the 'reader's' contiguities to the text are ontological rather than epistemological, as are the 'critic's'. The reader does not encounter or aim at objectivization, but at implication in the possibility, in the 'as if' of a real presence. He knows that the meanings which he obtains from his text are always partial, always ambiguously external, that they are, at best, a bonus of being. René Char puts it more concisely: 'La vitalité du poète n'est pas une vitalité de l'au-delà mais un point diamanté *actuel* de présences transcendantes et d'orages pèlerins.' Authentic reading momentarily fixes transcendence.

'Contiguities', as used above, need to be looked at. The critic keeps his distance. This retention is the condition of his ordering, magisterial focus. The reader attempts to negate the space between the text and himself. He would be penetrated by, immersed in its presentness. The reader strives for fusion with the text via internalization. And here we arrrive at a first disjunction in the general category and dialectic of reading. Internalization is eminently feasible in respect of texts and of music; but only partly so in the case of art objects. At its primary and most radical level, the thorough act of reading, the full apprehension of the *présences transcendantes* in language and music entails memorization. The act of learning *by heart* – an idiom of notable precision – is no technical auxiliary or carry-over from liturgical and pedagogical practice. It is of the essence of the reader's attempt to abolish or sublate that very distance which the critic stakes out. To memorize is, simultaneously, to enter into the text and to be entered into by the text (a process only partly realizable when one 'photographs' a painting or statue mentally). This dual motion of ingress and reception is formally and substantively the analogue of the dual motion of projection and withdrawal in the text or musical composition itself.

Commitment to memory is, in the first place, an individual phenomenon. It modifies the spaces and constructs of one's inner
being, as does the entrance of a 'high guest' (Hölderlin's simile)
into one's house. Very recent work in biochemistry even suggests
that such modification has its material counterpart, that the
augment of memory leads to delicate ramifications of molecular
fabric. But active remembrance is also a collective, a cultural
agency. It initiates and preserves a communion of shared echo, of
participatory reflex, pertinent to the notion of canon.

An unremembered text or piece of music exists in a penumbra of
anticipation as do the volumes currently untouched, where 'currently' can mean centuries, in the patient silences of the great
libraries. But a text can only enter into the full life of the canon
when it is woken by, housed within, the negated distance of precise
memory. It follows that 'total reading' has an inherent logic of
dispensation, that it tends towards a condition in which the materiality of the text is no longer required. The icon has been wholly
internalized. The executive recollection which makes it present in
and to the reader no longer depends on external confirmation. Such
orders of internality are no ideal fiction, though they may seem so
in our present climate of institutionalized amnesia. In other epochs,
societies or traditions, the commitment to memory, the availability
to total recall and reiteration, of massive bodies of texts – epic,
ritual, liturgical, historical, taxonomic – was, or still is, routine, as it
is routine, even among us, to numerous musicians who dispense
with a score and apprehend internally, in the soundless clarity of
mastered introspection, great stretches of polyphonic music. (I
have seen undergraduates switch off the sound track in a beloved
Bogart film and speak in unison long pieces of perfectly remembered dialogue.)

The negation of distance, of which memorization is the final logic,
brings on an extreme contraction of focus. Sense and spirit crowd
up, as it were, against the actual surface of the text. And here again,
instructively, the parallel with the apprehension of art objects begins to break down. In the case of the canvas, statue or building, we
must, to a greater or lesser degree, step back in order to see. But it
is in regard to texts precisely this contraction of focus which makes
of the single word or short sentence the crucial units of reading, as
they are of memorization. The practices of meditation and of commentary on the single word or verse, as they have been developed
by exegetes of revealed, of legal, or 'founding' texts – 'founding' in

the sense of being the documents of national identity, the epics and chronicles of inception – are not accidental or technical devices. Exegetic meditation on the minimal unit is the ultimate rationale of true reading. Reading and remembrance proceed word by word, a usage implicit in Walter Benjamin's proposal that the genuine translator, the translator who works furthest from the critic's paraphrase, is one who produces a word-for-word interlinear. With the Scholastics, the reader knows that 'God lies in the detail'.

It is in this entirely practical sense that the most evident records of iconic reading are exegetic: the letter-by-letter hermeneutics of the Kabbalists, the word-by-word commentaries of the Talmudists or Patristic readers, Karl Barth advancing sentence-by-sentence in Romans. But exactly the same contraction of perspective, with its attendant methodological extravagances and myopias, can be brought to bear on the secular poem, the philosophical text (Heidegger on Anaximander or Heraclitus), the legal statute. The difference is simply that the rabbinical exegete or Calvin on the Gospels can proceed without apology or rationalizing metaphor, 'as if' the real presence were unambiguously operative in his text. He can, in short, make explicit the assumption, implicit in all true reading, that the warranty of meaning, that which finally underwrites the capacity of language to have sense and force beyond sense, is of a theological order. The honest realist-critic, on the contrary, operates by virtue of immanent and secular presuppositions. It is these which give him the authority to judge, to consign 'inferior' works to non-remembrance (criticism is one of the means of forgetting).

In both its strengths and potential infirmities, a word-by-word reading will tend to be philological. It is philology, the literal 'love of the *logos*' which has been the natural instrument, the magnifying glass of the exegete. Likewise, musicology can dwell on each note or bar. Textual criticism is sharply 'critical', but in a sense almost antithetical to that of the critic's criticism. Textual criticism is the broom in the house of remembrance, sweeping away accretion of factitiousness in order to make presentness more translucid. It does not judge its text, as the critic must; it labours to restore it to exact mystery. That there are profound mirrorings as between philology and music, that both are disciplines of access to elemental energies of being projected towards and concealed from the intellect, was a fact familiar to Plato and recalled by Nietzsche. Philology and music pertain to the spheres of 'reading' rather than of 'criticism' (how much music criticism is there even worth forgetting?).

The critic prescribes a syllabus; the reader is answerable to and internalizes a canon. In practice, to be sure, the two will overlap. The 'syllabic' in a given culture will select and celebrate, will label as 'classic' the 'great books' around which a language and a society edify their codes of self-recognition. Such 'great books' may indeed be a part of the reader's canon (where criticism also focuses on revealed texts, this will be most obviously the case). But strictly considered, the inclusion in the canon of 'masterpieces' from the syllabus is accidental. Motivations towards the canonic are not, at their source, those of interested and prescriptive activity in the sense in which we found these to be fundamental to the critical exercise of ordering sight. The aim of the canon, and *aim* is precisely the wrong word here, is not that of stylistic exemplarity, in the way in which, for instance, the rhetoric of Boileau and Racine may be seen to have served as official 'weights and measures' for generations of French discourse. It is not nationally didactic in the sense in which much of Shakespeare had been for the Anglo-Saxon political community. In brief, the canon is not a catalogue of magisterially, circumstantially culled and monumentalized pre-eminence. A canon is the individually internalized cluster of crystallization of remembered, exegetically re-enacted texts or text fragments which result from (very often) unsought, unwilled encounter with and answerability to the 'real presence'. The authentic canon is not, or is not in the first place, the product of reasoned intention.

Its crystallization in the reader's inwardness results from a paradox of 'dynamic passivity', from the suspension of self which we experience when we pay utter attention to something, when we make acceptance and apprehension strenuous. This condition can produce a tensed openness which allows, which invites the text 'to read us' as much as we read it. Canonic are the texts and fragments of texts – criticism must seek to view the whole; reading can dwell on the smallest component – whose entrance into the reader's mind, and 'mind' is in this context a wholly inadequate, restrictive designation, whose immediacy to the reader's recall and revocation, come to alter the texture of consciousness. The reader revisits, comes back into awareness of the quick of his own augmented being through reference to, through silent colloquy with, through the citation of, texts and pieces of text. The archaic resort to *sortes*, the placing of a blind finger on some passage from a scriptural or poetic book, is an outward dramatization of this inward search for

essential insight, for an understanding of one's destiny. The canonic text enters into the reader, it takes its place within him by a
process of penetration, of luminous insinuation whose occasion
may have been entirely mundane and accidental – decisive encounters so often are – but not, or not primarily, willed. The 'high
guests' enter unbidden yet awaited.

There is nothing occult or mystical about this entrance, though
psychology has not, until now, given a convincing analysis of its
literal mechanism. The occurrence is banal to anyone whose mind
and body – both are involved – have been seized upon by a melody,
by a tune, by a verbal cadence which he did not choose by act of
will, which has entered into him unawares. It is familiar to whoever
has left a room – it need not be a museum gallery – only to discover
that there is lodged in his inner eye (the pun on *ego* is not entirely
trivial) some detail of an object, of a painting, some configuration
of tactile form or colour, which he has no awareness of having fixed
upon, of registering consciously. When fully accepted, when made
welcome and vital by virtue of precise remembrance and study,
such mastering entrants and trespassers take root. They mesh with
the fabric of the self; texts become part of the texture of identity.
Proust's notation and uses of the 'little theme' from Vinteuil's
sonata and of the yellow patch in Vermeer's view of Delft are
unsurpassed testimony to the origins and role of the canonic.

This particular set is instructive also in another sense. The Vermeer painting is, by critical consensus, a masterpiece; it figures
eminently on the syllabus. The Vinteuil theme, on the other hand,
is meant to evoke (so the scholars have found out) a particular
motif in a bit of chamber music by Fauré. Even committed Proust-
ians find it difficult to discern any particular excellence or mem-
orability in the original, let alone that central genius of
time-anulling beauty and meaning which the narrator attributes to
it throughout the novel. Thus, one fundamental element in Proust's
canon is of a sort which we would also find in the critical syllabus,
whereas the other is idiosyncratic and, by syllabic standards, insignificant, ephemeral, 'third-rate'. But it is to the minor, a classifica-
tion which it does not, in fact, recognize, that the canonic often
pertains. The canon which is the echo chamber of our personal
being, which is immediate to and consubstantial with those sum-
monses which give to our identity its individual weight and sa-
vour, is like a collage. The 'classic' and the 'syllabic' will figure in
it, as the Mona Lisa postcard figures in a surrealist constructivist

assemblage. But so will texts, graphic motifs, musical passages which are hardly respectable by the standards of critical judgement. A syllabus is taught; a canon is lived.

Indeed, he is no true reader who has not tasted the drug of the esoteric, who has not discovered that the song of the Sirens, maddening because it ironizes the brevity of personal existence, the insufficiencies of personal memory, is the silent call of the unread book. One would almost say, though this is sophistic hyperbole, of 'any unread book'. Exegesis, philology are, in pure extremity, value blind. Virtuosities of inwardness have been expended on inventories in Leviticus; A.E. Housman's readings, his vitalizing apprehensions, cut deepest in Manilius. The cheap tune haunts us. As Sartre recollects in *Les Mots*, the young person is 'read by', is woken and construed to identity by blood-and-thunder, by near-Valentines, or the memorable purple of travel and romance. (Hérédia's brassy sonnets and the somewhat saccharine memoirs and letters of Renan crystallized my adolescence.)

In turn, this primary inwardness and hybrid character of the canon will inflect the act of reading towards privacy, even secrecy. The critic must declare; this is his public and legislative ordination. The reader will often hold his illuminations mute. Or he will experience a contradictory impetus. He seeks to keep to himself the visitations by and internalizations of those texts or iconic objects which have most intensely affected his being. Yet, possessed of and by his talisman, the reader will want to inform others, where both meanings of *inform*, that of communication and that of shaping, are relevant. In the antiquarian, in the archivist, in the bibliophile and collector of works of art, this radical ambiguity and even duplicity of motives is a familar trait. The collector conceals his find in order to show it – a psychological reflex (lightly) analogous with what we have seen to be the pulsing dialectic of withdrawal and epiphany in art itself. It is from this divided stance that stem the 'schools of reading', the exegetic and hermeneutic disciplines, be they rabbinical, monastic, academic or simply familial, whereby a 'master' or first reader attempts to lay his disciples and collaborators open to the text. The opening of the text comes after the laying open of the reader. Literal repetition, transcription, commitment to memory often precede and will, at all times, be coterminous with exposition. The critic parallels mimetically or by paraphrase; he does not transcribe; he does not memorize the object of his judgement. The Kabbalist, the philologist, the musician must do so. Thus, when he invites others into the 'inner penetralium' of his sensibility – the phrase was St Augustine's before it was Keats's – when he invites others to make vital the canon which is a constituent of his own being, the reader reads *with* them. In the master critic there is, inherently, the bias to read *for* us.

Other disjunctions follow. The robust critic is a futurist. Whatever the acuity of analysis and judgement which he brings to bear on a past work, his aim, the test of his own antennae, must be the importation into the syllabus of the 'tradition of the new' (Harold Rosenberg's telling expression). He deals, to take up the simile of the *bourse* once again, in 'futures'. We have seen that it is in the measure of speculative risk, in the likelihood that some of his most costly investments will prove abortive, that lies the dignity of his craft. The true reader, on the contrary, is, almost unavoidably, a remembrancer. It is the ontological 'backwardness' of the canonic, in the fact that so many of the Eurydices on the reader's pilgrimage (*les orages pèlerins*) are in the shadows behind him, that lie the unworldliness, the dusty sorrows of his calling. This bent towards pastness is both individual and typological: much of the canon is given entrance to, is met with, in childhood or youth, when the inner spaces are as yet uncluttered and memory is rapacious. The great reader, and he is rare, is precisely the one who remains fully vulnerable, fully hospitable to the light and menace of the annunciation, in mature age. Much of the canonic is also historical. Therefore, it makes dangerous sense to the reader to intuit, to act on the prejudice, that there will be no texts produced in his lifetime or even thereafter to surpass, perhaps to match, those we attach to the anonymities of Homer or the Book of Job. The modern reader finds himself supposing, almost without examination, that certain 'transcendentals' in the canon, such as Aeschylus, Dante, Shakespeare, Goethe, represent singularities, compactions of totality of a kind which western culture, at least, will not regenerate. The critic's feeling on this must be one of rebellious doubt and contrary hope. When he visits the museum he must be present at the hanging of the new pictures.

III

The dualities which I have cited, and many others implicit in the argument, can best be subsumed under one fundamental antithesis. The critical act is a function of the ego in a condition of will. The critic wills his praxis. Even where his relation to the object of his focus is most affirmative, elucidative and heralding, this is to say where it is of the most patent service to the object, this relation is, nevertheless, structurally and dynamically egotistical (using this term in a non-moralistic sense). The yield is, as we saw, a counter-statement, a standing 'over and against' the text or art object which is the occasion of his proposition. The critic signs his perception no less than, often more emphatically than, the begetter of the original object. We saw also that there is in this ineluctable and legitimate egotism the constant potential of rivalry. Consciously or not, the critic competes with the text or art before him. Even celebration can, frequently does, come to eclipse its first cause. This, I suggested, is why the present-day inflation of the critic's status, vocabulary, didactic authority, idiom, media of dissemination and self-esteem are not accidental by-products of the mandarinization of literature. The prepotence of criticism over original composition, the interposition of the critic's persona between the text and the general light, are betrayals existentially rooted in the critical act. The impulse towards solipsistic sovereignty, towards the finding that there is really little left 'out there' worth serious criticism, or that what there is must be 'deconstructed' by the critic and immersed in Medea's cauldron, is no byzantine paradox. It is a thrust latent in all criticism. Finally, irremediably, the critic is *judge* and *master* of the text.

The reader is *servant* to the text. The genuine teacher, textual editor, scribe are called to a clerisy of service. The text finds out its condign reader. Often he would resist its peremptory ingress, even as the prophet seeks to shut his teeth against the imperatives of his calling (Jonah was a 'reader'). The reader's acceptance of the canon comports a trusteeship, mute and private except in those practices of collaborative reiteration, commitment to memory and heuristic commentary mentioned above. But whether singular or participatory, unspoken or communicated, the reader is 'in service' to the text. Roy Campbell recounts how the back of his spirit and the back of his body were bent when the text of St John of the Cross 'leapt upon him' from fortunate ambush. He became, as every true reader must become, a shepherd to the being of the text, a doorkeeper at the always closed and always opened gates to meaning. This latter simile is, of course, a borrowing from Kafka's parable of the doorkeeper before the threshold of the Law. In its seeming self-contradiction of closure and aperture, this fable illustrates concretely the process of dialogue with a canonic text. We understand and we do not understand enough; we grasp and that which we grasp eludes us. Again, there is nothing occult about the actual process, though it is difficult to paraphrase. It is the experience of the actor when the part which he has enclosed in memory springs to autonomous, mastering life; it is the ordinary experience of the performing musician in reference to the external or internalized score. Perhaps one might put it this way: *the critic's will acts. The reader's apprehension enacts.*

But if there is nothing occult in this process, there is in its motivation and pursuit a contract with the transcendent. In the final analysis, the reader has subscribed to a contract of implicit presence. He must 'enact as if' the letter is the vessel, however opaque, however fragmented, of the spirit. He must venture a Pascalian wager on the iconic potential of the work. The assumptions of such a contract have often been spelled out: by Novalis, when he urged that the 'true meaning of the World' had been lost but was recapturable in filaments of numinous discourse; by Péguy, when he identified *une lecture bien faite* with the unfolding of the blossom on the silent bough; by Heidegger when he asserted that 'the fate of western man' could well hinge on the right emendation of and answerability to a fragment of Anaximander. Or to put it in shorthand: the reader must suppose and accept that Flaubert was *not* indulging in rhetoric or baseless metaphor when he cried out, in the pain of mortal sickness: 'Why must I die while that tart Emma Bovary lives, and will continue to live?'

The contract with transcendence cannot be empirically validated. Its guarantor is theological, if this word is allowed its widest compass. As is 'theological' the warranty which underwrites the validity of metaphor and analogy (an issue closely argued in Pierre Boutang's key work, *L'Ontologie du secret*). This is the obvious weakness of the reader's theoretical position. The critic owes no hostages to mystery. The reader does. There is a necessary sense for him in the translation chosen by Luther in Revelation when he termed the 'Book of Life' to be an actual book. The reader must give almost literal weight to Mallarmé's conceit that the sum of being is *Le Livre*. This view can be felt to be at once exultant and a little mad – as so often are the practices of textual criticism, epigraphy, philology, heraldry, numismatics and exegesis in its pure being. Ecstatic, 'deranged' if you will, servants of the canon stand or dance 'beside themselves' because the text is now the sole and imperious lodger in the house of their being.

Of course, 'critic' and 'reader' as I have sketched them are near-fictions. Neither can be found at all readily in a pure state. There will be in even the most magisterial or narcissist of critics elements of disinterested acceptance, of apprehension beyond judgement. There have been in the most complete readers of whom we have record – an important qualification in view of the privacy of so much reading – critical reflexes, verdicts, impulses towards labelling. Even approximations to absolute types are rare. F.R. Leavis would stand near to the pole of unwavering criticism; Housman comes near to being the total reader (and neither of these two cases is altogether innocent of the pathological). In the ordinary run of things, 'criticism' and 'reading' interpenetrate and overlap. Nonetheless, it may be of some use to bear in mind the fiction of contrastive absolutes.

It is a platitude to observe the dishevelment in today's cultivation of humane letters. The self-satisfactions, assembly-line output of trivia, philosophic vacancy and histrionics which mark the academic profession of literature and its marriage to journalism are obvious. The debasement of the concept of 'research' in literary studies verges on scandal. Implicit in this essay is the hypothesis that much in this condition derives from a confusion between 'criticism' and the practices of exegetical reading from which the modern study of secular letters sprang. The notion that any but the most exceptional of human beings has anything *critically* new or re-evaluative to say of Dante, or of Shakespeare, or of Kafka, is cant. It is worse cant to institutionalize the belief that such rare ordering sight will manifest itself in the university undergraduate or graduate student. The present edifice of literary-critical studies (gossip in jargon) is a derogation, inevitable in view of the fact that the great majority of texts had been properly edited previously, from the exact arts of philology, historical linguistics, textual criticism, recension and collation. Today's undergraduate 'critic' and 'researcher in sensibility' is a high-wire acrobat who has not learned to walk.

What we need (I have argued this elsewhere) are not 'programmes in the humanities', 'schools of creative writing', 'programmes in creative criticism' (*mirabile dictu*, these exist). What we need are places, i.e. a table with some chairs around it, in which we can learn again how to read, how to read together. One aims at such a desideratum at the most literal levels. Elementary lexical and grammatical analyses, the parsing of sentences, the scansion of verse (prosody being the inseparable pulse and music of meaning), the ability to make out even the most rudimentary lineaments of those innervations and figures of rhetoric which, from Pindar to Joyce, have been the carriers of felt life – all these are now esoteric or lost skills. We need 'houses of and for reading' in which there is enough silence for the sinews of memory to awake. If language, under the pressure of wonder ('the surplus value') of multiple meaning, if the music of thought are to endure, it is not more 'critics' we require but more and better 'readers'.

'Great Readers', says Borges, who is himself one, are 'rarer than great writers.' The list would include Montaigne reading Seneca and re-reading himself; Coleridge reading Jacobi and Schelling, a reading whose motion of acquiescence and metamorphoric repossession Thomas McFarland has analysed with a tact equalling that of any other study of the stress of influence; Péguy reading Corneille and Victor Hugo; Walter Benjamin reading Goethe's *Elective Affinities*; Heidegger reading Sophocles and Trakl (not Hölderlin, whom he often reads wilfully and with opportunism); Mandelstam reading Dante and Chénier; Alexandre Koyré reading Galileo; Nabokov reading (not translating) Pushkin; Jean Starobinski reading Rousseau; William Empson reading complex words; Gianfranco Contini reading the Provençal poets, Dante and Montale; Pierre Boutang reading Plato's *Philebus*; Michael Dummett reading Frege, where depth and openness of reading are radically creative; D. Carne-Ross reading Góngora and Ariosto; Gershon Scholem reading the Kabbalists and reading Walter Benjamin . . . Servants to the text, scrupulous ecstatics, for in reference to the canonic, scruple and ecstasy are one.

A list of great critics? It would, no doubt, be longer and of greater public lustre. But is there need of such a list? Critics advertise.

A BRIEF POSTSCRIPT 1995

In the years since this essay was first published (1979), the exploitative arrogance and impatience of literary criticism, notably academic, has increased. Deconstructive, postmodernist, feminist, gender-oriented treatments of literary texts (where these are accorded any distinct status at all) are an industry. This industry can yield challenging, playful, indeed persuasive insights. Let me be absolutely clear on this. The rhetoric of 'absences' in deconstruction, with its precedent in Mallarmé and Nietzsche, with its roots in a Judaic rebellion against the unexamined authority of the canonic text, has generated excitement in what were, often, dusty quarters. Feminist readings have occasioned not only the revaluation of individual talents, but a sense of how much has been marginalized or passed under silence in our cultural history. Fresh and often bracing winds are blowing.

At the same time, much has been dispersed or, in its turn, marginalized. The arts of reading, as I tried to define and instance them in this paper, have been relegated to a mandarin, often defensive status. The instruments of lexicography, of grammatical and metrical analysis, of an awareness of rhetoric and historical context, now lie in rear-guard hands or lie broken altogether. These are the instruments of philosophy, which Gershom Scholen defined as the central science of meaning, as the sole authentic access to man's singular commerce with other men, with the past and with God.

Already in this essay, the notion of an ultimately theological underwriting of any coherent semantics is evident. *Real Presences*, which appeared ten years later, sought to argue this intuition fully. I persist, today, in feeling that the deconstructionist-Nietzschean provocation, that the subversion of the possibilities of verification of consensual meaning or 'meaning-fulness', cannot be refuted on merely secular grounds. The Derridean postulate (so radically Judaic) that a semantic marker can have meaning only if it is turned towards 'the face of God' and that there is no such 'face' – a nihilistic axiom to which the works of Levinas are a rebuttal – cannot, in my view, be falsified on psychological-rational grounds. No doubt such formulations and much of postmodernism are self-refuting in so far as they have to resort to the very linguistic means they deconstruct. But this is a formal quibble. The issue is ontological and fundamental. Ultimately, I believe, the act of faith in meaning, in the eventuality – always provisional, always postponed, always 'messianic' – of ascertainable sense, constitutes a kind of Cartesian wager (Descartes had to 'bet' on a benevolent Deity that would not have created an absurd, anarchic universe, arbitrary and thus indecipherable to human understanding). Hence my suggestion that it has, in our century, been the theologians or, to use Walter Benjamin's great image, those for whom some order of theology acts as the blotter underneath the page, who have been among the true readers. They and the philologists, 'lovers', as the word signifies, of the *Logos*.

The relations between my critical-scholarly work and my fictions is not one I can qualify objectively. But it is plain that the short novel *Proofs* (1992) 'imagines' the issues raised in this essay. They are compacted in the obvious play on words of the title: 'proofs' in the logical-evidential sense, and printer's proofs. In both, the concept of error, of the *erratum*, is capital. Talmudic and Kabbalistic speculations bridge the gap. It has been held that evil and injustice poured into creation via a minute error of transcription by the weary scribe to whom God imparted the Torah. There is a mystery, a spoor of holiness, in even the humblest, most everyday 'act of textuality' (the deconstructionist term *écriture* which would make all writing uniform in level or value is a deft reversal and travesty of this Talmudic axiom). The proofreader in my parable is convinced that messianic-utopian creeds – in his case Marxism – are simply an attempt to correct the script of history (the Italian version is entitled: *Il corretore*). To amend a printing-error, to 'get it right', is a profoundly 'religious' act even when performed by a militant atheist. That there is, finally, 'nothing to get right', that 'anything goes' – the current slogan in postmodernism, particularly in the American setting – is the exact antithesis to this credo. It can inspire a critic, not a reader.

Ideally, to be sure, these two attitudes should draw close. A serious critic ought to be a 'slow reader' in the sense I have tried to set out. For his part, the good reader should achieve a clarity of interpretation which renders criticism both possible and natural. Examples such as those of Coleridge, of Proust, of Péguy, a book such as Empson's *Structure of Complex Words* or Contini on Gadda and Montale, demonstrate the ideal. But my own intimation is, at present, one of a deepening division. In complicated but discernible ways, 'political correctness' has fed on this division. Reading, in the classical or thoroughgoing vein, is felt to be politically suspect. It speaks of 'order and degree', of solitude and inheritance.

It may be that the new electronics, that the Internet and 'virtual reality' – which is the contrary of any 'real presence' – will make this debate obsolete. The future of the book itself is now in question. The mere notion of 'reading', even as the postmodernist or the gender-ideologist still practises it, could alter fundamentally. But somewhere, I suspect, philology will endure in obstinate joy. Desert-fathers drinking deep.

2

So Little Do We Know of What Goes On When We Read

GEORGE CRAIG

It is always hard to get outside our assumptions, not least because we don't recognize them as assumptions. We may, through the intervention of others, discover that we are making assumptions, but we are most unlikely to get there on our own. In few areas is this so powerful and so widespread as in language itself. Walter Ong has brilliantly shown how difficult – one might say, for once without exaggeration or looseness, unimaginably difficult – it is for us to conceive a world without writing, to enter or represent the mental processes of those for whom writing is not, simply and overwhelmingly, there.[1]

Similarly, we take reading for granted. This is supported by the commonsense view that, if one starts to think about reading, it becomes hard, or even impossible, to read 'properly'. There is something in this of the discovery, usually made at about fifteen, that becoming conscious of one's walking had the most embarrassingly disabling effects. There is something in it too of the notion made familiar by rocketry, that there is a minimum take-off speed, below which the immediate goal (getting outside the pull of the earth's atmosphere) cannot be achieved. Think about reading, the view runs, and you'll be left sprawling clumsily on the verbal floor. Like all commonsense views, this is immensely plausible. But it rests on a prior assumption – that it is right, proper and normal for us to read easily, and that reading is akin to bicycle-riding. Once you've learned how to do it, you can never forget. More explicitly, you will always, barring injury or duress, be able to ride a bicycle. We have moved beyond the learner's, above all the child's, condition. For the last thing we would want is to find ourselves in that pre-competence stage again. Better to think that it is impossible, and that there is no way back. If reading becomes difficult in an adult situation, we prefer to think that the act of reading still remains easy, and that it is the reading material itself which is difficult.

It is of course tempting to think that there are clear distinctions to be made between easy and difficult, contrasting for example an elementary or basic activity – a child picking its way through *Janet and John* – with what goes on when an experienced reader engages with *Troilus and Criseyde* or 'Borges and I'. But we know very little of what goes on when we read – or of the strange continuities between these two, and indeed many other levels.

This is easily illustrated. What we adults call our response to a literary work includes elements as different from one another as, say, the perceived design of a text and temporary changes in our psychosomatic condition. It may be easy to give some account of the first (which is, ostensibly at least, something out there), but peculiarly hard to talk well or convincingly about the second. Everyone has, one imagines, experienced the shock of surprise, fearful or joyful; it is indeed one of the most important and power-ful signals we know. Yet our efforts to describe or catch it ('my heart missed a beat' or whatever) fall hopelessly short. Shifts of feeling, of energy, of absorption do not just accompany the act of reading: they are the form of that act for any given instance; and they are, unsurprisingly, at least as hard to describe as is surprise – since after all this last is merely one example of them.

However many other elements may be present in the act of read-ing, and even if all of them can be satisfactorily described, we are in the end left with a basic opposition: that between relatively describ-able complexities (the formal realities of a literary work, processes of appraisal, ideological determinants and so on) and something relatively indescribable but unarguably elementary (the excite-ments caused by inflections of our attention – fear, hope, joy, the stasis of blankness, the chill of despair). Even before literary criti-cism had achieved academic respectability this was an embarrass-ment; since that time it has been still less acceptable. If, as I want to suggest, that embarrassment is misplaced, the commonest way of dealing with it is the countervailing claim (implicit, for example, in the pejorative force attached to 'subjective') that the reader is a neutral witness more or less acute, more or less experienced. The most sophisticated version of this is that, with experience and guidance, the reader may attain the status of observer. But however the claim is elaborated, whatever concessions it may include (the reader as supremely sensitive receiving device, discriminator, active participant), its structure remains the same, dependent on an essentially romantic wish to be outside language in the moment of attending to it. For if we may indeed suspend disbelief, we may no more remove ourselves from the language-world than we can stop breathing, while our performance in the language-world is at all points uncertain. Whatever the reader may be a neutral witness of, it is not words. And the elimination of the false problem – the persistence of unwanted subjective elements in an objective process – allows sight again of a real one: the continuity between extraordinarily complex and extraordinarily primitive elements within a single process – the process of reading.

Psychologists inquiring into how people learn to read, critics writing about what they and others have read: both may enlighten us about reading in innumerable ways, but will leave us with the question of that continuity. Since most writing is about the complex end, we might turn rather to the other end, first of all. At once the scale of the difficulty is revealed: if there is this continuity, and if already we fail in accounting for psychosomatic change, can any discourse respect the continuity while not converting it into one more observable phenomenon?

A first clue comes from the earlier moments of reading as a learned practice. Once the beginner accepts the notion that he may make a connection between a given printed symbol and a given, presumably familiar sound, the possibility of something like a game exists, the more excitingly in that he will not yet know how big a game it is: it is too early to look for answers to questions like 'How many connections can I make?' or 'Does it always work the same way?' Success in a new venture of uncertain scope seems likely to associate, for some little time at least, deciphering with pleasure, particularly as acts of deciphering will be brief forays rather than extended scrutinies. There will be a point, however, at which the notion of a possible, even a necessary continuity (of deciphering and of what is to be deciphered) appears in the consciousness of the reader. From this point on the reader's situation is entirely different; he is faced with choices and decisions that are only marginally connected with deciphering. Brief forays, like muscle-flexings, sketch the possibility, even the imminence of a new activity, but without committing the venturer to the venture; the base, in our chosen example of the new learner, is still non-reading. What is next possible is prolonged absence from that base, from which a bit of reality is now explored indirectly via a book. Both elements are important in this development: the absence because it involves a serious redirection of attention (and in particular a turning-away from what other people are doing); and the indirectness because the decision to read is like a decision which puts the self at risk – a first dive, for example, or a musical solo – but unlike these, leads to no more direct involvement with the world, no externally sanctioned release. The indirectness restarts and extends a crucial process previously lived through only in preconscious experience: the infant's discovery that a known figure who has disappeared from view can reappear with the same characteristics. But what is new is that the apprentice reader has to decide to withdraw attention from the external world (including the book as object) *and* from his own internal world as a preliminary to an experience which is unpredictable and, in an important sense, unshareable. We can hardly be surprised that many gifted and sensitive children show reluctance to let reading get beyond the earliest stage. They are aware, even if not explicitly, that the recommended activity is one which involves a serious, because partial, lack of control, but brings no certainty of reward while offering no noticeable physical challenge (unlike, say, rock-climbing). The reader must agree to surrender before fighting the battle. It begins bodily: movement is to be avoided as far as possible; excitement or self-control are tolerable only from *within* a reading already successfully begun; awareness of the presence of others must be minimal; and consciousness of any or all of these constraints is seriously or totally inhibiting. The activity must be played out, at a first and yet also a permanent level, in the narrow limits prescribed by the eyes' ability to identify with certain black marks on a page. It is not my intention to make reading seem unbearably difficult or hazardous of access. But what is surprising is that, on the whole, these children do learn to read, sooner or later, for they have hit on a central and uncomfortable truth, one that we find again as part of the force of these words, from a rather more experienced word-user: 'Strictement j'envisage . . . la lecture comme une pratique désespérée.'[2]

The order of truth involved is uncomfortable in more than one way: the emphasis on struggle, risk, reluctance as readerly experiences tends to shut out the potential glories of reader–writer encounter; and the focus on decision, on boundaries (whether to 'go into' this partly alien territory or not) may have something of the effect which, I initially suggested, was produced by an unexpected intrusion of self-consciousness – like the causing of embarrassment over one's way of walking. Much teaching – and many assumptions underlying the language of an old-fashioned naturalistic criticism – will for obvious reasons play it down, or at least suggest that it is a consequence of inexperience, a mere stage, perhaps even an accident of mood or disposition. But there is a form of the discomfort which makes dismissal rather more obviously suspect: the concentration in the present argument is neither on the time before any given decision about reading has to be made, nor on the later time when a given reading is actually and successfully taking place, but on the segment of time between. Our general reluctance to linger on it should act as a warning signal: when we hurry away from any experience not already placed on some scale of social or moral acceptability, it is at least probable that more is going on than we are prepared to admit. Our language and our practice are, as ever, one: there is no familiar body of discourse concerned with this intermediate time; no equivalent of that branch of learning theory which bears on reading, or on the other side, of literary criticism. There are of course plausible enough practical reasons why this should be so: the activity of reading and all our other activities already generate and justify all the attention we can give them. But we are not yet clear what reading actually is; or whether there really is an alternative base which it offers. And it is this connection between the time of unease and the time of reading which we must get clearer, if we are ever to understand what the total process involves.

Think what happens when an experienced reader with a literary background sets out to read, say, the first page of a novel in a language which he or she knows much less well. We could sharpen the thought by positing that the reader has already read that page 'in translation', has read another version of it in another language and is embarking on *Der Tod in Venedig*, having read *Death in Venice* or *La Mort à Venise*. The very fact that the hypothetical reader is experienced makes likely a felt contrast (painful, one would guess) between familiar reading speeds and the rate of advance now. The experienced reader will know what it is like to read slowly in his or her own language: to engage, for example, with writing whose force, or charge, or complexity, or tonal unpredictability, make rapid, uni-directional progress unthinkable or undesirable. But the contact with the less-well-known language (distinct in this, of course, from a totally unknown and therefore finally unchallenging language) promotes, by contrast, estrangement. The effort to decipher ('looking up' words, trying to remember, to guess, to associate) brings its own excitement; but that excitement merely throws into sharper relief the intermittent awareness that deciphering is preliminary to reading. To the question, which may or may not be explicit, 'shall I ever be able to read this, in the way I can read other things?', no answer is given. Determination, patience, assiduity: these will in all probability bring about the desired result (in which case, as happens all the time with small children, the difficulty shrinks to invisibility, its urgency not only forgotten but inconceivable). But that doesn't affect the estrangement, the acute sense of lostness, while it is active (one thinks of that poignantly accurate title *Lost in Translation* which Eva Hoffman gave to her account of a brutal transition between post-war Poland and Canada). It is not a question of 'if I could only go faster'. Speed is only a factor within a relation. What is at issue is that there is, as yet, no recognizable relation. To read is to form a relation, only incidentally to put up a performance.

Deciphering may not yet be reading, but the time of deciphering is far from being dismissible on that account. For a start, it is a time in which the signifier (in Saussure's sense) cannot be immediately bypassed in favour of the signified. One stares at, tries to get the mouth round, consonantal clusters in German or Russian (or, for others, in English), rivers of vowels in the Romance languages, endless-seeming 'words' in Finnish or Hungarian. In these revaluings of alphabets, the tentative approaches to consonants, syllables and rhythms, we are given a chance to work free of illusions about the transparency, the 'naturalness' of language. And in so doing we are, among other things, moving in the terrain of poetry, where words have never been mere carriers of dictionary meaning. Strangeness is not just the desert of separation; it is also the ground of acquaintance, the indication of where relation might come about.

As soon as we turn our face away from the problems of the beginner, we can recognize that most, if not all, the elements can be found too in the experience of practised readers. Reading can never really become an automatic process, the unproblematic deploying of a learned skill. We should not confuse successful reading with reading *tout court*, or assume that there can only be either successful reading or none at all. Uncertainty in the first explorings of something written – and we may meet it, in line with our temperament, with anything from fear to irritated impatience – is rapidly dismissed or forgotten when the contact goes well. But we are perhaps too good at that kind of dismissing and forgetting: going through agonies before an important interview, then, if we have been successful, rewriting history to give ourselves a less unflattering role. But the uncertainty is not some ridiculous extra, some temperamental flaw: it is an unavoidable part of experience. We arrive at the possibility of easy, or easier, movement by living through (as distinct from willing ourselves through) the stage of inhibition or lostness.

We need think only of the writer with whom 'we can't get on', yet who evokes no easily discernible hostile feelings in us. The confidence of experience allows us to find ways of disguising failure: 'The words stay on the page', 'No matter how many times I read over the beginning I can't seem to get into it', and so on. But it is a failure to make the move from the first base to what for the moment we may still call the second, or from living to reading; and if it were to happen several times in succession with different writers we might be, at the least, seriously embarrassed. The embarrassment is interesting for the light it throws, not on us as variable individuals, but on the vague assumptions we appear to make about security. If defeat is a possibility, then the notion of the second base as a zone of ease is a hope, not a description; we are confusing our pleasure in successful reading with the activity as a whole. There is no question of denying that readings may be successful or unsuccessful; the point is to know what happens in reading such that 'successful' or 'unsuccessful' can be invoked at all. It must be clear that they cannot refer to an *event*, something that happens at a particular moment, but must bear retrospectively on a *process* – a process which itself is not clear. But if risk and challenge are involved as permanent factors whose distinctive force in this process is neutralized only when our reading is successful, then the notion of a base must be revised.

The first 'base' is simply that of our hold on the world: the particular state of readiness, sensory and affective, in which at any given moment we engage either with what we perceive as not-us (people, objects, weather changes, noise, whatever) or with drives or impulses arising from within us from below consciousness. Since all our responses and decisions, whether consciously formulated or not, must issue in performance here, it is not a state we can compare with anything else; this is what it is like to be alive and awake. It is of course by no means necessarily a comfortable state: our hold on the world may be or feel extremely tenuous. Among the forces constituting us are desires and fantasies that it should be otherwise, and these are fed and fanned by that part of our experience which takes us beyond base: sleep, and more specifically, dreams. Longings for omnipotence, for freedom from responsibility, for effortless fulfilment steer us in their turn towards certain kinds of activity which, belonging in real time, seem nevertheless to legitimize, through the establishment of their own internal rules, the switching of our attention away from the endless unpredictabilities of our world over on to a carefully delimited segment of it. Hence games, arts, gambling, soap operas, whatever. In the best examples, permission ('You may safely redirect attention') is reinforced by necessity ('You must redirect attention or you'll miss the pleasure'). But throughout the wide range of examples, we may distinguish those which allow, *inter alia*, direct expression of aggressive impulses and fantasies of omnipotence, or at least of potency and control (the *practice* of the arts, or of games, or of gambling) from those which entail a preliminary subordination of the self to the enterprise of another or others (listening to music, watching a play, looking at a picture).

Of the first we might say that they do not so much belong with the hope or illusion of an 'alternative base' as extending – and, it may well be, complicating – the primary base, since they offer instances of our hold, however partial, on the world. With the second we appear to be in a rather different territory: the handing-over, the deferring to another's venture have more about them of the yielding to daydream which bespeaks a loosening of that hold. But while they may foster this inclination to let go, they need not by any means do so. There is another, and equally relevant, sense of 'deferring' here: that in which, as a moment in a total experiencing which by definition is part of our positive action in the world, we agree in the first instance to wait for the performance of another. But whether we are listening to a story or a quartet or watching a dance or a match, there is an 'it' to engage with: the other's performance is offered in directly perceptible terms (however complex those terms may be). And that is where the difference from reading shows. Just as the severe physical constraints involved in reading can never be relaxed, even where a given act of reading allows access to intense experience, so we can say now that the other's performance will never be directly perceptible: only the written or printed symbols are immediately available. Neither of these facts might seem to weigh very much against the possibilities reading offers, but once again it would be a pity to confuse process with effect. What in reality they draw attention to is an extreme constriction occurring where two immeasurably large phenomena touch; where, for example, one imagination approaches another. What starts by looking like a mere convention, a rule of the game ('Just follow the printed marks and you'll . . .') reveals itself as a central structure, the physical and perceptual constraints imaging a basic human situation in which any contact we make with another person must pass through language.

To this intermediate situation in which one person's language-world is pointed towards another's, there is an immediate and necessary parallel. To want to meet someone face to face is to carry towards the projected encounter an indeterminate mass of hopes and fears, efforts and flaggings of the will, musterings and dispersings of energy; indeed the stronger the wanting, the greater will be the felt force of this alternation.[3] Success and failure lie some distance ahead, beyond a ground signposted with questions like: 'Will I be up to it?' But signposting, like any attempt at ordering, implies the other, less straightforward reality which is to be thus simplified. Wanting is so powerful an ordering that it will drive a path towards success and constitute that path as the dominant feature of the terrain. Such a venture will meet resistance, as will any move away from the already experienced; but where the goal, as here, involves a creature capable of independent choice, that resistance is much more intense, and may release very primitive feelings. The possibility that the hazarding of the self (explicable only in terms of desire) may be undertaken for nothing (meet no corresponding desire in the other) is a profoundly disturbing one, for in it desire is seen both as the only procurer of satisfaction and as that which may, once acted on, expose the self to humiliation and the denial of satisfaction. And with that we are back in the infant's world: wanting our wanting to be a necessary and sufficient condition. But, rare cases apart, we can't stay there. What one learns to do is to point a version of oneself towards the other, resolving the rest by focusing attention on his response so that tactical mistakes can be redeemed or surprise encounters accommodated. Suddenly in the present, two people are in conversation; anticipation is overtaken by experience; two mutually unknown worlds touch in an exchange of worlds, hallowed and governed by immemorial practice. Where

there has been no wanting on the part of the other there has been its
equivalent: the mustering of as many resources as seem necessary
to sustain the encounter without hurt or strain. The soundings and
explorations which follow are the constituents of a new reality, the
unknowable scope of which commands a new attention. Yet even
with the greatest possible goodwill from both parties, and however
wide the verbal territory each has covered before arriving at the
encounter, connection can be made only through the language of
each to the other.

Here, surely, we have our first serious clue to the nature of reading, which does not so much *resemble* what we have been looking at
as form one apparently eccentric mode of it. Such eccentricity as it
may have is in the *form* of the encounter, not in the forces at work
in it; and we shall see later that even that concession may be too
great and, for this and other reasons, misleading.

For the moment let us rather concentrate on the ways in which
connection is made: how the small range of gestural and spoken
language that makes up conversation, or the compressed offerings
and decipherings which join writer to reader, can carry enough of
the flow from each of two distinct personalities to allow even the
hope of pleasure. We can see straight away that there can be no
question of a direct exchange: although we talk of 'throwing ourselves into' this or that reading, we are unlikely, even in fantasy, to
conceive the possibility of ourselves ending up inside the writer's
reality, becoming one with him. We remain witnesses, and witnesses moreover to the product of that reality, not to the anterior
reality itself, however much the first may suggest about the second.
And of course the product is available to us in one form only –
written words. But if it is true that we do not in reading become the
originator of the words, it is also true that they are not simply made
over to us as some raw material which we might, gratefully receiving, transform into a private artefact. (We may and do play at this,
but this mild cheating hardly affects the general argument. Nothing
can annul the anteriority of the other's words; and, as we shall see,
the metaphor of raw material is illegitimate.) If, to put it more
simply still, we can neither offer nor absorb the words of another,
the connection must be indirect. It remains for us to see just how
indirect it is, and what form the indirection takes. One feature
perhaps deserves immediate attention: the way in which it is established in time. The other's words are, in both senses, there before
us; we follow them. This situation can be described in several ways,

but what is most interesting in it is that some of these ways not only may be but frequently are contradictory. In one version, for example, the writer has, by allowing the arrangement of words to reach us in his absence, given us, silent judges, all the evidence we need in order to formulate a verdict. From the writer as prisoner we pass to the writer as invader issuing an unbroken series of instructions for the direction of our attention; as procurer, knowledgeable in the illusory relations we crave; as isolate, arrogantly or humbly recording the inside of his head without reference to our concerns. And of course these and their like, with or without the caricatural edge, are not types of writer but kinds of relation between. So while the priority of the writer's words has, as we have seen, blocked any possibility of substitution and appropriation, it does not by itself determine the nature of the relation. What the examples make clear is that that relation has to do with *control*; with what might, at an appropriately primitive level, be pointed at in the question 'Who is doing what to whom?' (I ask or allow a clown to do his turn, and from my freedom laugh or don't laugh; I shiver and submit to the unexpected anger of an intimate; I behave erratically when faced with a behaviour I can't place; and so on.) Now this connotation of control, endlessly familiar from our direct dealings with others, is a little more puzzling in the indirect contact of reading. The priority in time of the other's words is given spatial expression as well: we hold in our hands the entire body of the words.

And of course it is not only in this sense that the connection is indirect: there is the question of address. We know one context where there is no mystery as to why connection can be such as to release the full play of dependent, dominating or submissive feelings: the reading of a letter from a valued other. It would be tempting to say that what really happens is that, wanting certain kinds of things to be said as tokens of a pre-existing relationship, we scrutinize the letter for their presence or absence, either of which, by setting off an echo in the continuing relationship, will belong to the mode of direct connection. But even in this instance, and however charged certain phrases may, by custom or desire, have become, there is no connection to be made except with the words, which here must take the strain of what, in face-to-face encounter, is carried by bodily presence: gesture and voice as well as word, experienced not only as immediate but as part of a history, a continuity. So since we can notoriously be led into intense turmoil by reading the words of the letter, while recognizing that these words

have no predetermined value, we move to thinking that the uni-
fying factor is our awareness of the other's characteristic linguistic
performance: shifts in tone, surprising emphases, familiar pattern-
ings perceived in a context shaped by habit and the assumptions
and predictions it generates. But, relevant though such developed
awareness is, it cannot give us the whole answer. We may know or
guess, for example, that venturing into writing is experienced by
the other as hazardous or even frightening; written performance
may then be so much at variance with spoken that it is to that fact
(maddeningly, saddeningly, fondly, embarrassedly) that developed awareness draws our attention. Now we have layer on layer
of indirectness: ultimately what we are seeing is not simply
the achieved performance of the other but the evidence of something more elusive – his relationship with his own words, the
extent to which this other that we know is vested in verbal representations, and the manner of that investment. In this connection,
the timorous letter-writer is not the least interesting example. The
general wish, however strong, to 'be in touch' with someone else is
only one of the factors at work, and is indeed unusual in being
positive; but then it arises from the non-particularized desires ori-
ginating in a relationship between persons. It functions, in fact, as a
simplifier, promoting the wish to be in some way directly available
to the other, without reference to the mode in which availability
can be realized. The other factors, however, bear on the mode as
well, and it is these which bring hesitation, constraint, even occasionally contrary desire (where the risks seem to outweigh the
pleasures conceived earlier; this is the letter that will not be written
or will be postponed). And they may turn on the writer's freedom
in relation to words. He may, for example, have been earlier
ravished by words from his other (may even, along the lines we are
pursuing here, have grasped how such excitement can have arisen
from reading them); but that offers no guarantees or even hints for
his own subsequent performance. Indeed the other's words have
introduced two new constraints: the felt need to do other than
borrow or repeat them, the felt need to be all the same 'up' to them.
These would be alarming enough if they were merely challenges to
ingenuity or range or capacity for intensity, issued to someone who
had all the same free access to words. But access is not free. Diction-
aries may suggest that words can be arranged in such a way as to
be, so to speak, equidistant from our central fears and desires,
sitting like tools on shelves. We may like to contrast the disturbance

produced in us by contingent verbal events with some ultimate possible equanimity about words, but we're unlikely to know many people who have ever found or even glimpsed this paradisal state. What starts for each of us with the unobserved chargings-up of certain words and phrases in early experience continues with the endless implications of our discovery that all others are other, and cannot speak even the same words as ourselves without being other. From this comes an unsought awareness of boundaries, of limits and limitations, and, with that, the notion of performance. Performing means risking: facing the double challenge of our private attitudes to words and of others' reception of those we utter. And while we may persuade ourselves that the exchanges of speech are so quickly over that the risk is bearable, we are likely to see writing as giving hostages to fortune.

If there is little we can do about unconscious or preconscious revulsions or preferences, we are quick to learn a way of apparently answering the other part of the challenge: anticipating the judgement of others by imagining ourselves to be receiver as well as sender of the words. This familiar and, on the whole, painful and unsatisfactory practice is, like many of those we are considering, profoundly ambiguous. In one conception of it we are close to the assumption of omnipotence: I predict and make bold to determine your response by the manner of my saying. In another we are closer to self-abasement: unless I can make this good enough – and perhaps even then – you will destroy me. And of course we could add other versions. Any or all of these will repay attention, but none has such general interest as the practice itself, however particular needs may colour it. Because it inevitably emphasizes the implied response of the other, it tends to play down the extent to which the imaginary judge is attending to the self. For here is not only 'What will he think of me when he reads this?' but 'What sort of me do these words suggest?'; not only an awareness, welcome or unwelcome, of the other's freedom, but an intuition, clear or confused, of the distance between intention and performance. Memory and desire may sustain the hesitant letter-writer for a while, the surge of unconstrained words momentarily drowning out hesitation, aligning permission with wish. But if the surge is over before the letter is finished and dispatched, the doubts return intensified. The writer's clear, if by no means necessarily exhaustive, awareness of intention reappears and is at once directed on to what has been produced during its brief abeyance. By a harsh symmetry, it is now the imagined permission which is withdrawn: the words written must stand alone to face the test of intention. Yet if desire cannot guarantee the desired result, intention, for all its implied awareness of self, of other and of the offering that purports to connect them, can do little more than make clear the size of the difficulty. The hesitant writer must either give up or move to a different conception of the enterprise. If he does finish the letter he will have made this move, even if he feels he has merely failed to satisfy the earlier conception. What he has done, however reluctantly, is to allow to go out a body of words which stands in a certain relation both to his own desires and to what he believes are the desires of the other, without being in a position to determine what that relation is. The body of words will be neither wholly justified by his desire nor wholly deprived of its informing strength; neither, since it is the body of *his* words, can it be wholly appropriated by the other. So it comes about that the writer of the letter, whatever his attitude to the relationship with the person to whom it is addressed, can work only on the words of his letter; and then only in hope, not in knowledge, of success. And with that, for all the weight of special circumstance (awareness of a particular other, shared experience, immediate desires and fears), he reaches the position of the writer *tout court*. By his work on and in the words, his provisional and simultaneous resolution of private attitudes to them, designs for them, reliance on them, all accompanied by his recognition of the necessarily partial hold on them (they are his words but they are also drawn from the common stock) – by this work he is establishing in words the constituents of a possible 'I'. It is as yet no more than a possible 'I'; there remains the perceiving of these constituents and the synthesizing of them; that is, the other work we call reading.

Of these two central notions, 'work' and 'I', let us look first at work. When we have reminded ourselves that even in letters to intimates, and despite the desire for immediate presence which impels the writing of them, there is no possibility of operating directly on the other, we reach a crossroads. The energy which accompanies and sustains the writing does not function in a void: if some part of it goes to feed the fantasy of direct connection, it must be part only. The scrutiny of our own words which we are drawn to is already evidence that something else is going on. The severity of our judgement will vary with temperament and circumstance, but these cannot account for the judging itself. Energy flows because in the moment in which we set about writing we re-enact in transposed form the irreducible human experience: a self confronting another self or other selves in the world. Just as the self cannot, outside madness, wholly determine its own reality, so it cannot, in the transposed encounter which is writing, exhaustively prescribe the terms in which the words are to be received. But this means, among other things, that writing is the ground of yet another encounter, located this time within the self: that between desire and experience. Whatever the form, intensity or direction of the desire, writing is inconceivable without it, while, at the same time, what we discover to be the impossibility of controlling the enacted form of that desire (the words written) entails its partial frustration. The blank page and the other's absence offer the writer an apparently total freedom; but whatever the nature of the relation with the other, the only way in which he can exercise that freedom is through the signs by which also the other's freedom can alone be expressed. Nor do attempts to break the pattern of indirectness ('Please believe me; I really mean this') have privileged force. To write at all is to settle for the desire over the fears of frustration. The 'work' is what goes into the resolution of a conflict in which not only these two elements but also residual longing for direct connection take part. Thus, against the odds, what starts out from a spontaneous wish to connect in the most personal way moves inevitably towards an exercise in composition; and the effort to reach the other, towards an argument with the self.

One extreme form of this argument (that in which the self, writing, tries to short-circuit response by assuming the judicial position of the other, reading) is so familiar in its barrenness that it has tended to obscure what in the central process is neither wasteful nor even avoidable. For the fact that our words belong to the common stock is relevant in more than one way. It is not possible for us to identify the moment at which, on the way to writing, impulsion issues in words. But, for as long as the prompting lasts, the emergent words are experienced as continuous with the impulsion. It is when, the prompting over, the words have taken their place on the page that the continuity is broken. The separation, symbolic and actual, allows renewed awareness of the words as having an existence independent of us, as being part of the common stock and so the property of none, as registering the absence of the previously sustaining continuity, as precariously viable, and so on. This moment is a node; through it pass in lines the several ways we apprehend it: the line that runs between intention and realization, the line connecting private-and-continuous with public-and-disjoined, the line from manic (the confident surge of creativity) to depressive (the verdict of the internal 'hanging judge'). But, as the metaphor suggests, the moment contains elements of all these oppositions. And because of that, the moment is dynamic, not static. The energy generated to deal with the tension between and across these operations must, if it is strong enough to overcome the paralysis or renunciation which is the only other resolution of that tension, catch up all the elements (temperamental, experiential, intellectual) in a single complex act. The territory of that act is, however, and can only be, words; resolution, therefore, however provisional, is accomplished in a stylization which promotes one of the elements to the central position: the opposition between language as private and continuous and language as common and disjoined. The 'work' is the effort to resolve, at each point of the writing and in the whole of it, that particular opposition. And because we arrive at verbalization in strictly private ways but are at the same time always aware of language as functioning outside us (as something we react to, have views on), the writing we do is not our considered 'answer' to a stated 'problem'; it is the form of our response to a situation we cannot control but find ourselves, through desire, involved in.

But if the writer's 'work', made necessary by the encounter of desire with the later oppositions, yields for the reader the form of the writer's response, it has by the same token achieved something else as well: the establishing, by way of words, of the writer's 'I'. For, whatever apparent permissions the intimate letter offers its writer for display of the *word* 'I' (or of course for coyness about such display), the controlling, intentional aspect is merely a component of the perceived 'I'. My words, the form of my response to desire and its oppositions as instanced in my struggle with language, in fact allow the reader of my letter to see the 'I' who is engaged in that struggle – whatever I am saying. But then my reader is not outside the struggle either. For that which enables him to perceive the 'I' of the letter is only partly memory and expectation (forms of attention which make of the letter a mere token or trigger); the other part is his awareness of how the form of my language struggle is related to his experience of his own. Locked for ever in the attempt to resolve our own language conflict, we watch, with the fascination of familiarity, the attempt of another. Thus, even in the most safely circumscribed of verbal relations – no doubt as to who is being addressed and who is making the address; shared experience; the justification of temporary absence and nameable desire – the relation between writer and reader is shaped by processes that have only indirectly to do with the person-to-person connection.

In turning, then, to the more open territory of poetry and fiction, we are not so much moving to a separate world as seeing the same ground with certain landmarks removed. Because contact must still be described in terms of the alignment of one individual's language practice with another's, it is a ground which will seem both totally familiar and wholly strange, like the landscapes we cross in dreams. The relationship, now hardly if at all compounded with direct experience, can be forged only by the play of one person's words on another's. For the writer this is an altogether more hazardous venturing, for the reader a far more problematic encounter. And this is likely to mean a steep increase in defensive activity. On the novelist's or poet's side, the argument with the self, the 'work', is intensified, since he or she can have no knowledge of the language practice of his or her putative readers. If freedom of movement is that much the greater, so are the risks attending that freedom. The writer is offering the terms of a notional relation, while being, until it is too late, the only witness to the adequacy of the terms. The temptations are many and familiar (the stridency of tone that marks a leading-with-the-chin, the recourse to self-distancing that invites collusion in 'knowingness', the attempt to short-circuit the difficulty by instancing verbal inadequacy within the fiction, and so on), but these are in the end merely variants of a single false hope: that one may both issue the challenge of words and, by an act of will, determine the response to that challenge. Indeed so false and yet so widespread is the hope (not only can the writer not resolve single-handed the question of reception, but the reader, who has his own temptations, may refuse to see challenge at all, preferring to take the words as a gift or an injection) that we must either assume most writers to be solipsists or conclude that there is being enacted in their words, whatever else these carry, the whole play of their desire and fear. The extent to which any given writer is aware of this may vary, but no degree of awareness will allow escape from the difficulty itself: the naming of central feelings may ease them, but it cannot resolve them. We are brought back to a final sense of 'work', of 'I' and of indirectness.

If we turn again now, before trying to suggest what that is, to the reader's side, it is less a postponing than a filling out. It may be tempting to see reading as, like swimming, an example of the kind of psycho-physical control we can, however painfully, learn. But, even when we have allowed for the extra difficulty which words bring into the experience, we are likely to forget or play down one factor. For if in one sense reading a new book is, as we have seen, like meeting a new person, and even though from the writer's side words have to do duty for everything else in that meeting, the fact is that they also take the reader, almost from the start, far beyond the terms of all but the most exceptional first meeting. Precisely because the writer has consented to the particular kind of coherence, of finishedness, that writers present, because he has, in so doing, revealed so much of his way of resolving his language conflict, his new acquaintance – the reader – is miles behind. The 'ordinary life' parallel, indeed, might rather be that of eavesdropping on highly charged words directed at someone else. One passes, within minutes of the beginning, from unfamiliarity to intimacy. Nor is this astounding result produced by the skill one has learned: that merely puts the overhearer, so to speak, in a position to eavesdrop. We cannot therefore draw up some simple parallelism between the writer's position and the reader's, in which, say, intention would correspond to expectation, active to passive, and so on. The reader's language practice is not simply aligned with the writer's: it has first to discover what that is and then, working from the signals generated by the discovery, accommodate the discovered practice. The challenge of irony comes readily to mind as an example, because irony is a specific testing of the capacity to accommodate: to discern it, to negotiate with it. And here too we meet an indispensable element of much earlier experience: the gradual emergence of trust. But trust too is no simple one-sided affair. In learning to trust the other, we are accepting a trust in ourselves in relation to that other. And with or without irony there will always be challenge. Even where the words carry reassuring labels (we have only to remember the force of titles like *The Body in the Library* or, for Wodehouse lovers, *Summer at Blandings*), it is still necessary to find out: disappointment, or worse, is always possible.

And so we come to the hardest question of all: how is it possible to map together these separate worlds in a conception of fiction that will not deny or merely wish away their autonomy and their separateness? It is not, after all, possible for us to 'map' human behaviour, settling for the imposition of the lowest common denominator; and perhaps fiction, too, is inconceivably diverse. But that diversity, that unpredictability, may supply the key. It is not mere perversity that keeps us, on the whole, living, even though 'life' is unmanageable; reading or writing novels and poems even though 'fiction' is unmanageable. If all the modes of language record and enact in transposed form our hold on the world, it is fiction which, with peculiar insistence, maintains the sense of that hold as *venture* rather than imposition: as adventure, as journey, as exploration in time and space. It continues to do so, and we continue to turn to it, because we are endlessly preoccupied with boundaries. Early representations of these ('enemy lines', 'the edge of the forest') may be simple, but the play of our excitement is rather less so. By way of these named boundaries we are led into the prereflective exploration and provisional redrawing of others (fantasy/reality, tolerable/intolerable, I/he or she, and, of course, reading/doing). Even in the immediate post-decipherment stage of reading, there is, as we have seen, room for preliminary discriminations, however inarticulate: reading itself felt as a possible adventure which in prospect disquiets some, attracts others. Here too we can discover trust: but that requires the risking, the venturing into uncertain ground, the acceptance of the danger of being lost or merely foolish. What is in any event set up is a possible connection between the words (written and read) and the provisional boundaries of the self, and that connection, indeed, is not wholly determined by the self.

Moreover, to the spatial emphasis in 'boundaries' we must add the temporal emphasis in 'exploration'. Novels in particular, whatever the ostensible complexities of their surface patterns (narrative direction, tonal variations and so on), can also recreate that formal continuity which is the other great feature of our venturing: that, with whatever halts or lapses, we *go on*. And it does so as experience rather than as demonstration: only by being 'in' the fiction can we know the shiftings 'in' the self, just as it is only the possibility of movements within the self which makes accessible the transpositions which are fiction. One example will perhaps serve: Alice and her looking-glass. When Alice passes effortlessly through the glass and into the other world, she is – we are to discover – in the territory we have known as dream, a territory in which assumptions about boundaries no longer hold. But we, in reading, are not dreaming; we are, *inter alia*, accommodating the vision by means of skills belonging in the non-dream world. Nor can Lewis Carroll write this dream without such skills. Even those of us who may prefer 'dreams' to 'reality' must, if we are to apprehend *this* 'dream', read these non-dream words. The venture which is reading with all its difficulties must precede the venture which is imaginatively following Alice; the words are reflecting surface *and* magic door.

In the end, *one adventure must stand for all*: that in which the reader, enmeshed lifelong in his attempt to verbalize 'I', meets the writer, who has issued an interim representation of his own attempt. When, for example, in *Oedipus the King*, after the unbearably charged exchanges between Oedipus and the Corinthian, Jocasta breaks her silence, she does not only warn of doom: she lets in, by the very act of speaking, the words which, we now know, her knowledge brought her during those very exchanges to which she had been helpless witness. Our sudden sensing of Sophocles' design, and of how our distracted attention had, Oedipus-like, filled us with unwarranted fancies, reminds us how far our reading is from the triumphant exercise of control, or even understanding. Yet at that moment of realization, it seems as if there is no distance between our words and the words of the other, and the distance between our struggle and the struggle inside the text has been for once abolished.

Unable to reach any reader direct, the writer works in the area between the subject (his whole self, forever unknowable) and the 'I' that he knows (writer, reader, comparer, aspirer); the work is a dialogue across the space between; the result is his language – provisional, opaque, other. By venturing out into a ground in which one's sovereignty does not run, a no man's land, the writer lays himself or herself open to every kind of response, including indifference; (s)he is also taking the step without which no contact is possible. This 'dialogue' – the transposed attempt to explore one's frontiers, however they have been established – is what the reader reads. Challenge, invitation, confession, demonstration: it is all of these, and more. And it at once puts under stress the language practice of the reader, bound, unless (s)he refuses the contact, to experience it as a testing of one's frontiers. Whether he or she is swept away, brought up short, briefly amused or gradually repelled will depend on how far, in the no man's land, the writer's 'dialogue' creates the conditions of a corresponding 'dialogue' in the reader. Only when each has had to forgo direct sight of the other can relation be established. To the form of one person's venture responds the form of another's: the unspeakable contact is made across the ground of fiction.

The process may go no further than the reader's initial scan: we may turn away in disgust or boredom; we may fail, angrily or ruefully, to make anything of a particular piece of writing. But if it does go further, it will be because we decide to relax our precautionary wariness so that the words of the other can be let in among our words. Each time we read on, we let in a Trojan horse. The subliminal scanning goes on, intense and continual (as in the most intimate of circumstances we are instantly aware of the minutest inflection of the presence of the other: a checked smile, a change of timbre, a sensed acceleration or slowing); but more and more the sense is that these are words that can be trusted, that have an autonomy that can connect with ours, can even, without necessarily destroying us, move beyond ours. We may not be able to describe the relation, but we can live in it, and when we do so, we are reading.

Notes

1.   Walter J. Ong, *Orality and Literacy* (London: Routledge, 1991).
2.   Stephane Mallarmé, 'La Musique et les Lettres', in *Oeuvres Completes*, Bibliothèque de la Pleiade (Paris, 1945), p. 647.
3.   Compare T.S. Eliot, 'Little Gidding', II, 'In the uncertain hour before the morning/Near the ending of interminable night':

> And as I fixed upon the down-turned face
> That pointed scrutiny with which we challenge
>   The first-met stranger in the waning dusk
>   I caught the sudden look of some dead master
> Whom I had known, forgotten, half recalled
>   Both one and many; in the brown baked features
>   The eyes of a familiar compound ghost
> Both intimate and unidentifiable.
>   So I assumed a double part, and cried
>   And heard another's voice cry: 'What! are *you* here?'
> Although we were not. I was still the same,
>   Knowing myself yet being something other –
>   And he a face still forming; yet the words sufficed
> To compel the recognition they preceded.

Part Two
Reading, Poetry and Vision

3

Two Essays at Human Assemblies

JOSEPH BRODSKY

HOW TO READ A BOOK
(THOUGHTS FROM THE TURIN BOOK FAIR)

The idea of a book fair in the city where, a century ago, Nietzsche lost his mind has, in its turn, a nice ring of madness. A Mobius strip (commonly known as a vicious circle), to be precise, for several stalls in this book fair are occupied by the complete or selected works of this great German. On the whole, infinity is a fairly palpable aspect of this business of publishing, if only because it extends a dead author's existence beyond the limits he envisioned, or provides a living author with a future which we all prefer to regard as unending.

On the whole, books are indeed less finite than ourselves. Even the worst among them outlast their authors – mainly because they occupy a smaller amount of physical space than those who penned them. Often they sit on the shelves absorbing dust long after the writer himself has turned into a handful of dust. Yet even this form of the future is better than the memory of a few surviving relatives or friends on which one cannot rely, and often it is precisely the appetite for this posthumous dimension which sets one's pen in motion.

So as we toss and turn these rectangular objects in our hands – those in octavo, in quarto, in duodecimo, etc., etc. – we won't be terribly amiss if we surmise that we fondle in our hands, as it were, the actual or potential urns with our returning ashes. After all, what goes into writing a book – be it a novel, a philosophical treatise, a collection of poems, a biography, or a thriller – is, ultimately, a man's only life: good or bad, but always finite. Whoever said that to philosophize is an exercise in dying was right in more ways than one, for by writing a book nobody gets younger.

61

Nor does one become any younger by reading a book. Since this is so, our natural preference should be for good books. The paradox, however, lies in the fact that in literature, as nearly everywhere, 'good' is not an autonomous category: it is defined by its distinction from 'bad'. What's more, in order to write a good book, a writer must read a great deal of pulp – otherwise he won't be able to develop the necessary criteria. That's what may constitute bad literature's best defence at the Last Judgement.

Yet since we are all moribund, and since reading books is time consuming, we must devise a system that allows us a semblance of economy. Of course, there is no denying the possible pleasure of holing up with a fat, slow-moving, mediocre novel; still, we all know that we can indulge ourselves in that fashion only so much. In the end, we read not for reading's sake but to learn. Hence the need for concision, condensation, fusion – for the works that bring the human predicament, in all its diversity, into its sharpest possible focus; in other words, the need for a shortcut. Hence, too – as a by-product of our suspicion that such shortcuts exist (and they do, but about that later) – the need for some compass in the ocean of available literature.

The role of that compass, of course, is played by literary criticism, by reviewers. Alas, its needle oscillates wildly. What is north for some is south (South America, to be precise) for others; the same goes in an even wilder degree for east and west. The trouble with a reviewer is (minimum) threefold: (a) he can be a hack, and as ignorant as ourselves; (b) he can have strong predilections for a certain kind of writing or simply be on the take with the publishing industry; and (c) if he is a writer of talent, he will turn his review writing into an independent art form – Jorge Luis Borges is a case in point – and you may end up reading reviews rather than the books themselves.

In any case, you find yourselves adrift in the ocean, with pages and pages rustling in every direction, clinging to a raft whose ability to stay afloat you are not so sure of. The alternative, therefore, would be to develop your own taste, to build your own compass, to familiarize yourself, as it were, with particular stars and constellations – dim or bright but always remote. This, however, takes a hell of a lot of time, and you may easily find yourself old and grey, heading for the exit with a lousy volume under your arm. Another alternative – or perhaps just a part of the same – is to rely on hearsay: a friend's advice, a reference caught in a text you happen to like. Although not institutionalized in any fashion (which wouldn't be such a bad idea), this kind of procedure is familiar to all of us from a tender age. Yet this, too, proves to be poor insurance, for the ocean of available literature swells and widens constantly, as this book fair amply testifies: it is yet another tempest in that ocean.

So where is terra firma, even though it may be but an uninhabitable island? Where is our good man Friday, let alone a Cheeta?

Before I come up with my suggestion – nay! what I perceive as being the only solution for developing sound taste in literature – I'd like to say a few words about this solution's source, i.e. about my humble self – not because of my personal vanity, but because I believe that the value of an idea is related to the context from which it emerges. Indeed, had I been a publisher, I'd be putting on my books' covers not only their authors' names but also the exact age at which they composed this or that work, in order to enable their readers to decide whether the readers care to reckon with the information or the views contained in a book written by a man so much younger – or, for that matter, so much older – than they themselves.

The source of the suggestion to come belongs to the category of people (alas, I can no longer use the term 'generation', which implies a certain sense of mass and unity) for whom literature has always been a matter of some hundred names; to the people whose social graces would make Robinson Crusoe or even Tarzan wince; to those who feel awkward at large gatherings, do not dance at parties, tend to find metaphysical excuses for adultery, and are finicky about discussing politics; the people who dislike themselves far more than their detractors do; who still prefer alcohol and tobacco to heroin and marijuana – those whom, in W.H. Auden's words, 'one will not find on the barricades and who never shoot themselves or their lovers.' If such people occasionally find themselves swimming in their blood on the floor of prison cells or speaking from a platform, it is because they rebel against (or, more precisely, object to) not some particular injustice but the order of the world as a whole. They have no illusions about the objectivity of the views they put forth; on the contrary, they insist on their unpardonable subjectivity right from the threshold. They act in this fashion, however, not for the purpose of shielding themselves from possible attack: as a rule, they are fully aware of the vulnerability pertinent to their views and the positions they defend. Yet – taking the stance somewhat opposite to Darwinian – they consider vulnerability the primary trait of living matter. This, I must add, has less to do with masochistic tendencies, nowadays attributed to almost every man of letters, than with their instinctive, often firsthand knowledge that extreme subjectivity, prejudice and indeed idiosyncrasy are what help art to avoid cliché. And the resistance to cliché is what distinguishes art from life.

Now that you know the background of what I am about to say, I may just as well say it: The way to develop good taste in literature is to read poetry. If you think that I am speaking out of professional partisanship, that I am trying to advance my own guild interests, you are badly mistaken. For, being the supreme form of human locution, poetry is not only the most concise, the most condensed way of conveying the human experience; it also offers the highest possible standards for any linguistic operation – especially one on paper.

The more one reads poetry, the less tolerant one becomes of any sort of verbosity, be it in political or philosophical discourse, in history, social studies or the art of fiction. Good style in prose is always hostage to the precision, speed and laconic intensity of poetic diction. A child of epitaph and epigram, conceived, it appears, as a shortcut to any conceivable subject matter, poetry is a great disciplinarian to prose. It teaches the latter not only the value of each word but also the mercurial mental patterns of the species, alternatives to linear composition, the knack of omitting the self-evident, emphasis on detail, the technique of anticlimax. Above all, poetry develops in prose that appetite for metaphysics which distinguishes a work of art from mere *belles lettres*. It must be admitted, however, that in this particular regard, prose has proven to be a rather lazy pupil.

Please, don't get me wrong: I am not trying to debunk prose. The truth of the matter is that poetry simply happens to be older than prose and thus has covered a greater distance. Literature started with poetry, with the song of a nomad that predates the scribblings of a settler. And although I have compared somewhere the difference between poetry and prose to that between the air force and the infantry, the suggestion that I make now has nothing to do with either hierarchy or the anthropological origins of literature. All am trying to do is to be practical and spare your eyesight and brain cells a lot of useless printed matter. Poetry, one might say, has been invented for just this purpose – for it is synonymous with economy. What one should do, therefore, is repeat, albeit in miniature, the process that took place in our civilization over the course of two millennia. It is easier than you might think, for the body of poetry is far less voluminous than that of prose. What's more, if you are concerned mainly with contemporary literature, then your job is indeed a piece of cake. All you have to do is arm yourselves for a couple of months with the works of poets in your mother tongue, preferably from the first half of this century. I suppose you'll end up with a dozen rather slim books, and by the end of the summer you will be in great shape.

If your mother tongue is English, I might recommend to you Robert Frost, Thomas Hardy, W.B. Yeats, T.S. Eliot, W.H. Auden, Marianne Moore and Elizabeth Bishop. If the language is German, Rainer Maria Rilke, Georg Trakl, Peter Huchel and Gottfried Benn. If it is Spanish, Antonio Machado, Federico García Lorca, Luis Cernuda, Rafael Alberti, Juan Ramón Jiménez and Octavio Paz will do. If the language is Polish – or if you know Polish (which would be to your great advantage, because the most extraordinary poetry of this century is written in that language) – I'd like to mention to you the names of Leopold Staff, Czeslaw Milosz, Zbigniew Herbert and Wyszlaw Szymborska. If it is French, then of course Apollinaire, Jules Supervielle, Pierre Reverdy, Blaise Cendrars, some of Eluard, a bit of Aragon, Victor Segalen and Henri Michaux. If it is Greek, then you should read Constantine Cavafy, George Seferis, Yannis Ritsos. If it is Dutch, then it should be Martinus Nijhoff, particularly his stunning 'Awater'. If it is Portuguese, you should read Fernando Pessoa and perhaps Carlos Drummond de Andrade. If the language is Swedish, read Gunnar Ekelöf, Harry Martinson, Tomas Tranströmer. If it is Russian, it should be, to say the least, Marina Tsvetaeva, Osip Mandelstam, Anna Akhmatova, Boris Pasternak, Vladislav Khodasevich, Viktor Khlebnikov, Nikolai Klyuev. If it is Italian, I mention Quasimodo, Saba, Ungaretti and Montale, simply because I have long wanted to acknowledge my personal, private gratitude and debt to these four great poets whose lines influenced my life rather crucially, and I am glad to do so while standing on Italian soil.

If after going through the works of any of these, you drop a book of prose picked from the shelf, it won't be your fault. If you

continue to read it, that will be to the author's credit; that will mean
that this author has indeed something to add to the truth about our
existence as it was known to these few poets just mentioned; this
would prove at least that this author is not redundant, that his
language has an independent energy or grace. Or else, it would
mean that reading is your incurable addiction. As addictions go, it
is not the worst one.

Let me draw a caricature here, for caricatures accentuate the essential. In this caricature I see a reader whose two hands are occupied
with holding open books. In the left, he holds a collection of poems;
in the right, a volume of prose. Let's see what he drops first. Of
course, he may fill both his palms with prose volumes, but that will
leave him with self-negating criteria. And, of course, he may also
ask what distinguishes good poetry from bad, and where is his
guarantee that what he holds in his left hand is indeed worth
bothering with.
　Well, for one thing, what he holds in his left hand will be, in all
likelihood, lighter than what he holds in the right. Second, poetry,
as Montale once put it, is an incurably semantic art, and chances for
charlatanism in it are extremely low. By the third line a reader will
know what sort of thing he holds in his left hand, for poetry makes
sense fast and the quality of language in it makes itself felt immediately. After three lines he may glance at what he has in his right.
　This is, as I told you, a caricature. At the same time, I believe, this
might be the posture many of you will unwittingly assume at this
book fair. Make sure, at least, that the books in your hands belong
to different genres of literature. Now, this shifting of eyes from left
to right is, of course, a maddening enterprise; still, a hundred years
hence, nobody's insanity will matter much to the multitudes whose
numbers will exceed by far the total of little black letters in all the
books at this book fair put together. So you may as well try the little
trick I've just suggested.

AN IMMODEST PROPOSAL
(INAUGURAL LECTURE AS POET LAUREATE OF THE USA,
1991)

About an hour ago, the stage where I stand now as well as your
seats were quite empty. An hour hence, they will be empty again.

For most of the day, I imagine, this place stays empty; emptiness is its natural state. Had it been endowed with consciousness, it would regard our presence as a nuisance. This is as good an illustration as any of one's significance, in any case; certainly of the significance of our gathering. No matter what brings us here, the ratios are not in our favour. Pleased as we may be with our number, in spatial terms it is of infinitesimal consequence.

This is true, I think, of any human assembly; but when it comes to poetry, it rings a special bell. For one thing, poetry, the writing or the reading of it, is an atomizing art; it is far less social than music or painting. Also, poetry has a certain appetite for emptiness, starting, say, with that of infinity. Mainly, though, because historically speaking the ratio of poetry's audience to the rest of society is not in the former's favour. So we should be pleased with one another, if only because our being here, for all its seeming insignificance, is a continuation of that history which, by some accounts floating around this town, has ended.

Throughout what we call recorded history, the audience for poetry does not appear to have exceeded 1 per cent of the entire population. The basis for this estimate is not any particular research but the mental climate of the world that we live in. In fact, the weather has been such that, at times, the quoted figure seems a bit generous. Neither Greek nor Roman antiquity, nor the glorious Renaissance, nor the Enlightenment provides us with an impression of poetry commanding huge audiences, let alone legions or battalions, or of its readership being vast.

It never was. Those we call the classics owe their reputations not to their contemporaries but to their posterity. This is not to say that posterity is the quantitative expression of their worth. It just supplies them, albeit retroactively and with some effort, with the size of readership to which they were entitled from the beginning. As it was, their actual circumstances were by and large fairly narrow; they courted patrons or flocked to the courts pretty much in the same way poets today go to the universities. Obviously that had to do with the hope of largess, but it was also a quest for an audience. Literacy being the privilege of the few, where else could a poet find a sympathetic ear or an attentive eye for his lines? The seat of power was often the seat of culture; and its diet was better, the company was less monochrome and more tender than elsewhere, including the monastery.

Centuries passed. Seats of power and seats of culture parted ways, it seems for good. That, of course, is the price you pay for democracy, for the rule of the people, by the people, and for the people, of whom still only 1 per cent reads poetry. If a modern poet has anything in common with his Renaissance colleague, it is in the first place the paltry distribution of his work. Depending on one's temperament, one may relish the archetypal aspects of this predicament – pride oneself in being the means of carrying on the hallowed tradition, or derive a similar degree of comfort from one's so well-precedented resignation. There is nothing more psychologically rewarding than linking oneself to the glories of the past, if only because the past is more articulate than the present, not to mention the future.

A poet can always talk himself out of a jam; after all, that's his métier. But I am here to speak not about the predicament of the poet, who is never, in the final analysis, a victim. I am here to speak about the plight of his audience: about your plight, as it were. Since I am paid this year by the Library of Congress, I take this job in the spirit of a public servant, not in any other. So it is the audience for poetry in this country which is my concern; and it is the public servant in me who finds the existing ratio of 1 per cent appalling and scandalous, not to say tragic. Neither my temperament nor the chagrin of an author over his own dismal sales has anything to do with this appraisal.

The standard number of copies of a first or second collection by any poet in this country is something between 2000 and 10 000 (and I speak of the commercial houses only). The latest census that I've seen gives the population of the United States as approximately 250 million. This means that a standard commercial publishing house, printing this or that author's first or second volume, aims at only 0.001 per cent of the entire population. To me, this is absurd.

What stood for centuries in the way of the public's access to poetry was the absence of press and the limitation of literacy. Now both are practically universal, and the aforementioned ratio is no longer justifiable. Actually, even if we are to go by that 1 per cent, it should result in publishers printing not 2000 to 10 000 copies of a poet's collection but 2.5 million. Do we have that many readers of poetry in this country? I believe that we do; in fact, I believe that we have a lot more than that. Just how many could be determined, of course, through market research, but that is precisely what should be avoided.

For market research is restrictive by definition. So is any sociological breakdown of census figures into groups, classes and categories. They presuppose certain binding characteristics pertaining to each social group, ushering in their prescribed treatment. This leads, plain and simple, to a reduction of people's mental diet, to their intellectual resignation. The market for poetry is believed to be those with a college education, and that's whom a publisher targets. The blue-collar crowd is not supposed to read Horace, nor the farmer in his overalls Montale or Marvell. Nor, for that matter, is the politician expected to know by heart Gerard Manley Hopkins or Elizabeth Bishop.

This is dumb as well as dangerous. More about that later. For the moment I'd like to assert only that the distribution of poetry should not be based on market criteria, since any such estimate, by definition, shortchanges the existing potential. When it comes to poetry, the net result of market research, for all its computers, is distinctly medieval. We are all literate, therefore everybody is a potential reader of poetry: it is on this assumption that the distribution of books should be based, not on some claustrophobic notion of demand. For in cultural matters, it is not demand that creates supply, it is the other way around. You read Dante because he wrote the *Divine Comedy*, not because you felt the need for him: you would not have been able to conjure either the man or the poem.

Poetry must be available to the public in far greater volume than it is. It should be as ubiquitous as the nature that surrounds us, and from which poetry derives many of its similes; or as ubiquitous as gas stations, if not as cars themselves. Bookstores should be located not only on campuses or main drags but at the assembly plant's gates also. Paperbacks of those we deem classics should be cheap and sold at supermarkets. This is, after all, a country of mass production, and I don't see why what's done for cars can't be done for books of poetry, which take you quite a bit further. Because you don't want to go a bit further? Perhaps; but if this is so, it's because you are deprived of the means of transportation, not because the distances and the destinations that I have in mind don't exist.

Even to sympathetic ears, I suppose, all this may sound a bit loony. Well, it isn't; it also makes perfect economic sense. A book of poetry printed in 2.5 million copies and priced at, say, two dollars, will in the end bring in more than 10 000 copies of the same edition priced at 20 dollars. You may encounter, of course, a problem of storage, but then you'll be compelled to distribute as far and wide as the country. Moreover if the government would recognize that the construction of your library is as essential to your inner vocation as business lunches are to your outer vocation, tax breaks could be made available to those who read, write or publish poetry. The main loser, of course, would be the Brazilian rain forest. But I believe that a tree facing a choice between becoming a book of poems or a bunch of memos may well opt for the former.

A book goes a long way. Overkill in cultural matters is not an optional strategy, it is a necessity, since selective cultural targeting spells defeat no matter how well one's aim is taken. Fittingly, then, without having any idea whom it is in particular that I am address-ing at the moment, I would like to suggest that with the low-cost technology currently available, there is now a discernible oppor-tunity to turn this nation into an enlightened democracy. And I think this opportunity should be risen to before literacy is replaced with videocy.

I recommend that we begin with poetry, not only because this way we would echo the development of our civilization – the song was there before the story – but also because it is cheaper to pro-duce. A dozen titles would be a decent beginning. The average poetry reader's bookshelf contains, I believe, somewhere between 30 and 50 collections by various authors. It's possible to put half of it on a single shelf, or a mantelpiece – or if worse comes to worse, on the windowsill – of every American household. The cost of a dozen poetry paperbacks, even at their current price, would amount to one-fourth the price of a television set. That this is not done has to do not with the absence of a popular appetite for poetry but with the near-impossibility of whetting this appetite: with the unavailability of books. In my view, books should be brought to the doorstep like electricity, or like milk in England: they should be considered utilities, and their cost should be appropriately min-imal. Barring that, poetry could be sold in drugstores (not least because it might reduce the bill from your shrink). At the very least, an anthology of American poetry should be found in the drawer in every room in every motel in the land, next to the Bible, which will surely not object to this proximity, since it does not object to the proximity of the phone book.

All this is doable, in this country especially. For apart from anything else, American poetry is this country's greatest patrimony. It takes a stranger to see some things clearly. This is one of them, and I am that stranger. The quantity of verse that has been penned on these shores in the last century and a half dwarfs the similar enterprise of any literature and, for that matter, both our jazz and cinema, rightly adored throughout the world. The same goes, I dare say, for its quality, for this is a poetry informed by the spirit of personal responsibility. There is nothing more alien to American poetry than those great Continental specialties: the sensibility of the victim with its wildly oscillating, blamethirsty finger; the incoherence of elevation; the Promethean affectations and special pleading. To be sure, American verse has its vices – too many a parochial visionary, a verbose neurotic. But it is extremely tempering stuff, and sticking with the 1 per cent distribution method robs this nation of a natural resource of endurance, not to mention a source of pride.

It is a truly remarkable phenomenon, American poetry. Many years ago I showed Anna Akhmatova, a great Russian poet, several poems by Robert Frost, from his *North of Boston*. A few days later I returned and asked her what she thought. 'What kind of poet is this?' she asked, in mock indignation. 'He talks all the time about what people sell and buy! About getting insurance and all that!' (I suppose she was referring to his 'The Star-Splitter'.) And after a pause she added, 'What a terrifying poet.' The epithet was well chosen. It bespoke the distinction of Frost's posture *vis-à-vis* the traditional 'tragic' posture of the poet in European and Russian literature. For tragedy, even self-inflicted tragedy, is always a *fait accompli*, a backward look, whereas terror is future-bound and has to do with apprehension or, more accurately, with the recognition of one's own negative potential.

I am sorely tempted to suggest that this terrifying aspect is indeed Frost's – and, with him, all American poetry's – forte. Poetry, by definition, is a highly individualistic art; in a sense, this country is its logical abode. At any rate, it is only logical that in this country this individualistic tendency has gone to its idiosyncratic extreme, in modernists and traditionalists alike. (In fact, this is what gave birth to modernists.) To my eye as well as my ear, American poetry is a relentless non-stop sermon on human autonomy, the song of the atom, if you will, defying the chain reaction. Its general tone is that of resilience and fortitude, of exacting the full look at the worst and not blinking. It certainly keeps its eyes wide open, not so much in wonderment, or poised for a revelation, as on the lookout for danger. It is short on consolation (the diversion of so much European poetry, especially Russian); rich and extremely lucid in detail; free of nostalgia for some Golden Age; big on hardihood and escape. If one looked for its motto, I would suggest Frost's line from 'A Servant to Servants': 'The best way out is always through.'

If I permit myself to speak about American poetry in such a wholesale manner, it is not because of its body's strength and vastness but because my subject is the public's access to it. And in this context it must be pointed out that the old adage about a poet's role in, or his duty to, his society puts the entire issue upside down. If one can speak of the social function of somebody who is essentially self-employed, then the social function of a poet is writing, which he does not by society's appointment but by his own volition. His only duty is to his language, that is, to write well. By writing, especially by writing well, in the language of his society, a poet takes a large step toward it. It is society's job to meet him halfway, that is, to open his book and read it.

If one can speak of any dereliction of duty here, it's not on the part of the poet, for he keeps writing. Now, poetry is the supreme form of human locution in any culture. By failing to read or listen to poets, a society dooms itself to inferior modes of articulation – of the politician, or the salesman, or the charlatan – in short, to its own. It forfeits, in other words, its own evolutionary potential, for what distinguishes us from the rest of the animal kingdom is precisely the gift of speech. The charge frequently levelled against poetry – that it is difficult, obscure, hermetic and whatnot – indicates not the state of poetry but, frankly, the rung of the evolutionary ladder on which society is stuck.

For poetic discourse is continuous; it also avoids cliché and repetition. The absence of those things is what distinguishes art from life, whose chief stylistic device, if one may say so, is precisely cliché and repetition, since it always starts from scratch. It is no wonder that society today, chancing on this continuing poetic discourse, finds itself at a loss, as if opening a book in the middle. I have remarked elsewhere that poetry is not a form of entertainment, and in a certain sense not even a form of art, but our anthropological, genetic goal, our linguistic, evolutionary beacon. We seem to sense this as children, when we absorb and remember verses in order to master language. As adults, however, we abandon this pursuit, convinced that we have mastered it. Yet what we've mastered is but an idiom, good enough perhaps to outfox an enemy, to sell a product, to get laid, to earn a promotion, but certainly not good enough to cure anguish or cause joy. Until one learns to pack one's sentences with meanings like a van or to discern and love in the beloved's features a 'pilgrim soul'; until one becomes aware, with Robert Frost, that 'No memory of having starred/Atones for later disregard,/Or keeps the end from being hard' – until things like that are in one's bloodstream, one still belongs among the sublinguals. Who are the majority, if that's a comfort.

If nothing else, reading poetry is a process of terrific linguistic osmosis; it is also a highly economical form of mental acceleration. Within a very short space a good poem covers enormous mental ground, and often, towards its finale, provides one with an epiphany or revelation. As a tool of cognition, poetry beats any existing form of analysis (a) because it pares down our reality to its linguistic essentials, whose interplay, be it clash or fusion, yields that epiphany or that revelation, and (b) because it exploits the rhythmic and euphonic properties of the language that in themselves are revelatory. In other words, what a poem, or more accurately the language itself, tells you is 'Be like me.' It tells you that your soul has a long way to go. For at the moment of reading you become what you read, you become the state of the language which is a poem, and its epiphany or its revelation is yours. They are still yours once you shut the book, since you can't revert to not having had them. That's what evolution is all about.

Now, the purpose of evolution is the survival neither of the fittest nor of the defeatist. Were it the former, we would have to settle for Arnold Schwarzenegger; were it the latter, which ethically is a more sound proposition, we'd have to make do with Woody Allen. The purpose of evolution, believe it or not, is beauty, which survives it all and generates truth simply by being a fusion of the mental and the sensual. As it is always in the eye of the beholder, it can't be wholly embodied save in words: that's what ushers in a poem, which is as incurably semantic as it is incurably euphonic.

No other language accumulates so much of this as does English. To be born into it or to arrive in it is the best boon that can befall a man.

To prevent its keepers from full access to it is an anthropological crime, and that's what the present system of the distribution of poetry boils down to. I don't rightly know what's worse, burning books or not reading them. I think, though, that token publishing falls somewhere in between. I am sorry to put this so drastically, but when I think of the great works by the poets of this language bulldozed into neglect, on the one hand, and then consider the mind-boggling demographic vista, on the other, I feel that we are on the verge of a tremendous cultural backslide. And it is not the culture I am worried about, or the fate of the great or not-so-great poets' works. What concerns me is that man, unable to articulate, to express himself adequately, reverts to action. Since the vocabulary of action is limited, as it were, to his body, he is bound to act violently, extending his vocabulary with a weapon where there should have been an adjective.

In short, the good old quaint ways should be abandoned. There should be a nationwide distribution of poetry, classic and contemporary. It should be handled privately, I suppose, but supported by the state. The age group it should be aiming at is 15 and up. The emphasis should be on the American classics, and as to who or what should be printed, that should be decided by a body of two or three people in the know, that is, by the poets. The academics, with their ideological bickering, should be kept out of it, for nobody has the authority to prescribe in this field on any other grounds but taste. Beauty and its attendant truth are not to be subordinated to any philosophical, political or even ethical doctrine, since aesthetics is the mother of ethics and not the other way round. If you think otherwise, try to recall the circumstances in which you fall in love.

What should be kept in mind, however, is that there is a tendency in society to appoint one great poet per period, often per century. This is done in order to avoid the responsibility of reading others, or for that matter the chosen one, should you find his or her temperament uncongenial. The fact is that at any given moment in any literature there are several poets of equal gravity and significance by whose lights you can go. In any case, whatever their number, in the end it corresponds to the known temperaments, for it can't be otherwise: hence their differences. By grace of language, they are there to provide society with a hierarchy or a spectrum of aesthetic standards to emulate, to ignore, to acknowledge. They are not so much role models as mental shepherds, whether they are cognisant of it or not – and it's better if they are not. Society needs all of them;

and should the project I am speaking of ever be embarked upon, no preferences should be shown to any one of them. Since on these heights there is no hierarchy, the fanfare should be equal.

For a poet to sink into oblivion is not such an extraordinary drama; it comes with the territory, he can afford it. As I said, he is never a loser; he knows that others will come in his stead and pick up the trail where he left it. (In fact, it's the swelling number of others, energetic and vocal, clamouring for attention, that drive him into oblivion.) He can take this, as well as being regarded as a sissy. It is society that cannot afford to be oblivious, and it is society that – compared with the mental toughness of practically any poet – comes out as a sissy and a loser. For society, whose main strength is that of reproducing itself, to lose a poet is like having a brain cell busted. This impairs one's speech, makes one draw a blank where an ethical choice is to be made; or it barnacles speech with qualifiers, turns one into an eager receptacle for demagoguery or just pure noise. The organs of reproduction, however, are not affected.

There are few cures for hereditary disorders (undetectable, perhaps in an individual, but striking in a crowd), and what I'm suggesting here is not one of them. I just hope that this idea, if it catches on, may slow down somewhat the spread of our cultural malaise to the next generation. As I said, I took this job in the spirit of public service, and maybe being paid by the Library of Congress in Washington has gone to my head. Perhaps I fancy myself as a sort of Surgeon General slapping a label onto the current packaging of poetry. Something like *This Way of Doing Business Is Damaging to the National Health.* The fact that we are alive does not mean that we are not sick.

It's often been said – first, I think, by Santayana – that those who don't remember history are bound to repeat it. Poetry doesn't make such claims. Still, it has some things in common with history: it employs memory, and it is of use for the future, not to mention the present. It certainly cannot reduce poverty, but it can do something for ignorance. Also, it is the only insurance available against the vulgarity of the human heart. Therefore, it should be available to everyone in this country and at a low cost.

Fifty million copies of an anthology of American poetry for two dollars a copy can be sold in a country of 250 million. Perhaps not at once, but gradually, over a decade or so, they will sell. Books find their readers. And if they will not sell, well, let them lie around, absorb dust, rot and disintegrate. There is always going to be a child who will fish a book out of the garbage heap. I was such a child, for what it's worth; so, perhaps, were some of you.

A quarter of a century ago, in a previous incarnation in Russia, I knew a man who was translating Robert Frost into Russian. I got to know him because I saw his translations: they were stunning poems in Russian, and I wanted to become acquainted with the man as much as I wanted to see the originals. He showed me a hardcover edition (I think it was by Holt), which fell open onto the page with 'Happiness Makes Up in Height for What It Lacks in Length'. Across the page went a huge, size twelve imprint of a soldier's boot. The front page of the book bore the stamp 'STALAG #3B', which was a World War II concentration camp for Allied POWS somewhere in France.

Now, there is a case of a book of poems finding its reader. All it had to do was to be around. Otherwise it couldn't be stepped on, let alone picked up.

4

Trances

LES MURRAY

As I see it, poetry exists to provide the poetic experience. Depending on whether you accept or reject the idea of purpose in things, that is either what it is for, or what it does. Everyone knows, and certainly anyone likely to be reading this essay should know, what the poetic experience feels like. It is a datum, a given thing, as distinctive as any other primary experience; it is easier to point to than to define or delimit, but at any intensity it is quite unmistakable. In its verbal form, it is what people read for, as much as for information, though they may be shy about saying so, in an age which distrusts 'mystical' talk and prefers to dissemble its spiritual needs. It is what people mean when they ask how much poetry a text has got in it, and it is not, of course, found exclusively in verse. In another way, it is that in a book or a piece of verse that can't be summarized, or put into other words; we feel a constraint about doing so, a feeling that we would violate something. Where the experience is intense, we find it extremely attractive, fascinating and yet quickly exhausting; if we stay focused on it, resisting this urge to take rests, it will itself seem to come and go. It is an experience we can have repeatedly, but find it hard to take in steadily, to sustain. The realms of gold, it would seem, oscillate – or our mind does, when we behold them.

'THE TRANCES'

Human beings have two main modes of consciousness, one that is characteristic of waking life, one we call dreaming. The former is said by psychologists and physiologists to be the province of the 'new' part of the brain, that recently evolved forebrain; the latter relates to the older, limbic level of the brain, sometimes called the reptilian brain. We now know from sleep studies that we need to experience both, and that we grow distressed if we are prevented from dreaming. Our dreams can invade the daylight realm of our life, and that is psychosis. In normal life, we experience a substratum of dream mentation running along just below our waking consciousness and seeping through it here and there. This is reverie, or day-dreaming, and if it is too markedly out of kilter with our daylight thinking, we find ourselves agitated and under stress. As we have known since Freud and other early psychoanalysts, neither of our two lives is wholly subordinate to the other – or, if it is, we are likely to be more or less severely ill. Harmony between our two modes of life promotes health, and it is my belief that aesthetic experience is the supreme case of harmony between them. To be real, a poem has at once to be truly thought and truly dreamed, and the fusion between the two represents incipient wholeness of thinking and of life. A poem, or any work of art, enacts this wholeness and draws us into it, so as to promote and refresh our own. We find the atmosphere of this fusion intensely attractive, and may even become addicted to it; this is the Good Addiction, which the other kinds merely point to and parody, and we can judge them by Jesus's test of examining their fruits.

What attracts us to art and poetry is probably, first of all, the signals it sends out that here the secret world is present; to put that another way we are drawn by the bloom of dream life that the work bears. If the work is too drily intellectual and forebrainish, we apprehend it as arid and not really worth the trouble, or else shallow. If it is too indulgently dreamy, we may gulp it greedily in search of sustenance, but finally find it arbitrary and unsatisfying, and if it is contrived to look dreamier than it really is, we will react to that, too, more or less quickly, depending on the strength of our need for dream-sustenance. In the long run, our unconscious will persuade us of the fraud, and reject it before we are aware the rejection has happened. This is frequently the fate of all but the best surrealist art, which apes dream mentation in order to invoke it. The danger, though, always, is that our need of the good, true harmony which the best art evokes and nourishes may be so great that we will fool ourselves as to the quality of what seems to be supplying it, or a sufficient measure of it. And since the fusion of dream life and waking consciousness, of dream and reason if you prefer, lies at the very wellsprings of human endeavour, extending far beyond anything we can recognize as art, it behoves us to be fussy about the nature and sources of inner equilibrium between the two which we attain. The artist Francisco Goya wisely observed that the sleep of reason produces monsters, and we have redoubled evidence for that in this century. The monsters we generated in part because the sovereignty of daylight reason we have extolled over the last past few centuries is an illusion, based on the delusion that we can ever fully wake up, and the further delusion that perpetual rational wakefulness would even be bearable. Our very evolution, I submit, doesn't tend that way, but towards a wholeness of which art is the model.

I have been convinced for several years that the fusion of our two modes of life is a prime datum of human life and action. Everything we make, beyond the immediately utilitarian and the trivial, and perhaps much of that, too, comes out of combinations of vision and reasoning. The thing has to make daylight sense, and have some sort of rationale, but it must also feel right, have the right sort of vibes as we say, and be acceptable to the contemplation of reverie.

The clue for the following poem, 'The Trances', came from tracing that curious set of occupations people hate to pay anything like a regular wage for: the nurturing housewife-mother, the poet, the priest, the soothsayer. There was a queer ancient comparability between these which got me going. A few more occupations seemed to be related, only recently secularized as it were: I saw this in the strong preference medicoes have for a fee rather than a wage. And scholarship was largely unpaid honorary gentleman-amateur work a century ago. I've known people, in Italy for instance, who held honorary chairs. The same is true of science: many there are still funded rather than employed. Money is *later* than humans' primal specialties and still dimly felt to defile them. Of course there's nothing wrong with prose, or ice: without ice, there would be no rain, and prose is normality. But nothing that we love or value begins in prose, or begins as prose for us. And there have been whole peoples, the Australian Aborigines for instance, which have shown a frequent preference for death rather than consenting to live in a fully prosaic world. The step down from a highly charged poetical reality to one where poetry, the dimension of spirit and trance, is scattered and half covert and unrecognized, is too terrible for many traditional Aborigines to take. We recognize this fitfully in their case, but may miss it in people of our own culture who belong to the same archaic continuity.

Les Murray

THE TRANCES

We came from the Ice Age,
we work for the trances.
The hunter, the Mother,
seers' inside-out glances

come from the Ice Age,
all things in two sexes,
the priest man, the beast man,
I flatten to run
I rise to be human.

We came from the Ice Age
with the walk of the Mothers
with the walk of the powers
we walked where sea now is

we made the dry land
we told it in our trances
we burnt it with our sexes
but the tongue it is sand
see it, all dry taste buds
lapping each foot that crosses
every word is more sand.

Dup dup hey duhn duhn
the rhythm of the Mothers.
We come from the Ice Ages
with the tribes and the trances
the drum's a tapped drone
dup dup hey duhn duhn.

We come from the Ice Age,
poem makers, homemakers,
how you know we are sacred:
it's unlucky to pay us.

Kings are later, farmers later.
After the Ice Age, they
made landscape, made neuter,
they made prose and pay.

Things are bodied by the trances,
we must be paid slant,
loved, analysed and scorned,
the priest's loved in scorn,
how you know he is sacred.
We're gifted and pensioned.

Some paid ones were us:
when they got their wages
ice formed in their mouths
chink, chink, the Ice Age.

A prose world is the Ice Age
it is all the one sex
and theory, that floats land
we came over that floe land

we came from the Ice Age
we left it by the trances
worlds warm from the trances
duhn duhn hey dup dup
it goes on, we don't stop
we walk on from the Ice Age.

'LIFE CYCLE OF IDEAS'

Poetry does have to be introduced and legitimized by prose till our
civilization is repaired. Here, perhaps, I should mention two terms
I have started using and which may be useful. I call properly
integrated poetic discourse Wholespeak, while discourses based on
the supposed primacy or indeed exclusive sovereignty of daylight
reason I call Narrowspeak. The former embraces all good poetry
including that of religion; the latter embraces most of the adminis-
trative discourse by which the world is ruled from day to day, as
well as most of criticism. We have come, over the last few centuries,

to think that we live in a prose universe, with prose as the norm of
all discourse. This is a cause, or a consequence, of the decline in
belief in creation (*poesis*). In fact, descriptive prose doesn't answer
to our own inner nature, and so cannot describe the cosmos adequately.

'Life Cycle of Ideas' was written a few weeks before 'The Trances'.

LIFE CYCLE OF IDEAS

An idea whistles with your lips,

laughs with your breath.
An idea hungers for your body.

An alert, hot to dissemble and share,
it snatches up cases of its style
from everywhere, to start a face.

An idea is a mouth that sells
as it sucks. It lusts to have
loomed perpetual in the night colours:
an idea is always a social climb.

Whether still braving snorts,
ordering its shootings, or at rest
among its own charts of world rule,
a maturing idea will suddenly want

to get smaller than its bearers.

It longs to be a poem:
earthed, accurate immortal trance,

buck as stirrups were,
blare as the panther.

Only art can contain an idea.

5

Poetry's Subject

DOUGLAS OLIVER

The forces that operate in our European cultures to limit 'poetry's subject' are often obscured. What's to stop poets writing whatever they want? Nothing, of course. At least, if you're only talking about 'subject-matter' and if the poet cares nothing at all for popularity. If an outright fascist poem would find poor audience, no doubt some fiend somewhere is writing one. But my question concerns not only cultural prejudice (justified or not) against the treatment of various poetic topics. Certain genres and prosodic styles may also be regarded as outmoded or undesirable. The field of popularly-welcomed genres limits, it seems, the possible subjects that can be written about: the jargon expression 'postmodernism' implies a limitation of this kind. But my title, 'Poetry's Subject', has more complicated aspects too. Poets, as 'subjects' from which poems issue, may find that social pressures constrict their perception of the broadest poetic 'subject-matters'. If we approach the borders of the socially permissible cravenly enough, we become half-blind and unable to perform our task frankly, which is irresponsible of us. This has been true in every age, so therefore in our own.

In discussing 'poetry's subject', then, I'm going to limit my meanings for 'subject' to three distinct definitions: first, the subject who performs the poem, either as poet or reader, rather like the personal subject who performs an active verb; second, the poem's subject-matter in a sense as active and broad as 'Invention' or 'discovery of the ideas and matter' in classical rhetoric; and third, 'subject' in a political sense – why do poets or readers in a given era become subjected to the sovereignty of limited definitions of good poetry? The old joke goes, 'I can make a pun on any *subject*.' There are two of my meanings. 'Make a pun on Queen Victoria.' 'She is not a *subject*': that's my third meaning.

Normally a poem is performed when it is originally written, or when it is read silently or aloud, or chanted, or sung by the poet or by a reader. Only at those moments can it be truly a poem, an artwork alive in time; otherwise, it remains just a text, closed up within a book or opened to critical attention, an object whose relations with time a critic may describe but which remain potential, not actual. When I talk about poetry as a poet, as an artist and not as a critic, I always focus upon performance of poems: artistically, that's where the action is, where the possibilities begin.

When poets become cultural critics they often narrow down poetry's vast potential into some version that accords with their own practice. Occasionally this is part of a scandalous grab for power, but usually it is just a natural consequence of the way artists focus on what they're doing. Among things I've read or heard are: poets shouldn't write full-blast political poetry as if they could change society; or, if they do they should keep clear of the specifics of news bulletins because the poetry will date; or they should write easily comprehensible poetry so as to regain the audience lost by modernist and postmodernist obscurities; or, only difficult poetry is interesting; or, formalist poetry is in and free forms are out; or, metaphor is in; or, metaphor is out; or neo-formalist poetry is conservative-academic and deconstructed texts are politically-radical; or neo-formalism is populist and postmodern deconstruction is academic-elitist; or, the poet should be a stage performer, a star like a rock or rap singer; or, the single, lyric voice is arrogant and false and the poem should be opened to the interplay of those manifold 'discourses' that constitute our sense of the world; or, such a discourse-textual approach is in danger of losing spirituality; or 'spirituality' suggests grand metaphysical claims that are no longer realistic in the dulled-out, British 'Thajorite' scene, the post Reaganomics scene, the post European Union, post World Trade Organization scene. A popular younger British poet was reported as saying: 'Most of us are trying to achieve a bit of humility.' And, '. . . if you're going to have the audacity to trash a few trees and publish work then you want people to read it.' Populist sentiments have helped to life a poetry revival both in Scotland and England, so I'll resist adding: 'Remember, Signor Dante: humility and trees!'

A familiar game suggests itself: we apply these tacit prohibitions to great poems down the ages: to some ancient epic like the anonymous *Inanna* ('narrative poetry is passé'), Homer and Virgil ('imperialist'), Petrarch, Villon, Louise Labé (too much emphasis upon the 'I' pronoun – and too confessional, Monsieur Villon), Pope

('We've had too much narrative satire'), Romanticism? ('Are you kidding?'), Emily Dickinson (the 'I' pronoun gone thoroughly metaphysical), Modernism (either 'too obscure' or 'Look, we're in the post-post era already'), Postmodernism (well, isn't that the problem we're all wrestling with anyway?).

Putting limits on the kinds of poem that can authentically be written in our own day always carries with it an attempt at subjection, that third meaning of my topic, of either poet or poetry reader. A poet of any integrity should have little difficulty in ignoring the efforts by colleagues, driven by their necessities, to define poetry's subject. In practice, we fall into schools. One of the literary critic's most vital jobs is to reopen these closed fields and to show the broader possibilities suggested by history, but unfortunately fashionable limitations rule criticism just as much as they do poetry. Hindsight makes this easy to see. The early healthy and corrective influence of Philip Larkin's anti-modernism – so essential to him in creating his remarkable and eccentric poems – gradually became one of the academic and journalistic orthodoxies, a conservative influence upon public perception of British poetry. His poetry will last, certainly. But the legacy of his insistence on crabby modesty is lasting longer than it should. A sly insult for Larkinesque reviewers in the 1990s is still to call a poet 'ambitious' – not 'too ambitious', mark you, just 'ambitious'.

For each installed orthodoxy, ambition is a threat and those of conservative mind view its restlessness with distaste. Dryden has memorably given this distaste its voice in his lines on Lord Shaftesbury, or Achitophel, who had led the Whig attempt to make Charles II legitimize his bastard son, Monmouth, so that Monmouth could succeed to the throne.

> Of these the false Achitophel was first;
> A name to all succeeding ages curst:
> For close designs and crooked counsels fit;
> Sagacious, bold, and turbulent of wit;
> Restless, unfixed in principles and place;
> In power unpleased, impatient of disgrace:
> A fiery soul, which, working out its way,
> Fretted the pigmy body to decay,
> And o'er-informed the tenement of clay.
> A daring pilot in extremity;
> Pleased with the danger, when the waves went high,

> He sought the storms; but, for a calm unfit,
> Would steer too nigh the sands, to boast his wit.

This Tory portrait of ambition has long fascinated poetry readers for the way it uses the speech apparatus when you perform it. Its consonants make you gag at the back of the throat or puff out little explosions of scorn or hiss or ffff – the way the sounds change place from lip to palate to throat twists the mouth – and the poem catches up the sounds into runs of speed, turned by contemptuous pauses, then spun onwards, so that Lord Shaftesbury's turbulence is mimed in a way that is both easy to describe and also transcends clear definition. To describe the effects fully would be to say something about the body–mind connection.

If the poem could be considered entirely as a text (no poem, of course, can), its sonic miming of contempt may be identified but remains inert. It takes a subject, the poet originally or a reader, to perform this contempt before the poem will live again. Only then, in performance, does the poem assume full artistic responsibility for what it is saying. Treating the poem as text, we may recreate Dryden as a figure in history; but in performance a quasi-fictional sharing of minds occurs between ourselves and a Dryden that our imaginations create. He almost rises before us, a figure who, we temporarily believe, spoke approximately in the verbal music we are creating and was responsible for it. The poem's politics live again in our own mouths, which in that suspension of disbelief have to mean the words spoken. So now it is both reader and the fictive Dryden who, together, are responsible for expressing scorn for Shaftesbury.

Responsibility for what we write can become a very complicated question, as a detour into the philosophy of 'intention' may suggest. In Elizabeth Anscombe's well-known thought-experiment, a man is pumping water from a cistern which supplies the drinking water of a house regularly used by evil politicians in control of a great state. Someone else has contaminated the water with deadly, undetectable poison. The politicians have Hitler-like, anti-Semitic projects and perhaps aim at world domination; the poisoner believes that if they and their families are destroyed, good politicians may gain power and usher in a political paradise. He has revealed his plans to the man pumping. Among the less-obvious chains of causation set going by this single action of pumping are the following: a number of unknown people will receive legacies because of the deaths of these families; the man's pumping will affect the relevant nerves and muscles of his own body; the moving arm is casting onto a rockery a shadow which looks like a face; the pump is making a rhythmic noise. And so forth.

Citing this example, Paul Ricoeur asks, What is the man actually doing? My own question is: what is he, and we may say she, actually responsible for? I want to transfer this question from Anscombe's little story over to the discussion of poetry.

A poet casting a poem into history by publication is responsible for sequences of events no less intricate than the man pumping. First, there are immediate sonic, semantic and emotional chains of consequence within the poem; ideally considered, they begin with the opening syllable and continue to the final one, until the poem's form looks back upon itself. This is accompanied by mental activity both physical and spiritual. Because of this mental activity, even at this fine level, too fine for reason to examine fully, the human processes involved imply responsibility at every juncture, a tiny responsibility, perhaps, arising in each small semantic, emotional and sonic change in the verbal texture. Considering the poem, now, as a whole, those human processes lead, of course, to many broader aesthetic, social, political, etc., fields of significance. For example, although observable real-life political effects of a poem may be rare, the poet is still responsible for every poetic detail that could have such effects, or indeed do in the spiritual activity accompanying performance.

In its original creation the poem is alive as art. The author reperforms it immediately after it is written, and the art comes alive again. Publication sets the poem loose and, with each new reading in each new era, history shines its different lights upon it. A reader in any century reperforming the poem experiences some version of the enchaining of causation, therefore of responsibility, down the poem's length and outwards into society. Simultaneously, an aesthetic transaction takes place between reader and imagined poet across the centuries. The consequences may be different from anything the poet could have intended. Yet, as Auden realized in censoring his own poem, 'Spain', the poet is still, almost unfairly, involved – even perhaps in any reasonable misreadings of the poem.

Dryden was writing with his nose to news bulletins, for Shaftesbury was awaiting trial for treason when the poem was published in 1681. 'Nose to news bulletins'? I recently read in a great modern poet's essays that political poems should not be written like that. They will date. True, history eventually ran against Dryden's Catholic viewpoint: the Stuart royalty went out; Britain's protestant constitutional monarchy came in. Shaftesbury, in another liberal view of history, turned out to be if not thoroughly enlightened, at least prophetic of the ideologically tolerant constitutional monarchy of today. The poem certainly has dated in that respect. But much in the *Divine Comedy* has dated even more extremely, as have some best moments in Shakespeare's plays (the porter's speech in *Macbeth*, for example), not to mention Marvell's wonderful 'Upon Appleton House'. What rescues Dryden's poem from mere datedness? The Biblical parallels? Somewhat, but just as forcibly, it is Dryden's nose-to-news-bulletin contempt for Shaftesbury that twists his vowels and consonants into the snarl that gives the poem its peculiar and lasting artistic resonance and form.

Once we perform a poem, our questioning takes on a quite personal fervour: the question is not just whether it is a great poetic text or what its politics were; we sense how truthful or untruthful we ourselves are being as we speak it. Performing Dryden's lines I intensely realize that some of their scorn could be directed against myself, for – to my shame or credit – I have something of a Shaftesburyan restlessness with my country's present politics. This realization leads me to desire that my restlessness be fully responsible, that is, to use a dubious word, patriotic. In that wish, I meet my imagined Dryden as an opponent but as one who is complicit with me.

Of modern British poets, few have taken the notion of responsibility in such Puritan seriousness as Geoffrey Hill. He once wrote that one of the 'indubitable signs' of Simone Weil's greatness was her suggestion that anyone discovering avoidable errors in texts or broadcasts should be entitled to bring an action against the perpetrators before special courts whose sentencing powers would include prison or hard labour on conviction. Hill does not go on to recommend this frightening system but, more moderately, cites W.K. Wimsatt's belief in 'the fullness of [the poet's] responsibility as public performer in a complex and treacherous medium'. This was what Simone Weil was trying to get at.

Were I to write a critical article about Hill's own poems as text, I imagine I should find myself at a political distance from him. When, one day, I heard him read from *Tenebrae* I was entranced, as ever, to hear a genuine artist at work, for his voice seemed to wrest the vowels out of his conscience. I am a sympathizer with Jean Jaurès's stand in France against World War I and cannot read without anxiety Hill's poem about Charles Péguy, whose writings in a manic phase may have encouraged a fanatic to assassinate the great pacifist. Hill, who regards Péguy as one of the great souls of our century, also calls Jaurès the great socialist; so I would not like to refer to this elusive poem without appreciation for Hill's tenderness and efforts at rectitude. What constitutes an 'exemplary death' has much fascinated Hill. A lyrical section in the poem associates Péguy's patriotic sacrifice in war with the 'exemplary' aspect of his 'defeat', to combine two items of Hill's terminology; it is the 'great work' of his small body's death. David Gervais reminds us that Péguy had written in *Eve*:

> – Heureux ceux qui sont morts pour la terre charnelle,
> Mais pourvu que ce fût dans une juste guerre

in which the native soil becomes a charnel house and that is rhymed with 'a just war' to make a sacrificial conjunction. Hill lifts the phrase and sets it into a more complex sense of sacrifice, half in his own voice, half in Péguy's, and thrilling with Hill's characteristic impregnation of rural nostalgia with violence:

> Happy are they who, under the gaze of God,
> die for the 'terre charnelle', marry her blood
> to theirs, and, in strange Christian hope, go down
> into the darkness of resurrection,

> into sap, ragwort, melancholy thistle,
> almondy meadowsweet, the freshet-brook
> rising and running through small wilds of oak,
> past the elder tump that is the child's castle.

In that patriotic marriage of blood, native soil and eccentric Christianity, half-attributed to Péguy, Hill takes away any sure standing ground: it is the 'Mystery of the Charity of Charles Péguy' that he is inviting us to consider. The words 'die for the "terre charnelle" ' suggest a death that Péguy might have found 'exemplary'. Then Hill bloods a revived, pastoral countryside with this phrase so as to create a hope of renewal. As Hill knows, we have to beware rhetoric which sentimentalizes patriotism and sacrifice, and I re-

main uneasy whenever response to violence is seen as the final test
for a person; many exemplary lives are too gentle to confront
violence very staunchly and have their own different courage.

But performing the poem, I can't distance myself as I just have
from the very words that distress me and probably Hill too: 'die for
the "terre charnelle" '. Their consonants happen at the back of the
teeth and then, when images of resurrection come, dental consonants return in 'almondy' and 'meadowsweet' and the breath comes
through the teeth until 'charnelle' is transformed into 'freshet'.
Performing those lines, I am briefly forced to live through this
religious politics because the sacrificial death and the Christian
hope in resurrection are brought so vividly together in my own
speaking voice. It rather flusters me, frankly. To illustrate what
'vividly' means there, I spent a summer in New York, once, tran-
scribing on to computer interviews with HIV-positive homeless
people, some of whose lives had been so deprived that more than
one said that being identified as sero-positive was the best thing
that had happened to them. They had never been permitted exemplary lives and deaths. Because their voices came intimately
through my headphones, it seemed as if I were speaking myself;
when they drank a glass of water it travelled down my own throat;
and so there were times when I had to pause in my typing because
I was overcome by having to perform their life stories with them.

What happens when I perform Hill's lines parallels my experience of Dryden's: poetic responsibility for each word, each conson-
ant, lives again, within myself. This is why I only partly agree when
Anthony Hecht says Dryden's move from Cromwellian to Catholic
politics doesn't affect our sense of his poetry's quality. This is true
when we reflect upon the poem as text, for then our personal
political judgements stand a little away from the poem; partly,
good criticism aims at such objectivity. But the more fully we enter
our performance of the poem, the less true Hecht's remark
becomes. If the politics, for a moment, come alive in our mouths
that must affect our sense of the poem's quality – we aren't made of
wood; poetry, of course, is never pure. Yet this is a living experience and trapped within its moment. Only by emerging from our
performance and becoming critics again can we restore reflection
and balance to our aesthetic judgement; but then the poem has
become inert in time and Hecht becomes correct again. This is
frustrating, but so is all human experience of time. As Paul Celan
wrote to a schoolteacher, 'In a poem, what's real happens . . .'

My concentration upon individual performance is mere self-reflexive humanism, say certain postmodernists, employing what is supposed to be an evident slur. Individuals are defined in relation to the vast social, political and historical elaborations of language that allow us our own speech and self-definition. The political and economic dominance of our use of language needs to be challenged by poetry that avoids Narcissistic indulgence, that opens out to the play of language itself and removes self-reflection from the poem's pool. Let me accept for a moment the cogency of this approach.

To take one example of many, the African-American poet Nathaniel Mackey interestingly suggests that bringing into poetry traditional, communal and collective wisdom may act as a corrective to a subjective lyricism that is compromised with the history of oppression; and very ancient roles for the poet are also implied here. He is thinking of slavery, mostly. For the African-American, Indian-American cultures I can see the healing potential in the suppressed wisdom. Then again, as a Jewish friend remarked, in Fascist Germany you can see the dangers of an appeal to the deep conservativism in certain folk cultures. What might be a stricture in one sense against Fascism can become in another cultural context, that of Mackey, an opening-out.

But even in the most radical intertextuality, even in complex literary collaboration, issues of responsibility will arise as before. They will follow the poem down its length and extend outwards into society before the lines of force created by artistic form draw back again upon the poet(s). As a poem nears the borders of clear meaning, however, this becomes harder and harder to see, and the question of individual responsibility for what is written becomes increasingly fudged although it never goes entirely away. So those who write difficult, experimental poetry which attempts to purify language politically take on a difficult task; they know that they will not easily get approval either from the widest readership or from poets who seek that readership. Utmost possible clarity is always desirable, but poetry needs all the shots in its armament, from populist broadsides to experimental *tirs-en-avance*.

Many postmodernist theories of consciousness and language rest upon a fundamental linguistic paradox. When, through language, you seek to discover the origin of language you are setting a snake to bite its own tail. What you discover is more snake. Plus a moment when the snake is not sure whether to bite or not. Similarly, when through examining language you hunt down that origin of personal language, the subject, the 'self', you discover not the 'self' but more language: you can't escape that conundrum any more than you can escape any other form of linguistic scepticism that is radical enough. To put this into my own terms, you are then treating the 'self' as a text, and you find it as a text, not as a performance set into time. You convert into puzzles about language the self's actual temporal difficulties concerning its own origination, intention, responsibility and moral action. Criticism, however subtle its analysis, has supplanted lived-through experience: lived-time, so to speak, has not yet started; nor has the responsibility of the poem, as opposed to that of the criticism, really begun.

I have used those difficult words, 'moral action'. Not least since Heidegger's criticism of Husserl and developments since in the hermeneutic philosophical tradition, we are supposed to have lost all our absolutes: absolute presence, absolute transcendental ego, absolute ethics, absolute meaning in texts, and much that we used to mean by 'moral'. I fear Stanley Fish has captured all too well this anti-foundationalist position:

> Isn't it the essence of truly responsible behaviour – legal or any other – always to be looking beyond the horizons of the local and contingent to more general principles (of logic, ethics, reason), principles that would add a level of constraint higher than that already built into practice? The answer is 'no,' and the reason is that there are no higher or more general constraints, only constraints that are *different*, constraints built into practices other than the one whose reform is now being contemplated.

I do not suggest that the following is how Fish would apply his ideas, but if we took his remarks most exorbitantly, we should fail to place anything but a transient value upon value, as if we no longer had the dialectical thesis–antithesis–synthesis but just antithesis–antithesis–synthesis – which, I might wickedly add, will do in economics as a definition of the global free market. I notice that Fish doesn't use such common words as 'belief' or 'conviction'. These, the appropriate terms for describing why we feel responsible, inconveniently relate to the mysteries of private experience and to the performance of our lives. Where they are not appeals to dogmatic faiths, they become annoyingly individual in their foundation. Instead, we find in my quotation from Fish the philosophically more adaptable term, 'constraint', a restriction that can be written down as moral precept or as law. If you talk of constraints, instead of beliefs, you ensure that everything you discuss can become a matter of competing discourses, texts and hermeneutical interpretations. I am not setting against this an absolutist, Platonic or religious notion of values or morals; rather, I'm suggesting that it is only in the various performances of our lives that beliefs and values arise as living – not textual – issues, and then they revive their true dialectical ambiguity between stasis and transience.

Now I'll broaden these twin concepts of performance and responsibility to as wide a definition of artistic practice as possible. A poet's full performance is the whole life's work; it is for that he or she finally takes responsibility. After the poet's death, individual poems will be seen as part of that overall project, even if they didn't seem so at the time.

It's an ideal, but in the project of my own life's writing, I hold to the analogy of a strawberry plant. Individual projects may grow out of other projects in the life-work rather as by a propagating shoot. Any restrictions that contemporary poets or critics seek to place on the craft I try to ignore: the shoot plants itself wherever the growth process – that overall performance – leads it. What might be left is a various life-work including genres as different as may be necessary: some easy for readers to comprehend, some more difficult, some high-toned, some light and comic so that the fuller human life of the writer may be incorporated. To adapt Henry James's image of the 'House of Fiction', a life-work may have many windows, but also many doors for readers to gain access to rooms they feel most challenged by. This time, I do *not* want to imply ambition but surely Boccaccio or Shakespeare, on their grander scale and each in their own treacherous medium, worked in a similar way.

Since poetry in its performance is primarily a human activity, what is at stake is our definition of what being human means. Here is my principal aphorism: *Each narrowing of what contemporary poetry is supposed to do bears with it an equivalent narrowing in the definition of a human being.* If an aphorism is so blatantly truthful that it makes us a little weary to hear it, ten-to-one that truthfulness is in danger of being overlooked.

The most breathtaking example of narrowing, of course, is that it has taken millennia to redefine poetry in such a way that women writers have any equality. Other large-scale forms of contemporary blindness would include nationalistic chauvinism, especially in dominant nations, and access to the very highest levels of esteem (not to levels just short of the very top) being restricted mostly to poets whose voices suggest variously privileged racial, educational or class backgrounds.

In the smaller details we have to beware narrowing too. For example, the return in Britain and America to traditional formalism usefully appeals to that wider general public which is put off by unexpected metrics. Stated like that, neo-formalism can encourage a welcome, democratic broadening of readership. My own laboratory experiments persuade me that conventional forms promote confidence about how to read the poem. I have often got inexperienced readers to perform poems in different genres into linguistic recording machinery. The resulting spectrographs separate out the vocal patterns that are perceived by listeners as pitch, loudness, voicing (laryngeal activity) and rhythm. Greatest agreement between readers' performances of the vocal music seems to occur with the most tightly ordered verse forms such as Pope's heroic couplets.

But promoting such confidence is not always the most interesting thing for a poet to do – sometimes ambiguity in the music is more creative. Stated like that, there's a risk that if neo-formalism should become a fashionable dogma it will narrow poetry's 'subject'. I recall a respected English critic claiming long ago, dogmatically, that Robert Creeley's poems did not respect the integrity of poetic lines. When I performed a Creeley poem with slight, Americanized hesitance into linguistic machinery, the spectrograph traces confirmed what my ear told me: the line endings are terrifically delicate. The poet-figure as subject, inflected with hesitance, becomes interestingly uncertain. The dashes that rhythmically structure Emily Dickinson's poems would surely create an analogous delicacy, for typography enters this too. One may give a sense of line closure in complex ways, using lips, nose, tongue, palate, throat, larynx, breath and silent suspense added to measure, meaning and emotional significance in a multitude of combinations. Voicing at the larynx plays an especially complex role. To insist on formal metrics alone is just to take a particular road towards defining line closure, not, of course, a minor road. Conventional formalism cannot easily accommodate long, syncopated lines like this by Denise Riley:

This thick body can't dim its brilliance though it vexes the car of my
　　flesh . . .

Nor can it cope with the jazz of such African-Americans as Amiri Baraka or Quincy Troupe or with the younger, rappy, hip-hoppy African-Americans such as the sharply amusing Paul Beatty from Los Angeles.

Broadening our definition of poetry becomes essential at a time when publishers, faced with a chancy market, welcome tighter definitions to suit the populist taste. Bad art, feeble jokes, jingoism and outright murder are also within the broader human repertoire, and we are not, as artists, to give all kinds of poems equal weighting in value or to fail to excoriate the bad. But nor are we to scorn audiences, especially the widest poetry ones, which prefer the conventional modes to those which elites find more imposing; taste depends partly on educational opportunities and different audiences need their own poetry.

Haven't I trapped myself between populist and elitist positions? When we perform poems without distinction of genre or consideration of contemporary taboos, all these questions fall away: we either enjoy or take profit or we do not. A poem either exalts us or it does not. I'll illustrate this from a poem by a writer of highly refined poetic philosophy and from a poem by one of the most rock-star like poets which seems to yield a similar insight.

Since we are foundering in moral relativism as societies become more and more multicultural, the constraints – to use Fish's word – upon good action are too important for poets to fail to consider. J.H. Prynne, in his book *Her Weasels Wild Returning*, writes about the original moment of an event or act of mind:

> So far the slope drifts in, often it does. Furnishing
> a new track or late to consult, all by the way brought
> together, a trial to go on.

This is typically dense but I'll risk an interpretation. First, I am not going to separate mind and event, or, necessarily, animal from human mind. An event, including an act of mind during an event, is fed by content from the past. The input is imaged as a sloping, a concentration of detail, drifting into the very moment of the mind-act. Part of this process is habitual or frequent ('often it does'): part is casual, occasional or uncontrolled ('drifts'). Each time, this content is presented to the mind in a novel form which is suggestive ('a new track'), but there may be effects from the inevitable time-drag of thought ('late to consult' – combining both 'delay' and 'future retrospection'); yet despite these time-delays the act becomes unified through the actual event ('brought together'), 'by the way' offering puns on 'way' as 'path', as 'casual place of occurrence', as 'manner' and as the expression 'incidentally'. This creates the partly tentative, partly bold experimental tone of an authentic mind-act, expressed in at least four meanings of 'trial' in play all at once: an essay or attempt to continue, a testing-out that we may rely on, a burden (as in 'It's such a trial') and a judgmental proving of responsibility. Could any two and a half lines be more accurate about the dynamics and responsibilities hiding within a mental performance?

Prynne's words are high-toned and intellectually very complicated; they are more intensely correct and yet tentative than the confidence in Fish's moral relativism. Prynne's bookishness and allusiveness can easily put us off, although we are nonetheless ready to admire a torturous, bookish density in the exquisite, knotty diction of Paul Celan. Celan's poems are surely among the most beautiful written in any country postwar so full as they are of the suffering that characterized the post-Auschwitz generation.

Strange as it may seem, a similar mind process to that described by Prynne may be expressed powerfully for a more popular audience, as in Linton Kwesi Johnson's 'Sonny's Lettah'. The poem starts deceptively as a letter written from a London prison by a Caribbean:

> Dear Mama,
> Good Day.
> I hope dat wen
> dese few lines reach y'u,
> they may find y'u in di bes' af helt.

The poem/letter becomes a little masterpiece of delayed and displaced information as we learn that the letter-writer is apologizing to Mama for letting his younger brother get arrested under the old British 'sus' laws, whereby the police used to be able to stop and question anyone who in their eyes looked suspicious. Meanwhile (and the letter-writer reports this as if it were less important) he himself reacted so fiercely to the way the police handled his brother that he is being charged with murder. This is an extraordinary, straight-sung demonstration of a social dynamic that Prynne has expressed otherwise as an act of mind. The drift of racism in a culture, the sharp encounter ('a fresh track') that results on the road and partly by hazard ('by the way'), the literal murder trial to come, all those other meanings of 'trial' as burden and test and so on, and the retrospection with such kindliness towards the mother ('late to consult') – these are lightly suggested in two or three elegant, snappy pages. To perform Kwesi Johnson's poem in your head brings to your active mind complex uncertainties not so dissimilar from those raised by Prynne's poem, along with deep cultural disquiet.

Why should we make exclusive claims for either of these styles, Prynne's or Kwesi Johnson's? I've already implied that we need the most intense intellectual inquiry and we need the affecting, popular appeal to the sense of justice; both are part of what it means to have a humane society with each *poet contributing what they can best do.*

For some years, I have been greatly taken with Paul Ricoeur's attempts to bring together the analytic and hermeneutic traditions in philosophy. Most recently, he has tried to define the relation between the human 'self' and the outside world. As I am not a philosopher and could hardly presume myself to define what is human, I shall avoid Ricoeur's complexities.

What I find congenial is that at every point where other philosophers have attempted to freeze these discussions into the linguistic-analytical on the one hand, or into never-ending, anti-foundational, relativistic hermeneutical discourses on the other, Ricoeur keeps insisting that the description of human behaviour has no true *temporal* existence without a self to act it out and without a *relationship* with what is other. Only relationship set into temporality makes the dialectic come alive. Talking about linguistic analytics, he says that what has been omitted in such an approach is not just one important dimension among others but an entire problematic, namely that of personal identity, which can be articulated only in the temporal dimension of human existence.

This is humanism but of a rich kind because it is united authentically with our lives set into time, into performance.

Left out of so much contemporary, post-Wittgensteinian philosophy is the private world of our individual consciousness. I am not speaking religiously or even metaphysically. We tend to redefine private mind-acts, our beliefs and emotions, into functions that our language can more objectively discuss, quasi-scientifically. Thus 'emotion' (what we actually feel) is often redefined as 'attitude' (what we think about what causes those feelings); or 'human action' (what we actually did as persons) is redefined as 'event' (what happened, viewed somewhat impersonally); or we have seen Fish not use the word, 'belief' (what we feel to be right to think), but 'constraint' (restrictions on thought or action); or, in related theories, 'speech' (an 'I' putting language into action) is regarded as logically, though not literally, anterior to 'writing' (text-like creations whose mysterious connection with the metaphysics of the present is via the 'trace' and whose 'I' becomes a textual subject). With each redefinition, real-time temporal process bleeds out of the description, temporal paradoxes take its place, and we seem to become a little less responsible for what we do.

Ricoeur's description of human activity is rich enough for me to map on to it most contemporary styles of poetry, for he relates quite workaday conceptions of the self both to the analytics of everyday language and to the queasy marshes of hermeneutics. And this leads him to discuss the ethics and then the morals of living a good life within a just society. Mapping poetry on to that, we may say first that in our ordinary wish for a warm, neighbourly, just society, we need ordinary, clear poems capable of touching people's hearts; or, we need perfect lyrics too; or we need poetry's grand monuments; or, at the sharp end of politics, we shall look to the 'exemplary' courage of an Akhmatova or a Mandelstam or to South Africa's Dennis Brutus and Arthur Nortje, or to Malawi's Frank Chipasula and Jack Mapanje, or more recently to Nigeria's Wole Soyinka (in the forefront of courageous protest against political injustice yet again). Few clearer moments were sounded in postwar poetry than when Brutus wrote about cruelly treated prisoners on Robben Island working barefoot on sharp-bladed rocks:

> the bloody flow
> thinned to pink strings dangling
> as we hobbled through the wet clinging sands
> or we discovered surprised
> in some quiet backwater pool
> the thick flow of blood uncoiling
> from a skein to thick dark red strands.

or when Malawi's Chipasula wrote dramatically and hyperbolically about life under Hastings Banda:

Your streets are littered with handcuffed men

For these are poems dignified by their performance in a poet's real life, and this adds to their quality as we reperform them in a way impervious to judicious criticism of them as text. Such poets keep alive in their own tongues and circumstances Akhmatova's great purpose and subject-matter, similarly dignified, during Germany's invasion in 1942:

> We will preserve you, Russian speech,
> from servitude in foreign chains,
> keep you alive, great Russian word,
> fit for the songs of our children's children,
> pure on their tongues, and free.

(Trans. Stanley Kunitz with Max Hayward)

So the verse may acquire a political or ethical tonality and this may be direct and activist, nose to the news bulletins, more distantly historical, comic, satirical and so on. Or poetry may strike the grand tone of some of our culture's monuments. Or it may happily provide more contained entertainments to fill anthologies. And, again, poetry needs its experimental wing, whether mainstream publishers like it or not, because the history of poetic cultures has sufficiently shown that the avant-garde is ignored at peril and that it is always vilified by populists. Identifying the avant-garde is fortunately difficult; its final definition will be spoken unpredictably by an increasingly technologi-cal future, and furthermore, it has often turned out, either during or after an epoch, to be the mainstream after all. Without intense ex-perimental inquiry poetry becomes complacent, especially politically complacent; without popular outreach, poetry risks becoming driven in upon itself, another kind of complacency. Only by somehow en-compassing both tradition and novelty will it achieve its bedrock qualities: beauty, truthfulness, wisdom, prescience.

Yevgeny Yevtushenko, introducing an anthology which grouped together the warring schools of modern Russian poetry, prayed 'O Lord, when will we at last understand that writers are not race-horses competing for first place but workhorses pulling in common harness the common cart of literature.'

Let me exclude too easy a notion of democracy. Since any poet's judgement is partisan, not everyone else seems to be pulling in the

same direction or with the same exalted purpose. In my reading I
naturally go for that poetry which opens out the highest spiritual
and musical awareness I myself can experience. It depends what
topics a given prosody is capable of representing in whatever degree of finesse.

Questions of a poem's spiritual status always arise in performance whether we like it or not. By 'spiritual' I mean (in this
context) 'whatever relates to our performance of a poem that
cannot be fully explained through language itself or through
other forms of analysis'. This fierce concentration is quite different
from anything I have said about narrowing the general field of
poetry.

Poetry published in Britain right now often has insular concerns
– the Larkinesque spirit again, perhaps. I have a fear about my own
participation in the national poetry. What if a legendary poor person hoves in sight, no longer the peasant behind King Wenceslas's
back, but, say, an educated African from a desperate country. He
asks how I see myself as poet, what my poetry's subject-matter is
like, what relation it bears towards world economic subjugation of
poor nations with repressive political systems. There we have my
three meanings of subject again. I would not like to reply that I was
just writing for the Anglo-American market, or to apologize that, as
a compromised Westerner, I couldn't address such topics at all, or
to quote Auden's famous dictum out of context as usual, to claim
that poetry only survives in the valley of its own making where
executives 'would never want to tamper'. The African is already
walking away, muttering, 'I was talking about world poverty.
Some of our writers landed up in jail, so the executives who did that
certainly wanted to tamper.'

I don't want to get out of this on a cheap appeal to sentiment, but
I've come to think that we cannot limit either our poetry's concerns
or genres. Our culture stands too greatly in danger of rotting. In
this impasse of European- and world-wide squandered democracy,
to raise any shout at all is hard enough. John Ashbery pinpoints our
problem, set into another story, in an image also symbolic of the
partial autonomy of text from writer:

> This severed hand
> Stands for life, and wander as it will,
> East or west, north or south, it is ever
> A stranger who walks beside me . . .

I have recently taken a step to restore urgent speech to my work. It's not very dramatic. It's to pass outside my Western body and to regard my poetic position from the Third World standpoint. I have, for example, been reading the grand UNESCO history of Africa, which with all it can and cannot say politically about modern African countries gives me a fresh view of the shape of the world. So much of what I'm doing poetically then seems trivial; so much that remains to be done seems culpably left undone – irresponsibly left undone.

Agreed: we have no right as Western poets to vaunt our opinions about Third World matters. But I can define one neglected subject-matter for us Westerners. Mightn't we just accept the Western subject-self as a fouled entity and expose it (and ourselves) in as great an honesty as we can bear, so that those who live in less privileged parts of the world may criticize us, because they *should*? And can't we then *still carry on*, unredeemed, deadly unredeemed in fact, not seeking profit, trying to quell our literary pride, our condign self-justification, as well as we can? Am I being theological? Not in the least. It's as simple as this: a child has five apples, another child has only one. The minute the child with five starts talking a blue streak about anything else but the disparity you know he or she's avoiding the issue. If he does talk about the disparity and still doesn't give any apples back, at least there's no doubt about his selfishness and, who knows, the other child's hostility might make the apple thief ashamed. Out of that correct, necessary hostility, an honest dialectic might be restored, and spirit might rise. You'll say that's sentimental after all but it is not.

Mandelstam wrote:

As a child can answer equally:
'I'll give you an apple' or 'I shan't give it to you,'
While his face is an accurate cast of his voice as he utters the
words.

(Trans. Bernard Meares)

Selected references

Anna Akhmatova, 'Courage', in the Yevtushenko anthology below.
John Ashbery, 'Worsening Situation', in *Selected Poems*, New York: Elisabeth Sifton Books, Viking, 1985.

Paul Beatty – see, for example, his *Joker, Joker, Deuce*, New York: Penguin Poets, 1994.

Dennis Brutus, 'Robben Island Sequence' in Adewala Maja-Pearce (ed.), *The Heinemann Book of African Poetry in English*, London: Heinemann, 1990.

Frank Chipasula, 'A Love Poem for my Country', in the Adewala Maja-Pearce volume, above.

John Felstinger, *Paul Celan: Poet, Survivor, Jew*, Newhaven, Conn.: Yale University Press, 1995.

Stanley Fish, *Doing What Comes Naturally: Change, Rhetoric, and the Practice of Theory in Literary and Legal Studies*, Durham, NC and London: Duke UP, 1989.

David Gervais, *Literary Englands: Versions of 'Englishness' in Modern Writing*, Cambridge: Cambridge UP, 1993, pp. 235–8.

Anthony Hecht, *The Hidden Law: The Poetry of W.H. Auden*, Cambridge, Mass: Harvard University Press, 1993.

Geoffrey Hill, 'Mystery of the Charity of Charles Péguy', *Collected Poems*, Harmondsworth: Penguin, 1985. My account is influenced by Gervais.

Linton Kwesi Johnson in Neil Astley (ed.), *Poetry with an Edge*, Newcastle: Bloodaxe Books, 1993 edn.

Nathaniel Mackey interviewed by Edward Foster, *Postmodern Poetry: The Talisman Interviews*, Hoboken, NJ: Talisman House, 1994, p. 69.

Osip Mandelstam, 'The Finder of a Horseshoe', in the Yevtushenko anthology below.

J.H. Prynne, 'Well Enough in Her Riding After', in *Her Weasels Wild Returning*, Cambridge: Equipage, 1994, p. 7.

Paul Ricoeur, *Oneself as Another*, trans. Kathleen Blamey, Chicago: University of Chicago Press, 1992.

Denise Riley, 'True North', in *Mop Mop Georgette*, Cambridge: Reality Street, 1993.

Yevgeny Yevtushenko (Selec., Intr.), *20th Century Russian Poetry: Silver and Steel, an Anthology*, New York: Doubleday, 1994.

6

Triumphant Obstination:
Reading Adrienne Rich and Elizabeth Bowen

HESTER JONES

In her essay, 'How Should One Read a Book', Virginia Woolf begins by reminding her readers that reading and methodology are uncomfortable partners. It is, as she says, impossible to prescribe patterns for reading: 'The only advice, indeed, that one person can give another about reading is to take no advice, to follow your own instincts, to use your own reason, to come to your own conclusions.'[1] Independence, Woolf confidently asserts, is 'the most important quality the reader can possess', yet in order to enjoy that freedom, 'we have of course to control ourselves.' This pattern of initial open-mindedness, followed by the punctilious practice of discipline, turns out to characterize the essay itself, as well as anticipating the pattern Woolf recommends when it comes to reading. Her advice is simple: one should read first as the author wrote: 'Do not dictate to your author; try to become him,' she commands her reader. Such an immersion in the author's identity, however, must be quickly followed by a second response: 'we are no longer the friends of the writer, but his judges.' Receptivity must be balanced by strenuous and thorough assessment. In short: 'We must stress the value of sympathy; we may try to sink our own identity as we read. But we know that we cannot sympathize wholly or immerse ourselves wholly.'[2]

Woolf here sets out the parameters of reading theory. As Patrocinio P. Schweickart has pointed out, 'mainstream reader-response theories are preoccupied with issues of control or partition – how to distinguish the contribution of the author/text from the contribution of the reader'; feminist approaches, by contrast, according to Schweickart, emphasize the need to establish communication and relationship between the female reader and author, and are

103

less threatened by the possible encroachments on the identity of both which may occur.[3]

Schweickart argues that Adrienne Rich's essay about Emily Dickinson, *Vesuvius at Home: The Power of Emily Dickinson*, exemplifies such a celebration of female community and mutual endeavour, in contrast to the 'patriarchal' tendency to antagonize and polarize the reading experience. I shall suggest in this essay, however, that Rich's account of reading, and in particular, reading Emily Dickinson, is in fact much more complex than this. I shall also propose that Rich alludes to and transforms Virginia Woolf's model of reading which operates around the antithesis between friendship and judgement; and, further, that Rich uses and complicates the metaphor of possession (the reader is possessed by her text, and struggles in turn for possession of and over it) – to adumbrate the complex and intricate relation between author, reader and the wider reading community, whether wholly female or female and male.

I shall also make several comparisons between Rich's account of reading and the account which is to be found in Elizabeth Bowen's essay on Rider Haggard's *She* – an essay which offers an 'explanation', to use Bowen's own term, of the experience described in her short story, *Mysterious Kôr*. More importantly, though, it also offers an account of how reading Haggard's story gradually led to an understanding of what Bowen calls 'the power of the pen'. The end of the essay states nothing explicitly, but leaves us to assume that the book therefore also contributed to Bowen's growth as a self-aware and powerful writer. In her essay, Rich also discusses an author whose writing is particularly important to her personally, and to her growth as a writer; so important, indeed, that distinguishing between her own and Dickinson's character has become virtually impossible. Rather than analysing her, Rich consequently conducts a conversational exchange. In this, as a reader and writer, she also, rather surprisingly, resembles Elizabeth Bowen. She speaks of the 'vibrations', Bowen, of the 'echo-track', which pass between author and reader and which bring author and reader together. As Rich says in her recent collection, *What is Found There*, a writer 'depends on a delicate, vibrating range of difference' between author and reader.[4] Both authors, here and elsewhere, struggle to maintain amidst the revelations of a 'reading' what Bowen calls in her essay 'The Roving Eye', the 'core of naivety', without which both reading and writing become false. This 'faculty for experience', as Bowen says, is characterized by its freedom, its not being 'imposed upon'. This freedom, as Bowen makes clear in her essay on *She*, was also experienced as an unexpected power, a power to follow the artist's 'roving eye' regardless of convention or social custom.

Rich's essay falls into two parts, the first of which takes the form of an autobiographical journey towards the person of Emily Dickinson, the second comprising a sequence of readings of some of Dickinson's poems. Unsurprisingly, perhaps, given the nature of Rich's own political and ideological beliefs, these readings are characterized by their interest in the relation between an artist and her talent, her power. Rich finds in the poems the consciousness of an artist essentially at ease with her own powers, aware 'of her own measure'. Dickinson, Rich reminds us in the first half of the essay, occupied the most desirable room in her father's house, the room with the most views; Rich deduces from this that Dickinson, far from being a domestic prisoner, actually enjoyed a kind of domestic sway. Rich celebrates the courage with which Dickinson embraced her own power: 'To recognize and acknowledge our own interior power has always been a path mined with risks for women; to acknowledge that power and commit oneself to it as Emily Dickinson did was an immense decision.' It is this, fundamentally, which draws Rich to Dickinson, and it is this aspect of the essay which interests me and which it has in common with my second focus of discussion, Bowen's essay on *She*. For Rich admires Dickinson's power and is empowered by it, without losing her self-possession. She allows herself, in the course of the essay, to admit that she is 'possessed' by Rich; yet such is the generous exchange with which she reads Dickinson that such self-loss is not felt by the reader as an encroachment on individuality, but rather as an extension of personality.

Rich's essay opens with the following paragraph:

I am traveling at the speed of time, along the Massachussetts Turnpike. For months, for years, for most of my life, I have been hovering like an insect against the screens of an existence which inhabited Amherst, Massachussetts, between 1830 and 1886. The methods, the exclusions, of Emily Dickinson's existence could not have been my own; yet, more and more, as a woman poet

finding my own methods, I have come to understand her
necessities, could have been witness in her defense.[5]

In commenting on this sentence, Patrocinio Schweickart draws
our attention to Rich's use of the judicial metaphor, and says: 'The
feminist reader takes the part of the woman writer against patriarchal misreadings that trivialize or distort her work.'[6] This remark
underestimates the potential threat which such an action might
offer Dickinson. The authority of Woolf's image of acting as a
writer's 'judge' is tempered to the less ambitious and more personal image of being a 'witness'; the wholehearted warmth, however, of losing one's identity, even momentarily, in 'friendship' for
the author similarly becomes the more considered action of
'defense'. Friendship and judgement have fused, to become the
action of serving as 'witness for the defense'. Furthermore, the two
are not separated into consequential actions, but are one action.
And, most importantly, it is an action which is somewhat stridently
and awkwardly placed in the past tense: 'could have been witness'.
   For all its suave intimacy, the rhetoric of Rich's essay is carefully
managed; its effects are not arbitrary ones. The phrase 'could have
been witness' feels uncomfortable and uncannily familiar because
it is reminiscent of the many poems by Dickinson which describe
an action which has not in fact happened, but which might happen
or might have happened. Dickinson invests the cluster of alternative paths around an experienced fact with a potency all her own.
One example of this will suffice:

> Our journey had advanced –
> Our feet were almost come
> To that odd fork in Being's Road –
> Eternity – by Term –[7]

So in saying that she could have been witness in Dickinson's
defence, Rich seems to invest the 'past-which-did-not-happen'
with a power and allure worthy of Dickinson. Dickinson's poems
like to begin with an assertion of impotence, a willing declaration
of her own limits. One of her most famous poems, 'Because I could
not stop for death', leads thus from powerlessness to discovery: the
poem stops short of reality, but makes its vision out of its own
disempowerment. Yet in saying that she 'could have been witness',
and thus referring intimately to a verbal formulation with which

Dickinson would be familiar, Rich is in fact articulating the central difference that exists between herself and Dickinson: she 'could' have done all sorts of things denied to Dickinson. But it is in going against this image of powerful compensation, and in imitating Dickinson's own process of stopping short of action, that Rich in fact hopes to approach the poet.

Throughout the essay, Rich maintains a clear sense of who she is: she is looking back at her own past, through the light of Dickinson's poems. The 'I' never quavers, its assurance gives the essay its compelling authority. But the present tense of the essay is taken up by the authority of that I also continually giving itself over to independently reimagining, revisioning, Dickinson, through her historical context and through her poems. Everything else comes second.

It is not as though Rich needs to take Dickinson's part, as Schweickart suggests, for the essay is powerfully aware of how the feminist reader/defender is as likely to distort or belittle as the patriarchal reader. The zealous desire to make Dickinson conform to a pattern of feminist oppression and liberation may be as misleading as the wish to sentimentalize, marginalize and trivialize her. Rich 'could', before fully realizing the significance to her of Dickinson's example of powerful independence, have rushed to Dickinson's defence. The thrust of Rich's essay, however, is to say that Dickinson needs nothing like this; she presents Rich, in fact, with an image of a self-determination, independence and self-respect which did not preclude responsiveness to other people.

Rich later says: 'she was, and is, a wonder to me when I try to imagine myself into that mind.' The centre of the sentence, 'a wonder to me', sounds charmingly gawky and deliberately unprofessional, uncritical in its terms of judgement, challengingly colloquial and impressionistic. It explicitly offers 'wonder' in place of the forms of criticism which have the effect of 'narrowing down' the genius of Emily Dickinson. But in countering the reductive effects of such criticism, Rich produces a remark whose essence is itself comically 'quaint', however much she prefaces it with a guarantee of consistency in this view across the years ('was and is'). This creates an awkward and yet also curiously truthful amalgam of responses. It is as though, while apparently remaining herself, Rich actually uses herself in order to find something more or someone other than herself, now registered inside that self. Such, Rich suggests, is the use of imagination in reading, so complicating the issue of possessing and being possessed that they become virtually indistinguishable.

Such a complex and almost animate movement between what constitutes Adrienne Rich and what remains of Emily Dickinson characterizes the essay as a whole, and gives it the remarkable and powerful appearance of being an easy conversation between friends in which much is said and exchanged, and in which no one minds too much who said what. Both are responsive persons, whose characters are mutually informing though discrete and distinctive. The sentence 'More and more, as a woman poet finding my own methods, I have come to understand her necessities', confirms this impression. 'My own' and 'her' are in complex relation. That word 'necessities' is also carefully chosen: had Rich said 'needs', this word might have endorsed the image of weak and uncontrolled dependence; but 'necessities' makes objective and also grand the personal state. It makes of personal need something akin to fate: Dickinson's need was in fact her destiny, and it confirmed her role as a genius. In making her necessity her fate, Rich goes on to suggest, and in taking control of her limited environment, Dickinson provided an example for subsequent women caught up in a situation which seems to lack promise. The 'necessities' of Dickinson's character and life are comparable to the sense of necessity in a poem; the sense that a poem makes its own way into existence, and that the artist must recognize this truth and respond to it. Further, by using the word 'necessities' of Dickinson, Rich highlights their forceful effect on her, the reader: Dickinson's powerful presence has made itself felt by her, and driven her – as if by necessity – to write the essay about her. Such an approach displaces attention from Rich herself to Dickinson: Dickinson provides the initial drive, which Rich feels obliged to respond to with her pilgrimage of homage.

And the metaphor of the journey which governs the essay is similarly complex. As I have indicated, the opening sentences suggest something long-drawn out and driven in Rich's relation to Dickinson; like Dickinson, she uses the puritan image of the soul in quest to elevate and aggrandize her own project. Yet, also like Dickinson, the tones of the essay ironize and lighten this purposive expedition. The pilgrimage to the place of Dickinson's 'existence' is also a social call, a visit: not only is Rich literalizing the feminist's belief in contextualization, but she is also portraying herself as a charmingly amateurish, slightly eccentric, belle-lettristic literary tourist, not presuming to pass judgement on the poet, merely hoping to offer worship at her shrine. And, again, Rich assumes this mask deliberately, I think: for later in the essay, she talks powerfully of what she calls Dickinson's 'little-girl strategy', her adoption of a mask of 'innocuousness and of containment.'[8] Rich's own mask lies in the charming directness of her use of the first person, which is at once both unashamedly herself and also the strategic use of herself.

'I have been hovering like an insect', says Rich, 'against the screens of an existence which inhabited Amherst'; later on in the essay, too, she repeats this image: 'I become again, an insect, vibrating at the frames of windows, clinging to the panes of glass, trying to connect.' Schweickart comments on this passage: 'In trying to read Dickinson, Rich seeks to enter her mind, to feel her presence. But the text is a screen, an inanimate object. Its subjectivity is only a projection of the subjectivity of the reader.' And of the phrase 'trying to connect', Schweickart says:

> Feminist readings of female texts are motivated by the need 'to connect', to recuperate, or to formulate – they come to the same thing – the context, the tradition, that would link women writers to one another, to women readers, and to the larger community of women. Of course, the recuperation of such a context is a necessary basis for the nonrepressive integration of women's point of view and culture into the study of a Humanities that is worthy of its name.[9]

Although this provides a useful and plausible account of the difference between feminist and conventionally patriarchal methods of reading – and helpfully stresses the 'necessary basis' of feminist reading – I am not sure that it is an exact or full description of Rich's procedure and position in the essay. For a start, the phrase 'trying to connect' remembers E.M. Forster's famous imperative 'only connect': Rich's language, if it is to be even a 'partly common' one, cannot help but connect to a non-feminist, even anti-female, tradition, as well; any determination to touch an exclusively female tradition and audience must contradict her own statement from the essay 'Someone Is Writing A Poem': 'I can't write a poem to manipulate you; it will not succeed.'[10] Furthermore, several different movements are actually at work in the images of 'hovering against

the screens' and 'vibrating at the frames'. To begin with, the image
is one Dickinson herself used to powerful effect.

In her brilliant poem, for example, 'I heard a Fly buzz – when I
died', the last stanza reads:

> With Blue – uncertain stumbling Buzz –
> Between the light – and me –
> And then the Windows failed – and then
> I could not see to see – [11]

The fly's 'stumbling Buzz' – a mixture of seeing and hearing – is the
last thing Dickinson imagines experiencing before death. The fly is
a little like Charon crossing the river of death, and is also therefore
the self's point of contact with both this world and the next. Obed-
iently, Rich uses the image as a way of recrossing that river of
difference, imitating Dickinson's use of participles in 'stumbling' to
suggest the element of shapeless and indeterminate uncertainty.
But while Dickinson's fly was pathetically unwanted and unpurpos-
ive, Rich's more generalized 'insect' knows what it's about. No
longer held 'between', it beats 'against' and 'at' the limits which
contain it: it has become a revolutionary in its maturity. Dickinson
made mock of the myth of a climactic, progressive death: to her,
death is no accomplishment, it is rather a gradual 'failing'. Her
poem takes place 'Between the Heaves of Storm', just as the fly
'interposes' between herself and the light. Definition occurs between parameters, in the stillness between one 'heave' and the next.
Dickinson pre-empts criticism by contrasting its 'uncertain stumbling' with the stark clarity of her own vision. Rich, implicitly,
accepts the uncomplimentary role of intruding insect, but skilfully
transforms it, suggesting that criticial interpretation need not be a
rude 'interposition' between the poet and her vision, but may
rather be a polite 'vibrating' in place of Dickinson's failing sight.
The 'Windows failed' for Dickinson; they have for Rich become
recalcitrant panes of glass. Rather than 'uncertain stumbling' she
offers 'hovering', 'vibrating', as imperfect but repeated attempts at
persistent poise. For 'hovering' involves moving away from, as
much as moving towards, its goal: indeed, in order to stay put, such
an alternation of advance and retreat is essential.

Such a movement between identification and distinction could be
described as 'dialectical', and Patrocinio Schweickart does indeed
contrast the characteristically 'dialectical' relation between female

reader and text with the 'dualistic' tendencies of much androcentric criticism, particularly that of Jonathan Culler and Wolfgang Iser. But 'dialectic' as a term formalizes and, more importantly, makes rigid a movement which for Rich and Dickinson is ceaseless and without a determined form. A dialectic has a known and firm trajectory; 'hovering' only a rough and sketchy arena. Similarly, a dialectic is determined by its poles of reference; 'hovering', however, looks to itself, and is more tenuously related to its focus of interest. For me, the word suggests a greater modesty and deference (servants and suitors hover around their beloved object) and also indicates an awareness of the scope and difficulty of the project Rich is 'trying' (the word is repeated frequently) to accomplish. A dialectical relation between text and reader puts both firmly in their place. Rich doesn't, at least at the outset of her journey, want to do this. To Rich, Dickinson is 'a Vesuvius'. Who would dare to harness a volcano?

And there's one further point to make about Rich's choice of metaphor here. At least three times, she uses a plural case to describe the thing she finds herself up against: she is hovering against *screens*, she is vibrating at *frames*, she is clinging to the *panes*. The three words resonate, as if their repetition were an attempt (nothing more forceful or assertive than that) to imitate the reiterative and re-visionary nature of reading, something which in fact gives the lie to the metaphor of the journey which underlies the whole essay. Writing the essay is an extension, a continuation of and in line with the process of reading the poems which Rich finds herself immersed in. It seems like a perpetual process; in fact, looked at more closely, the process involves numerous and repeated 'attempts' at the recalcitrant 'existence' of Dickinson and her poems. Dickinson is contained by the facts of her existence: she is closed in by those dates, 'between 1830 and 1886', facts which, like the notorious dashes in her poems, look like forms of containment, yet yield to nothingness on closer view. In generalizing and making plural the obstacles Rich finds herself confronting, she acknowledges their metaphysical, partly abstract quality.

So in that case, given the glassy recalcitrance of material existence, why is Rich travelling to Amherst when Dickinson herself disparaged such earthly facts? In using these images, Rich deliberately keeps the nature of the problem surrounding Dickinson ambiguous. She declines to ascribe the problem either to Dickinson herself or to the myriad interpretations and myths which have

sprung up around her. It is enough, for Rich, as it is often enough
for Dickinson, to be aware of a barrier, of many impediments to
clear understanding, and also to be aware that the difficulty is
related to Dickinson's superb incandescence, to her visionary trans-
lucence. Like light, she is, and is not, there. By recognizing the role,
the 'necessity', of the screens and panes in Dickinson's life, Rich
suggests, we may perhaps also understand the necessity of chaste
inscrutability to her creative life.

As if in answer to the 'screens', 'panes' and 'frames', then, early on
in the essay Rich has actually offered three more or less mutually
exclusive images of reading: we have the image of the romantic
quest, with its well-defined destination and breathless, excited style;
we have the 'hovering'; and we have the judicial metaphor of serving in Dickinson's defence. All, perhaps, are inadequate models for
reading; all, true to Dickinson, 'tell the truth but tell it slant'; all stop
short of the reality, the 'existence' that was Dickinson's. Approach
towards the object of veneration is held off by proper caution and
obstruction: the two are poised in precarious tension.

Rich's grandiloquent and swelling rhetoric ('for months, for
years, for most of my life') prepare us for the intense moment when
the encounter between text and reader occurs, the moment when she
will 'see' her, when the poet's presence will descend like a god
on her humble acolyte. I cannot feel that we are expected to take
this tone altogether seriously: but its almost naive fervour and
swelling emotion nonetheless make a point: reading is powerful, it
involves the emotions and it leaves its mark. Rich's style expertly
holds in tension the gusto which gets books read, and the minute
analysis which is used to justify and explain this experience. It is
hard to produce praise of a writer which conveys the spontaneous
enthusiasm of an individual and private response without that
response being enervated by strident assertion ('this is what *I*
think') or dulled by weak reference to an authoritative view ('this is
what is thought'). Rich falls into neither trap, however, sustaining
the warmth of fervent and felt admiration, while ballasting it with
articulate and engaged commitment. She readily admits, unlike
Woolf, that neither admiration nor assessment came first; they have
always coexisted in emulous companionship. She endorses no pho-
ney detachment from the text, for without engagement at the centre
of a response, it will not live. She hovers *against* the pane; her
engagement combines commitment with antagonism, and the two
need not be disentangled. Such possible antagonism is indicated in

the humorous, almost Swiftian, contrast between the volcano-poet and the insect-reader: it's a contrast which ironically acknowledges the hopelessness of 'trying to connect', of trying to establish a relationship between the creator of translucent texts and their hovering, vibrating reader.

However, in locating Dickinson 'at home', Rich is going at least some way towards trying to pin her down, to identify her 'natural' situation and context, and publicly to understand her elusive and determined privacy. Conscientiously, however, she looks first to Dickinson's own somewhat negative definition of what 'home' was: 'home', she wrote, 'is not where the heart is, but the house and the adjacent buildings.' Dickinson's anti-romantic definition distracts attention away from the conventionally comfortable, emotionally charged idea of 'home' towards something cooler and also more specific. She moves from the material thing – the house (which is important) – to the 'adjacent buildings'. Home is a matter of orientation, of direction and attitude, not of simple feeling. Dickinson is almost, I think, making a religious point: 'home' is to be found in the attitude and deportment of the individual, just as religious faith is as much a matter of inclination and willing attention as a matter of emotional transport.

And it is this reorientation that Rich uses against the danger she knows she herself offers: the danger of so taking possession of Dickinson in Rich's own terms as to domesticate her in a way troublingly comparable to those patriarchal critics who, Rich says, narrowed Dickinson down, cut her down to size and believed her genius to be of a kind which could be 'enclosed' by a mere situation. Even in writing an essay which tries to transform the continual process of reading and rereading into a single artful 'reading', an ending-place, a home for the experience of many moments and years, Rich knows she runs the risk of joining the ranks of appropriating critics. A piece of criticism is likely to want to make something more general and representative, though not necessarily larger, out of a life's works. So Emily Dickinson sits like a lady 'at home', awaiting the rush of public inspection, transforming her private being into a public spectacle, while Adrienne Rich, with conscious and scrupulous self-irony, pays her call and waits on her attendance. If one is not careful, warns Rich, the volcano may be thus reduced to quaintness.

But Rich's next move is to turn Dickinson's refusal to be domesticated inside her work, in the very creating of it, into a means of offsetting the danger of Rich herself critically redomesticating the opus. 'I have a notion that genius knows itself', writes Rich, taking the thought in particular from the Dickinson poem which begins triumphantly: 'I'm ceded – I've stopped being Theirs –' and which ends by celebrating her own 'Will to Choose, or to reject,/And I choose, just a Crown –'. Rich applauds Dickinson's active use of the 'will to choose': she recognizes in her the talent for survival, portraying her in fact as a kind of Anne Frank, a refugee in the closet, writing for posterity amidst adverse circumstances: 'she was determined to survive, to use her powers, to practise necessary economies.' Instead of being a 'soft cherubic' gentlewoman, with 'dimity convictions', Dickinson turned her creative powers forcefully on her own self and life. Such an action could seem unwomanly in its apparent selfishness; Rich's point in the essay is that such self-knowledge and self-confirmation was not only not selfish but 'necessary', both for her own survival, but also, as the end of the essay makes clear, for those women who came after her, women such as Rich, who need a model of woman-centred activity. Generous and unqualified acceptance of and interest in Dickinson is tempered by a brisker and more honest use of her. There is no mimsy aesthetization; Dickinson is no good if she cannot do some good.

And from this the essay finds its point of poise, as Rich moves from celebrating Dickinson unconditionally, towards asking how she can transform her into a template, a model, for subsequent women writers. The lasting achievement of the essay is its superb combination of admiration and respect, a respect for the separateness of Dickinson, a distinction which *itself* gave Rich power and strength. As a model Dickinson's separateness engenders that of others without endangering her own. For as Rich wrote to Dickinson, in her own poem, 'The Spirit of Place': 'strangers are an endangered species' but:

> This place is large enough for both of us
> The river-fog will do for privacy
> this is my third and last address to you
>
> with the hands of a daughter I would cover you
> from all intrusion even my own
> saying rest to your ghost

with the hands of a sister I would leave your hands
open or close as they prefer to lie
and ask no more of who or why or wherefore

with the hands of a mother I would close the door
on the rooms you've left behind
and silently pick up my fallen work[12]

Dickinson leaves room not only for readings but also for the creation of future writings.

The bringing together of a moment of direct apprehension and the following need to objectify and appropriate the moment can be expressed in ways other than those Adrienne Rich uses. For the remainder of this essay, I shall consider a reader whose terms of reference are different from Rich's, but who in her writing demonstrates a surprisingly similar combination of bare wonder and objectivity.

When asked to discuss for a radio programme the book which had most affected her when young, Elizabeth Bowen chose Rider Haggard's thrilling romance, *She*. She also, I suggest, reflected on her reading of this book, and the cardinal role it played in her 'accession to power', as she described it, in her short story, *Mysterious Kôr*. The talk, which appears in an edited form in the collection of essays entitled *Afterthought*, resembles Rich's essay in a number of respects, though the two essays are in cultural and historical terms otherwise very different. Both essays are discussing works which have long had a profound influence on their minds, and which, in Bowen's case at least, started to affect them before they were fully capable of rational assessment or analysis. They are both trying to present accounts of works that have been close to their hearts, and which perhaps therefore particularly resist an 'objective' analysis. Like Rich, consequently, Bowen seems almost to exaggerate the emotional nature of her response to the book. Unlike Rich, Bowen is not explicitly concerned with questions of gender, let alone of feminist or lesbian allegiance. But she is, I think strikingly like Rich, concerned with the experience in which an object inspiring wonder becomes 'a wonder to me'; when receptive 'reading' breaks into 'a reading'; when a book ceases to be distinct from the reader, and becomes an inseparable part of their mental scenery. Bowen remembers the time when she read *She*, the prewar era in fact, as 'a dull, trim back garden, in which only trivial games could be played'. Reading, and particularly the reading of *She*, her first quasi-adult book, interrupted a world which lacked clarity or the colour of revelation: a world 'hemmed in', as she says, by a tediously factual objectivity, in which the 'myths of childhood' were exhausted, but the full experience of adulthood was still on the horizon. It was this liminal nature of the book which made it memorable: it brought Bowen, as I have said, 'accession to full power', just as Dickinson brought Rich to an understanding of the need to recognize and respond to the power and force of her own, distinctively female, talent and needs.

Bowen is specific and very interesting about the way in which this revelation, this sudden understanding, came about. Externally, as she says, the book promised little, with its 'pink-brown cover', suggesting 'cocoa or milk-chocolate'; it had a homely and comforting lack of pretension or ambition to educate its reader. But it was, in fact, a 'book of promise', its style giving 'the effect of wellsugared cocoa laced with some raw and subtle intoxicant'. In other words, *She* brought the civilized and the wild enticingly together. Bowen acknowledges the sensationalism of the book and even imitates it with heady, even gushy, enthusiasm: 'But Kôr, Kôr, the enormous derelict city, whose streets the Amahagger dare not read, is ever on the horizon. My impatience to visit it was immense.' She slips thus into the present tense as the memory of reading the book returns to her. Towards the end of the essay, she writes of the 'echo-track' by which this kind of memory operates, and thus makes an important point about reading. We do not read books in isolation from our own lives: not only, as Rich points out, do we need to explore the context of the author's lives, but our rereading of books also helps us to remember our past lives: things, even the look of a book, carry intense memories which lie buried until reawakened.

When remembering the effect of *She*, Bowen is puzzled for a moment for an explanation of its tremendous effect on her. She consequently reminds herself and us of the nature of Kôr:

> Court upon court, space upon space of empty chambers, that spoke more eloquently to the imagination than any crowded street. It was a wonderful sight to see the full moon looking down on the ruined fane of Kor. A wonderful thing to think for how

many thousands of years the dead orb above and the dead city below had thus gazed upon one another.

This image is powerful, I think, and spoke to Bowen, not least because it expressed for her the relation between the self and the unknown, or even the divine, which was to become a central theme in her work. Martin Buber's *I and Thou* employs a strikingly similar image to describe a similar experience: man at first has 'only the dynamic, stirring image of the moon's effect streaming through his body', an effect which gradually becomes 'an object', a 'He or She' out of the unknown 'Thou'. Bowen's *Mysterious Kôr*, I will argue, takes this process, again embodied by the moon, further.

The book, for Bowen, was experienced as an epiphany: she tries to rationalize this experience by observing coolly, 'whatever happened, buildings survived people', and by referring to the book's interest in reincarnation, but eventually she realizes that her fascination with the book was more than this:

> It was the idea of obstination, triumphant obstination, which became so obsessing – want any one thing hard enough, long enough, and it must come your way. This did strike deep: it came up like a reinforcement, because in my day, my childhood, all polite education was against the will – which was something to be subdued, or put out of sight as though it did not exist. Up to now, I had always expected books to be on the side of politeness.[13]

Bowen even reanimates an obsolete word, 'obstination', to convey the exact force of her meaning. The word combines the senses of 'obstinacy' and 'determination' and even 'destination', thus conflating goal and journey into the one word, as well as making the morally negative term (obstinacy) laudable, converting it into 'determination'. Although Bowen's sense is not easy to follow, she seems to mean that the book reinforced something she privately felt but dared not acknowledge, let alone express, and that concerned the connection between art and will, creation and power: to create, she suddenly realized, the self must feel free to pursue what it wants and needs. This conflicted, as she says, with what 'polite education' told young women.

So just as Rich found in Dickinson's poems confirmation and self-assurance, so too Bowen reads this apparently innocuous, even rather sedate, Edwardian romance as undercover propaganda, a book which allowed her to confront the possibly destructive force of her own creative will. The shift from 'obsessed' to the implicit though not used term 'obstinacy' and on to the composite term 'obstination' charts, I think, a movement towards self-under-standing and self-acceptance which reading *She* triggered and fa-cilitated, and which many of Bowen's best novels, in particular *The Death of the Heart*, similarly explore. Bowen rejects, in other words, the restrictions both of contemporary psychoanalysis (and its pre-occupation with obsession) and also the outmoded Victorian mor-ality which chided obstinacy and recommended politeness. (And of course, such an emphasis on politeness also led to compensatory obsessions.)

Helped by the revelatory experience of *She*, Bowen finds herself looking to a kind of purposive selfishness which has an end in view, a form of art not enclosed in the self of the artist (as an obsession might be) but not committed to a system of pseudo-objective morality either. Obstination, instead, determines a form of reading and writing which derives from the drive of the individual, yet which does not allow the individual to indulge in licentious escapism. Before reading *She*, Bowen had expected books to be on the side of politeness, a covertly repressive force, against self-affirm-ation or self-discovery. *She* proved that cocoa could be laced with alcohol, that politeness and the wild could be brought together. Reading the book made her feel at home; yet it also violently propelled her beyond the boundaries of the familiar 'home' and gave her an intoxicating sense of possibility. As she says at the end of the essay: 'After *She*, print was to fill me with apprehension. I was prepared to handle any book like a bomb.' It was, in short, writing that she had discovered: 'what it could do!' And still more, 'the power of the pen', the power to anchor and to transmute the reading self. And again, as in Rich's essay, this experience is de-scribed in terms of a 'revelation'; the encounter with *She* is, as in *She*, an encounter with another.

Martin Buber, as I have suggested, expresses this experience in terms of a dialectic: 'A time comes when it [the 'I'] bursts its bonds, and the *I* confronts itself for a moment, separated as though it were a *Thou*; as quickly to take possession of itself and from then on to enter into relations in consciousness of itself.' Bowen and Rich, however, choose to use the 'echo-track' of reading, in which a continual process of exchange and vibration between past and present prevent a more rigid pattern from emerging.

At the beginning of Bowen's short story, *Mysterious Kôr*, we are presented with a scene rendered ghostly and inert by the flattening light of the moon: 'Full moonlight drenched the city and searched it; there was not a niche left to stand in.'[14] As Buber said in *I and Thou*, the moon's effect is personified, yet at the same time its agency is curiously formless: the light, not the moon, is 'full', the city is 'drenched' as well as searched. Bowen's remark in the essay on *She* that she read the book at a time when 'there was no undiscovered country' and when she had 'developed a grudge against actuality' is relevant here. History, objectivity, academic precision had robbed the world of romance. In the essay 'The Roving Eye', Bowen describes the writer as an 'inattentive learner in the schoolroom of life' and goes on to say:

> Concentration on any one writer's work almost always ends by exposing a core of naivety – a core which, once it has been laid bare, seems either infantile or august. [. . .] Somewhere within the pattern, somewhere behind the words, a responsive, querying innocence stays intact.[15]

The moon's omnipresence in the story makes every presence insubstantial, depriving each figure of its own individuality, blurring distinctiveness like a blot of ink, arresting the development of all three characters whom the story describes. And yet, their innocence is also a precondition of the story's creation, and without it, the significance of the story's moment will be lost. Callie, who guards the hearth and waits for her friend Pepita and Pepita's lover, Arthur, to return to their shared 'flatlet', has a virginal purity. It is an irony, therefore, that she clings unquestioningly to family values, even though she seems to have no intention of putting them into practice. This purity gives her, like the moon, a poignant but cool isolation in the story. Pepita, by contrast, has the company of her soldier-boyfriend; but she too looks for a way out of crowded modernity, clinging to the imaginary world of 'Kôr'. Both, therefore, are revealed by the story to have a 'core of innocence' which the moon both reveals and represents.

However, the narrator describes Pepita and Arthur's romance as a 'collision in the dark'; passion and sympathy in the story (Pepita expressing the first, and Callie the second) have become divorced from one another, the one turning to the loss of identity, the other leading to isolation. Unless these two coalesce, the story suggests, the characters cannot reach a state of self-determination; their progress remains arrested. In the story there is no explicit moment of revelation or disenchantment for Callie. And yet, as Callie returns to bed after talking, in the middle of the night, to Arthur, she discovers to her dismay that her romantic belief in love and high values has not been justified. Instead she tries 'to compose her limbs'; and with the 'composition' comes the end of innocence and the beginning of something in her analogous to art. Without the moon's mysterious eye, life is, as Callie says, 'not so strong'; yet the waning of idealism is a necessary preliminary to self-creation and artistic fashioning, two processes that are seen to coincide.

Shadowing the story is the myth of home, the myth of the 'abiding city' whose towers and streets, though 'void', still remain, if viewed with closed eyes. Like Rich in her reading of Dickinson, Bowen found in *She* a place of power. In *Mysterious Kôr*, a vision of perfect 'answering', a communion in which solitude and responsiveness perfectly coexist, is regretfully seen to be beyond the 'making my own', beyond possession. Adrienne Rich turns from her vision of Dickinson, floating ghostlike down the stairs, and starts to ask how she can transform her into a model for the present. Similarly, Bowen's heroine seems to start rebuilding for herself the vision she has lost.

Both these, then, offer a model of reading that moves beyond the opposition between immersion and judgement, adoration and criticism. Bowen's essay on *She*, however, also brings home to its reader the importance – the 'power', even – of reading which maintains or rediscovers the 'core' (or 'Kôr') of innocent responsiveness within complex literary creation. Bowen's account, as the points about 'obstination' suggest, draws a parallel between this core of innocence and the artist's need to follow his or her 'roving eye'. Like Rich, in other words, she perceives the essential need for self-knowledge, freedom and the power to remain deliberately susceptible to whatever the text (in the case of the reader) or the subject (in the case of the author) demands. If a scrupulously, self-consciously ideological reading threatens or disrupts this process, the reading will lose its power.

Notes

1. Virginia Woolf, 'How Should One Read a Book', *The Common Reader* (London: Hogarth Press 1932), p. 258.
2. *Ibid.*, pp. 267, 268.
3. See Patrocinio P. Schweickart, 'Reading Ourselves: Toward A Feminist Theory of Reading', *Gender and Reading: Essays on Readers, Texts, and Contexts*, edited by Elizabeth A. Flynn and Patrocinio P. Schweickart (Baltimore, Maryland: Johns Hopkins University Press, 1986). Henceforth referred to as Schweickart.
4. Adrienne Rich, 'Someone Is Writing a Poem', *What Is Found There* (New York and London: W.W. Norton, 1993), p. 84.
5. Adrienne Rich, 'Vesuvius at Home: The Power of Emily Dickinson (1975)', *On Lies, Secrets, and Silence* (London: Virago 1980), p. 158.
6. Schweickart, p. 46.
7. Emily Dickinson, *The Complete Poems*, edited by Thomas H. Johnson (Trowbridge, Faber & Faber 1970), p. 303. Henceforth *Poems*.
8. 'Vesuvius', p. 169.
9. *Gender and Reading*, p. 48.
10. Adrienne Rich, p. 84.
11. *Poems*, p. 223.
12. *A Wild Patience Has Taken Me This Far*, collected in *The Fact of a Doorframe* (New York and London: W.W. Norton 1981), pp. 300–301.
13. Elizabeth Bowen, 'She', *Afterthought* (London: Longman 1962), pp. 111–12.
14. *Mysterious Kôr, The Collected Stories of Elizabeth Bowen* (London: Penguin 1980), p. 728.
15. 'The Roving Eye', *Afterthought* (London: Penguin 1962), p. 193.

Part Three
Reading and Teaching

7

Reading about Things:
or Hannibal Goes for the Mail

JOHN BAYLEY

During my years as a university teacher in English I have often wondered how the job should ideally be done, only to conclude that, as with most other human arrangements, there are no ideal ways, and perhaps not even any particularly good ones. So much depends, as with all levels of the teaching process, from the earliest study of books onwards, upon the individual teacher. English is most unusual as an academic subject in that good instruction, and reception, does not really get more complex or sophisticated as time goes on. Good books, bad books too, remain much the same; and the will, or the wish, to read them probably does not change very much between the ages of 12 and 20. English can never truly count as an academic subject for this reason. There is no natural progress, as in other kinds of study.

Nor is there any true closure of technique. Reading remains the same, although it may come to be called 'close reading', detailed study of a text. And do any texts, at university level, really get studied more closely than things once read in childhood? A habit of reading has to be learnt, and an old immediacy grown out of. What is in books ceases to be the most exciting thing in life. The helpless and engrossing privateness of reading disappears.

But none of this happens totally; and in any case the exam question about *Hamlet* is much the same at school as it is at the end of a university course. There is a *childishness* still haunting the subject. Hardly surprising that two of the most charismatic of its teachers – C.S. Lewis and J.R.R. Tolkien – wrote childrens' books, adventure stories, texts that can be 'read at all ages'. Nor that another charismatic teacher, F.R. Leavis, continually and often pet-ulantly stressed the notion of *adulthood* in literary studies. To be on the side of life, through the proper study of books, is to become mature.

125

This openness, and even more what seems this threat of a kind of permanent adolescence, has often troubled those teachers who take the subject most seriously. It accounts for the hint of scorn and patronage in early reactions to an English School. A subject for young women, and for the not very bright? An attempt at closure was at first made by emphasizing the study of Old English. Here was some sort of mystery which required orthodox tuition, and which could not be discredited by the profane layman who himself read English literature – up to a point anyway – and who was apt to deride the idea of a difference between reading it and studying it.

But eventually of course something far more effective was devised. Literary Theory. Here was a mystery inaccessible enough not to be discredited by the ignorant, and at the same time exciting in the promise it held out to the student of magic understanding, true revelation. It could dissolve, surely, the thickness and stodginess of a literature course, substituting key texts and insights for the great mass of event and contingent personification which wearied the compulsory, if not the compulsive, reader. Also, it had to be taught; and, like all instruction in mysteries, this could be a stimulating process.

Literary Theory also possessed cosmopolitan and continental prestige: no small assets to a subject whose mere Englishness could seem naive and provincial, as well as increasingly out of favour as the social and political climate changed. Nor did it strike the intrigued student as in any way dry as dust. It was, or could be made, full of sex and violence, as well as being relevant, challenging and contemporary. And had not Roland Barthes endearingly preached the doctrine of *jouissance*? In his cheery Gallic way he linked the concept, linguistically and metaphysically, with sexual gratification, which could only seem to make the reading of texts more acceptable (indeed more adult). Some might have found *jouissance* harder to come by when they were actually grappling with the formulaic complexities of *S/Z*, Barthes's famous commentary on a story of Balzac, or with his other writings. But the concept remained a heartening one, and with a curious significance in view of that unspoken, for in a sense embarrassing, connection between reading – helpless, gluttonous reading – and the study of a text. Perhaps the two could be brought together, or at least into a more harmonious relationship? This might depend less on taste than on raw ability, the ability of those who master grammar and the problems of mathematics, who enjoy solving crossword puzzles and legal difficulties. The person who can do these things is not just a reader, and for such a person this new form of intellectual reading may come easily. He might well be able even to find *jouissance* in it. For the ordinary reader, dependent on the things, events and people in books, it would continue to be a task of some difficulty.

But it would be a task, if an arduous one, and of an exclusive kind, which may be what the student of literature is often, if unconsciously, hoping to be set. Reading Trollope to answer a question on him ('Is Trollope more successful with his male or his female characters?') is hardly a task, and to study a whole brood of novels by reading them incompletely, or too fast, is not the natural way to read. A real promise in literary theory is to excite the student by offering a new version of the excitement originally immanent in print. Here its offer of a key, or several keys, to the reading process is a real asset, and one which the good student can make an impressive use of.

He will have to forfeit, of course, any neutrality which he might have thought himself to have possessed, again probably unconsciously, in the reading process. *The Wind in the Willows*, or *Treasure Island*, will become transformed into texts full of political and social significance. No harm in that, except that an innocence in reading, once overlaid, is not easy to recover. It can be recovered, none the less, and a new reading experience can restore it, at least briefly. Philip Larkin once said that writing a poem was rather like trying to recall a tune that had gone out of the head, and even while there was a recollection of it, seemed hardly to have existed. The poem, if it comes off, recaptures the tune and sets it down. But then commentary can overlay it and make the original tune difficult to recapture. Everyone has had the experience of finding a piece of music tied inextricably to words that were subsequently written for it. A peculiarly exasperating case is that of Holst's Jupiter, in the *Planets* suite, which was set to bad, but alas memorable, words in 1915 or thereabouts by the British Ambassador to the USA. Holst detested them. The listener who finds his verbal memory firmly in charge of his musical memory may do so too. The verbal impress of a literary theory, in practice and in action, may have the same effect. A primal reading of *The Wind in the Willows* does not even quite extricate itself from the later 'discourse', which suggests the social significance of the Mole and the Rat, the Toad, the Badger and the Wild Wooders.

My *tendance* here may seem towards primitivism, childish primitivism. A first reading may none the less be connected with a
subsequent kind of vivid indifference, expressive of the true joy of
print. Primal reading is a thoroughly irresponsible activity, and this
irresponsibility can persist, and very often does so secretly, though
it may be schooled by a literature course to keep itself quiet. The
counter-argument to what might be called neutrality in reading
(though I think 'indifference' is the more expressive word) is of
some interest, as well as having great importance for the exponent
of any kind of Theory.

The line he takes is that uncommitted reading does not, and in the
nature of things cannot, exist. Of course this is true in the obvious
sense that we cannot be other than the products of our culture and
age. But the exponent of Theory goes much further than this. So-
called uncommitted persons, who are not against the politics of
Theory, but either unaware of them or uninterested, are really in
the grip – equally unawares maybe – of another and rival Theory.
They are just as much participants, even if involuntarily, in the
ideological struggle. Indeed one valuable function of Theory politics is to wake them up to the reality of the obsolete assumptions to
which they are unknowingly committed. As Terry Eagleton has put
it, they 'seem unaware that theirs is just another form of politics',
for 'a conservative politics is usually one which denies the very
category of the political itself.'

It follows that literature can only be properly read and understood if it is seen in terms of politics, of warring ideologies. In one
sense again this is a commonplace. *The Canterbury Tales, Paradise
Lost, The Faerie Queene* are obviously full of the politics of their time
and of their individual authors. So is Shakespeare. This has always
been taken for granted: but it has not been seen as the essential area,
not only for study and research, but for the consciousness of the
ordinary reader. The notion of the past and its writing as *different*,
an experience outside our own, used also to be taken for granted:
indeed the sense that it was so constituted a primal experience in
reading. 'The past is a foreign country: they do things differently
there.' A vital function of ideological Theory is to assert a uniformity of approach from the standpoint of the present and its preoccu-
pations. Readers, it is assumed, will only feel at home in the past if
they see it in terms of contemporary *idées reçues*.

The resulting naturalization of literature in the interest of ideologies which, although sometimes in competition, share the same

assumptions of unchangeable correctness, has produced readers of what has become a meta-literature, a system of clues and pointers to be recognized accordingly. Where the university teaching of English is concerned, this has led to professionalization based in the 'state of the art' of Theory. A state of the art approach, in imitation of other technologies, has replaced what used to be the virtually static principle of scholarship, recognized alike by scholars and amateurs. It would not have occurred, say to C.S. Lewis, however ideologically dedicated a man in his own fashion he may have been, that technical skills and vocabularies were needed for scholarship, or for teaching. Himself an effective writer and natural stylist he would have held a gift for polemics an asset, though not as essential, for a good teacher of literature; but it would have been a face-to-face polemics, in the lecture room or on the page, without recourse to the technology of a profession.

The sense that readers of literature should know, or find out, what they should be looking for is common today, and carries the implication that reading is itself becoming a kind of technological skill. The alert student is reading to identify what the climate of Theory has taught him. There are instances in this context where the technological approach and vocabulary has virtually superseded the ideological and functions on its own, sometimes producing a criticism whose conclusions seems strangely old-fashioned and familiar, because similar to the kind of comments that might all artlessly have been made by readers in a pre-technological age. A former student of mine, who became interested in the novels of Elizabeth Bowen, has produced in collaboration with a friend a brilliant study of her work, based, as they put it, 'on a new kind of literary critical writing', in which this novelist's 'personal experience, imagination, and feelings' are transmuted and reinterpreted into the sphere of Theory.

The results are striking and to anyone unfamiliar with the novels the might well seem to give the essential Bowen: that is the wholly theoretical Bowen. For her readers, in the normal sense, the charm and pleasure of her novels lies in their humour and observation, their distracted intelligence, the sardonic absence of a coherent point of view. The theoretical reader transforms this impression by turning it into his own sort of higher coherence. In the resulting as it were meta-novel, the 'text' is 'loosened', 'so that words and figural processes induce a hallucinatory logic counteracting experiential readings.' In other words, as it would perhaps be fair to say, the *apparent* experience of reading Elizabeth Bowen is not the *real* one. Finding itself unable to assign her to a political or socio-historical category, correct or incorrect in this context or that, Theory gives her high marks in terms of its own fallback formulae of indeterminacy, *aporia* and dissolution. Formally speaking, she was exploring a new and original kind of logic in terms of her fiction.

The point to stress, I think, is that this 'new kind of critical writing' is based on real and acute perceptions with which any 'normal' reader of Bowen would agree, but which are used by the two critics to produce a meta-Bowen who can then be formally installed in the pantheon of Theory. The writer herself has become denaturalized, in the fashion predicted by Mallarmé in his sonnet on Poe. Theory, like eternity in the sonnet, has changed her at last into her true self. With the result, at least where students of literature are concerned, that she must in the future be studied, not read, on these critical terms. The natural or unsophisticated reading of a novel by Bowen will only be possible outside the scope of literature studies.

From the point of view of the Theorist his techniques can only impose the absolute necessity of taking over books, reading matter, in this way. Their freedom to be their merely apparent selves cannot be recognized. This necessity also explains, of course, the necessity of attributing a similar strategy, however unconscious it may be, to the view that a simple natural, indifferent or unstrategic reading is ever possible. But in claiming this the theorist and his disciples inevitably paint themselves into their chosen corner. However swarming with unconscious prejudice his own reading attitudes may be, the untrained reader is helpless before what seems to be on the page: he has no standardized technique for dealing with it. Hence it is this ordinary reader who actually receives the freedom of what is in the book, instead of supplying his own ready-made lock-up for himself and the book to inhabit.

Anyone who has had to give a course of classes in individual texts will recognize in the guidelines he finds himself having to lay down for himself and his students the beginnings of the situation from which Literary Theory ultimately derives. Anarchy, and the innocent abuse of that happy freedom, is what the class-giver soon finds himself coming to dread. 'I don't like that Rupert Birkin', obstinately remarked a young women in a class I once gave on *Women in Love*. In spite of the danger signals here, which my previous experience warned me of, I was rather struck by this com-

ment and weakly asked her to say why. She was unable, or disin-
clined, but in a flash an aimless wrangle had broken out between
her and other students who wished to treat Lawrence in terms of
textual orthodoxy, and the formal to-ing and fro-ing of moral and
aesthetic criteria. We were not on to Literary Theory in those days,
but the need for its guidelines could be said to have loomed large
in the background of the discussion. We were, after all, studying
the text, and not just reading it for fun.

On the spur of the moment I recently produced some pieces at
random to a class, giving out photocopies of them to read as a
prelude or *hors-d'œuvre* to the main text we were studying. There
was no rhyme or reason in the selection: indeed no coherence at all.
I was just curious to see what immediate responses would be, and
what participants would regard as the object of the exercise. The
object of the main exercise, the study of *Silas Marner* as a text, was
already obvious and had in a sense been predetermined by their
week's reading. So instead of *Silas Marner* we spent the period
discussing the pieces I had produced. These were not anonymous.
I said who each piece was by, and what more or less were the
circumstances in which it was written.

We started with a short piece of Livy, describing Hannibal's
crossing of the Alps. Not much to say about that. Everyone knew
more or less about it, but what to say about it in terms of the study
of literature? Could the point be to decide Hannibal's political
status in terms of historical materialism? What about the fires and
the vinegar to crack the rocks? How was that significant then? Well,
perhaps it wasn't, but didn't it stay in the mind? Was it not compelling to read about? Yes, but in terms of the historical process, to
which Livy must be giving expression, Hannibal was a negligible
factor. Literature as history was making this point clear. His efforts
in the end were wasted. Is the effort that becomes heroic legend
ever wasted? Why describe the achievement in such detail?

The pursuit of Hannibal soon looked unprofitable, and already
seemed to cause suspicion. We moved on to some stanzas from Dr
Johnson's poem 'On the Death of Mr Robert Levet, a Practiser in
Physic'.

> Well tried through many a varying year,
>   See Levet to the grave descend,
> Officious, innocent, sincere,
>   Of every friendless name the friend.

> Yet still he fills affection's eye,
>   Obscurely wise and coarsely kind;
> Nor, letter'd Arrogance, deny
>   Thy praise to merit unrefined.

The sigh of relief that went up was almost palpable. Now everyone knew what to do and the sort of things to say. We were soon on to the sense of 'tried', of 'officious', and of the methods by which an eye may be filled. (With water, or with an image, present or in the past.) Ambiguity abounded: even irony; for no doubt Dr Levet was a stout, coarse sort of person, however benevolent, who would fill an eye – quite an eyeful in fact – as he would fill a suit of clothes. Was the physical picture of the man that was emerging further strengthened by the unexpectedness of the adverbs that qualified his wisdom and his kindness, without of course contradicting them? No doubt it was: and it was in the art of the poem to use such elaborate devices of language (the rhetorical oxymoron) to confirm, as it appeared, its own rugged simplicity, and that of the man who inspired it. But could the poem be falsely pretending to a simplicity it did not possess? Placing itself in an unwarranted way on the side of a person who knew nothing of poetry, while pretending scorn for the people who did?

So one of our number was ingenious enough to think, and animation became general. Johnson might have been surprised, and probably displeased, to find his poem treated as so much an object for study of this sort. He had hoped it would make its point more simply? He was trying to give a voice to the inarticulate, and to the silent good they might do in their lives? But in our context his poem had become only a fruitful source of study.

And so, it turned out, had the next piece, although it had come into my head quite contingently and without any idea of a parallel.

> I have made fellowships –
>   Untold of happy lovers in old song.
> For love is not the binding of fair lips
>   With the soft silk of eyes that look and long,
>
> By joy, whose ribbon slips, –
>   But wound with war's hard wire whose stakes are strong;
> Bound with the bandage of the arm that drips;
>   Knit in the webbing of the rifle-thong.

I have perceived much beauty
> In the hoarse oaths that kept our courage straight;
> Heard music in the silentness of duty;
> Found peace where shell-storms spouted reddest spate.

This turned out an *embarras de richesse*. There seemed almost too much to say. We were soon on to the use of Keatsian romance in the grim situation of trench warfare, whose properties could be used none the less in much the same way as the former conventionalities of romance. 'Oaths' were similarly consecrated by a poetical context. Was 'Apologia Pro Poemate Meo' a good poem? Most of us emphatically thought not. Why then was it being so much argued about, and providing so many interesting points in terms of close reading? How much did it tell one of Wilfred Owen's character and personality? There was silence on this point, which may have appeared inappropriate to a discussion of the mechanism. But didn't 'I have perceived much beauty' say something about Owen's openness, earnestness, lack of humour about himself and his verses? Didn't it touchingly convey something involuntary about his nature – naive, sheltered, shocked, priggish? But no, no – all the technique was ironical, putting old poetic conventions into a new form, unsuitable for them, and *therefore* effectively shocking. To emphasize the horror of war, and the suffering and separation of those who had to be a part of it? Yes, but that wasn't the point of the poem, which was a piece of elaborate technique, highly crafted (look at the metre) but not necessarily successful.

What disappeared in studying the piece was its intention, the significance of its title. Someone did indeed point out the 'ironical' similarity – Latin epitaphs and things – with *Dulce et Decorum Est* ('it is sweet and glorious ... to die for one's country'). But what about the vivid image of the poet himself? One girl in our group interestingly said that she thought the poem protested too much. But perhaps, I wondered, was it the point to protest too much, to make a reader rightly feel uncomfortable, if accidentally embarrassed?

Did not both Johnson and Owen – however different their approach – want to make you aware of people who weren't able or anxious to attempt their own awareness of things? Was the human side of the poetry more important than the way it was done? How could that be, when the way it was done was the point of studying it?

A slight sulkiness descended upon our group as a whole at this point, nor was it in any way diminished by the final extract. This was from the Diary of the Revd Francis Kilvert, 10 August 1871:

> I went to the post and walked in the lime avenue till the postman came. Two wood pigeons were cooing to each other aloft in the limes. The sheep grazed in the grassy avenue or lay under the trees grunting and groaning with their bright red bodies panting in the heat and their white foolish curly horned faces stretched out upon the ground. Now and then came up the avenue the tinkle of the wandering bell.
> 'It's warm,' said I to the stout flushed bearded postman.
> 'Ah Sir,' he said, ' 'tis something more than that.'
> The two Miss Barnes came from Tillworth to spend the afternoon and play croquet.

I explained more or less who Kilvert was, and where he lived and worked. Someone observed that it didn't sound much like work, and the social point was taken up by someone else, who said with a slightly cunning look that the postman called the diarist 'Sir'. The value of the passage, if any, could lie in its unconscious and therefore revealing indication of the class habits and structure of the period? Another suggestion was that the parson seemed to imply that the sheep and the postman came into the same category of inferior beings. The same young woman who had thought the poem protested too much said the diarist certainly managed to convey what a hot day it was. It made her feel quite hot herself. There was some laughter at this, but she pressed her point, wondering why the sheeps' bodies were described as red – surely they couldn't have been red? I said perhaps they had been shorn recently, and the shorn skin appeared inflamed in the sunlight. They now looked expectant but rather irritated, as if I had been keeping the real significance of the passage up my sleeve.

I told them that the reason I had remembered this extract was not directly to do with the diary, but because I had seen it quoted years ago in a small magazine article. It had been a discursive essay, in the fashion of the time, about reasons why we remembered bits out of books. The writer was unable to say why this extract from Kilvert's Diary had particularly struck him, but thought it had something to do with two factors: the sense of something recalled being far more vivid than the original happening itself, and the feeling of an exchange of words that had passed into time and acquired the significance of a gnomic utterance, like words found carved on stone. Reading that, I remembered having seen Kilvert's own tombstone in the churchyard at Bredwardine by the river Wye. It had on it a quotation from the Book of Hebrews. 'He being dead, yet speaketh.' Kilvert had died young, and quite suddenly, a few weeks after he had got married and given up writing his diary.

The attention of the class had wandered, but the girl who had remarked on the heat of the day in the passage asked whether the Diary could be obtained easily, and she told me later that she had become hooked on it. The next week we were back on *Silas Marner*. George Eliot's loving if somewhat over-emphatic reconstruction of past habits and customs in a Midland village made something of a contrast with Kilvert. The novel was the perfect subject for close criticism, almost as if George Eliot herself had intended it to be read that way.

My brief informal experiment in what used to be called Practical Criticism had not been much of a success, though it had at least resulted in Kilvert himself acquiring another addicted reader. It had also shown, perhaps, that I.A. Richards's barely concealed sense of impatience and bafflement over those original 'protocols' (the written responses of students faced with a poem they had never seen before) was something that might still be experienced, almost unchanged, today, although our contemporary group of students had a much better idea of how they were supposed to view a passage and what kind of things they should say about it.

But it also made me think, not for the first time, that Richards's gloom over the bizarre reactions and confusions of his subjects was as out of place as were the vigorous steps which he then thought should be taken to end that kind of confusion. My own end feeling was that no guidelines to informed and educated reading should ever be necessary, at any stage of the process. Illuminations came out of anarchy and went back into it: nor could there be any such things as irrelevance or correctness in response to reading. The only cause for feeling downhearted, as it seemed to me, was that many students were, or had become conditioned to be, all too anxious to find out, or to be told, a proper way of doing things. It was their dissatisfactions that seemed incongruous with the process of reading, and with its pleasures and rewards.

Literary Theory could, and often did, assuage those dissatisfactions. There was indeed some irony in the fact that Theory had no trouble in taking in, even consecrating for its own line and its own purposes, the kinds of genial anarchy that seem to suit discussions of literature, and to be natural in the reading of books. It had the vocabulary to formalize all those feelings and responses. It could establish for its own purposes how already these students removed the author from the work, and the concept of truth from his language. By the application of logic to the many varieties of reading and response the theorists could demonstrate how things really were. And this could bring a feel of success and reassurance to students who were looking for a regime to live under, a course whose technology could be mastered: even excelled in, because it was properly understood and accepted by those who taught it, and so by the students who took the course.

Abandonment of Theory today would probably be like trying to abandon the motor-car. It has come into existence because of the need to instruct in the reading of literature by rules of some sort, if it is to become an academic course. But I doubt whether the realities of Kilvert's postman ('something more than that'), or of Hannibal's mountaineering in Livy (the girl who remarked on the heat of that 10 August was also struck by the Carthaginian general's use of vinegar) can ever come in to the compass of Theory, or become more real to the reader because of it. It will give him something else as a substitute, of course. But discoveries in reading are like the feeling that Kilvert the diarist makes us share, and become aware of, in another of his entries. He has just met some friends of friends in Wales, been shown over their house and given their hospitality. When his party sets out again, the hostess walks with them a little way. 'Then she wished us goodbye and went into the house, and I was sorry to see the last of her though an hour before I had not known there was such a person in existence. Her maiden name I find is Prescott.'

8

Micro and Macro

PHILIP DAVIS

I

The pioneers of psychoanalysis, wrote Bruno Bettelheim towards the end of his life, came to their subject out of their own personal and emotional experience, necessarily having to find their own way without formal training. Today, in contrast:

> An elaborate course of study is required of people wishing to become psychoanalysts and much of the highly personal excitement psychoanalysis once created is gone; it has become an institutionalized discipline . . . . I am not suggesting that today's analysts approach their patients differently than mine did me because they lack human decency. I believe, rather, that their attitudes largely reflect the institutionalization of psychoanalysis as a highly skilled therapeutic specialty, and by certain rigidities resulting from the long, demanding, and complex training psychoanalytic institutes require of candidates.[1]

My concern is not with psychoanalysis as such but with the depersonalizing tendency that Bettelheim describes as the natural result of the evolutionary development of a specialization. In so far as a subject can be defined and taught, it spreads itself wider – even if in any one particular participant it does not always go deeper. But in the name of a discipline's general progress, individual efforts are harnessed, sensibly enough, to a collective enterprise. Perhaps only a nostalgia for individualism would deny the continual, small but cumulative gains that can be made through the collective work involved in the establishment of a discipline, particularly in the sciences.

I am in favour of the teaching of reading in universities. To read seriously, with real thought and attention, is a practice that benefits from analytic study, collaborative help and excited discussion. But of course, studying literature is not concerned with progress in research as a science is. Moreover, the study of literature is radically unlike other forms of educational study in the humanities and social sciences: for we teach how you need never be dependent upon secondary textbooks, but can always go directly to the *original* material – the books themselves. Your specimens, your field trips, your primary sources are always with you. Ideally – and it is not altogether a paradox – we can *teach* the possibility of individuality, with readers regularly feeling like those original pioneers and personal discoverers that in other more organized disciplines can rarely ever exist again. Thus, while working within institutions, I have always trusted that the reading of literature might escape the fate of quasi-scientific institutionalization and not suffer the separation of work from individual personality.

I have always assumed too that any attempt to make reading, and thinking about one's reading, into a separate closed discipline would be contradictory. A secondary means – reading – should not be made into a primary study; but instead, just like that which it studies – namely, literature – it should always be looking outside itself. It still seems to me a golden rule that all literary activity has at times to work against itself, using literature precisely to get access to things outside literature. According to a long tradition, the letter can kill if it does not give way to a sense of that meaning in the service of which it exists. Fitting *things* to *words*, wrote Wordsworth in an 'Essay on Morals', is no more than a juggler's trick: the 'noble employment' lies rather in 'fitting words to things'. However complex the actual relation between words and things, that shorthand way of putting it remains Wordsworth's working priority.

It is a mistake if reading and thinking about reading become an autonomous subject, separating words from things. Readers should not be thinking of themselves as 'readers': first of all they should be thinking about what they are reading. Moreover, we are not just to learn *about* books and writers, we are to learn *from* them. We should read in order to try to think outside the books even as writers do inside them in the very writing of them. Wordsworth himself urged readers to become what he called 'silent poets', seeking to use their imaginations in the same way that writers do:

> O reader! had you in your mind
> Such stores as silent thought can bring,
> O gentle reader! you would find
> A tale in every thing.

What would that be like, to find a tale – not in 'everything', mere grist to the writer's exploitative mill – but more precisely, in every 'thing', where 'thing' is that which sheerly and singly exists there, prior to articulate consciousness?

For Wordsworth, it would be like this.

An old man is struggling to pull up the root of an old tree. A young man comes by, sees his hopeless attempt, and pulls the rotten stump up for him – effortlessly. The old man thanks the young man profusely for his help. The stump is out, the young man has been kind, the old man is better off. And yet, oddly, the old man's expression of immense gratitude, for what the young man did so easily, upsets the young man very much indeed. The weak old man had cried while thanking him, as though in further weakness.

Wordsworth was not scornful of prose paraphrase: he thought it usefully disclosed what he called a poem's undercurrent or bare skeleton. To a poet, with 'such stores as silent thought can bring', just such an unremarkable and seemingly prosaic scene might be where poems come from – because of the odd, disproportionate upset it caused. A poem could come out of the street. It would please the Tolstoy of *What is Art?* if a Wordsworth poem made you look differently at old people.

I shall return to that apparently simple poem, 'Simon Lee', later. But it is important to return to it only after establishing what is at stake in coming back to it in one mental state rather than another. In the institutionalized mental package of today, the age of Cool, readers too often start by *resisting* what Wordsworth asks them to do when he seeks the collaborative loan of the reader's store of experience and feeling. You're imagining that the events in this poem *really* happened, they say, with suspicion. Yes, is the reply: but that is what imagination does. I know that art is not the same as immediate reality, but it exists, as Samuel Johnson says in his 'Preface to Shakespeare', precisely to 'bring realities to mind'.

Modern objectors speak dismissively of sentimental fictionalizing, of humanism's ersatz religion of literature. And these may well be salutary warnings against a reader's therapeutic cultivation of secondhand feelings and substitute fantasy life. But it is still a poor and mean do if the first response to a call for imaginative generosity is one of resistant suspicion in the face of what is merely held off by calling it comfortable sentimentality.

For why does modern intelligence so often mean a separated intelligence, putting in mental distance and, in instances like this one, declaring coolly from outside the text that the poet is trying to 'manipulate' the reader? Perhaps people are right to be sceptical, but I would prefer it if they were worried about what they were doing even while they were doing it, rather than instead of even trying. It is a contradiction if to start from scepticism only serves to keep people all too comfortably confident of what they think. It is bad if thought exists only to stop people from attempting anything risky, wrong if thought keeps people outside the inner experience of reality.

The danger of education in general, and of reading in particular, is that it may produce a race of secondary human beings, using verbal intelligence as a substitute for experience. We know that advanced societies can reach a point of decadence where practices that were originally a means become professionalized ends in themselves; where the practice and study of literature, for example, becomes a speciality in its own right rather than retaining a relation to living. This is, I believe, a general Western problem now – even in 1987 Saul Bellow had his protagonist say in *More Die of Heartbreak*:

> Educated opinion in the U.S.A. envies the East its opportunities for more cultivation and development because *there* they suffer more deeply. Here suffering is trivial. Nobody gets hacked to pieces for his ideas . . . Russian suffering was, in a large historic view, suffering in its classic form, the suffering mankind has always known best in war, plague, famine and slavery. Those, the monumental and universally familiar forms of it, must certainly deepen the survivors humanly. My temptation was to try to make [people] understand that the sufferings of freedom also had to be considered . . . . Inside the sealed country Stalin poured on the *old* death. In the West, the ordeal is of a *new* death.[2]

When societies and their institutions become over-comfortable, they view with envy the dramatic hardship abroad that they have not got at home for the renewal of their lost purposes. Hence the displaced English and American lip-service paid to Mandelstam and Primo Levi, to Havel or Soyinka. We want their spirit without their fight. What is extraordinary in them seems all too ordinary and passé in us; for we covertly suspect that their extraordinariness is partly dependent upon a regressive political oppression to keep it alive and practically relevant. Further on from 1987, with the destruction of the hold of the USSR, the abiding problem in the new Europe and the USA will be to find purpose here and now – not by turning away from the unheroic situation of relative comfort but by translating back down into it the original sense of literary importance we claim to admire elsewhere. Otherwise, new death. What Saul Bellow says can be found before him in the nineteenth century in Kierkegaard and in George Eliot: that the great heroic human actions must now go on within that apparently small human ordinariness, which literature itself exists to recognize as not really that small or that ordinary. But because he has not himself completed the twentieth-century translation he describes, even Saul Bellow is in danger of depending upon the very threat of spiritual death he rails against if he is to defy the charge of being an irrelevantly old-fashioned literary man.

It is better to start further down, not loftily talking about things, but personally involved within them at a more microscopic level. Intensely small is usually deeper. For persons embody more thoughts at more levels in more deep and authentic configurations than does any overall theory or ideology. When his protagonist inhabits trouble in less dignified and more messy ways, Saul Bellow is himself more honest. So it is, for example, with Herzog.

Saul Bellow's Herzog is at once an academic intellectual and an old-fashioned emotional type, whose very intellectual task is to seek a union between those two modes. In a world that no longer seems to value emotion, Herzog thinks of the (ineffectual) feeling he still has in his heart and cries: 'Doesn't it mean anything? Is it simply a joke? A false hope that makes a man feel the illusion of worth?' To avoid becoming a joke, he knows he needs some structure of thoughtful belief to rescue personal emotion from shame – for 'consciousness when it doesn't clearly understand what to live for, what to die for, can only abuse and ridicule itself'. As it is, the only unity Herzog can see for the present is an ironic one: that both as a thinker and as a family man he has failed and is coming apart. Yet manically he still seeks a synthesis of all he believes in, even as the very effort causes him to fall further apart. For Herzog has his

large project, a spiritual project defying history and fashion, which
is disguised and concealed – or is it perhaps buried and lost? –
within the microcosmically small realm of the stubbornly personal:

> He, Herzog, . . . had characteristically, obstinately, blindly but
> without sufficient courage or intelligence tried to be a *marvellous*
> Herzog, a Herzog who, perhaps clumsily, tried to live out mar-
> vellous qualities vaguely comprehended.[3]

In art you don't just get the mere washed-up opinions or gross
assertions you too often hear from people in life; in art-speech, as
D.H. Lawrence calls it, you are immersed in the melting-pot from
which the thoughts of human beings first emerge within the felt
presence of all the rest of their lives. 'Literature is the personal use
or exercise of language,' said J.H. Newman in *The Idea of a University*: it is a language or a tone cast by the individual like his shadow,
correspondent to the shape and movement of his inward life.[4] If
only that art-speech, that shadowy aura, could be reproduced outside the realm of art. Perhaps that is what critics might be for today:
to produce a form of writing that learns from art and yet is itself
outside art; that exists to show you how you can learn from art
without being an artist; that, finally, goes beyond the language of
paraphrase and opinion and tries to create a resonant personal
arena to work within, disclosing what the writer means and stands
for, without the cumbersome mediation of apology or explanation.

For literary critics, I believe, are middle-men and middle-women;
as readers, they are the translators between writing and living, and
should be the personal testers of the troublesome relation between
the thoughts and feelings they get from books and the lives they
lead even so. Sometimes these translations go on too comfortably,
too crudely, as if reading something simply allowed one to *have* a
book's meaning without further experience. But warning examples
notwithstanding, nothing is more urgent now in the West than the
whole varied enterprise of carefully tested translation – translation
from old ways to new ones and back again; movement to and
fro from the religious to the secular, from the public to the private,
from extraordinary to ordinary ways of being, from literary practice to practice within the world; a shifting from the physical to the
mental and then from the mental to the physical, from practice to
theory and back again, from thoughts about feelings to feelings
about thoughts – in short, all the work that keeps untying and

retying the subtle knot which makes up man, to see how it goes. That is Herzog's uncompleted project, the best project of all. 'Doesn't it mean anything?'

II

But I return to my starting point. The *first* task of readers is to put literature not into theory, not even into translation, but into imaginative practice in its own microscopic terms. So like a writer, let me at least try to *do* something here, instead of merely talking *about* something. What I will do is simply ask you to read with me, as though aloud, part of Wordsworth's poem in order first of all to learn and recreate its language:

> One summer-day I chanced to see
> This Old Man doing all he could
> About the root of an old tree,
> A stump of rotten wood.
> The mattock tottered in his hand;
> So vain was his endeavour
> That at the root of the old tree
> He might have worked for ever.
>
> 'You're overtasked, good Simon Lee,
> Give me your tool,' to him I said;
> And at the word right gladly he
> Received my proffered aid.
> I struck, and with a single blow
> The tangled root I severed,
> At which the poor Old Man so long
> And vainly had endeavoured.
>
> The tears into his eyes were brought,
> And thanks and praises seemed to run
> So fast out of his heart, I thought
> They never would have done.
> I've heard of hearts unkind, kind deeds
> With coldness still returning.
> Alas! the gratitude of men
> Has oftener left me mourning.

Of course, unless they are lucky enough to be beginners, most serious readers inside and outside universities will already know well enough that poem, 'Simon Lee'. Do I wish to insult you by taking you through this apparently simple and familiar work again?

Not at all. But let's not suppose that because we may be attempting higher work than a first-year undergraduate, we start from some different place. The people I teach are surely right to have as their first question: How do I get into a poem? *not* How do I get out of it? We too must always start by trying to make the poem come back to life, in its own time again, through the primary reality of living performance.

'Faithfully reading out a poem, a poem that one admires,' said Leavis, 'one should think of oneself as both the violinist and the violin.'[5] Critics are not actors or orchestral musicians, but in the field of literary education we are an equivalent: the re-performers, the keepers-alive. Being at once the violinist and the violin suggests something of the complicated relation between the mental and the physical that goes into the true conceiving of literature when one doesn't merely remain outside it as an observer. For in reading aloud one struggles to get it minutely right, where saying it, hearing yourself say it, and thinking about what you hear and say – what Wordsworth calls 'the mind's internal echo of the imperfect sound' – are all having to go on within the same living instant of time. Institutionalized thinking separates things out and makes academics prefer the clarity of single and static thoughts; poetry does not work like that. There is a richness as well as a limitation in poetry's gift of making many things happen at the same time: in reperformance of a poem you have to make choices, emphases, in the midst of competing options.

Thus, even as the force of grammar, rhyme, metrics and tale takes the reader on past, Wordsworth is very good at making you want to dwell for a microsecond longer than is possible upon one particular word within a line. For example, I know I want to colour that word 'single' – 'and with a *single* blow I severed' – playing it off both against the 'long' and 'vain' efforts of the elder described a line or two later *and* against the earlier line 'This Old Man doing *all* he could'. We need, while reading, to think up and down the lines as well as along them. Moreover as you read:

> I struck, and with a single blow
> The tangled root I severed,
> At which the poor Old Man so long
> And vainly had endeavoured.

that innocent-looking hinge 'At which' outwardly enforces a merely *grammatical connection* at the same time as, inside, you are feeling a hidden *emotional contrast*. That is poetry's second, tacit, and hidden language.

Or there again, Wordsworth sometimes loves quietly to single out not just a word but a whole line, mentally, in implicit poetry, while the life of the stanza goes on prosaically past it. So while I read of the old man's tears:

> I thought
> They *never* would have done

I am also thinking back to:

> That at the root of the old tree
> He might have worked *for ever*.

There are half-hidden relations and secret places in poetry, and readers have almost to make themselves like a poet to catch them.

Thus, for example, the poet Les Murray describes a friend once saying to him, 'I came to that place in the poem, and clunk! my mind turned inside out': inside out as in:

> I've heard of hearts unkind, kind deeds
> With coldness still returning.
> Alas! the gratitude of men
> Has oftener left me mourning.

'Huh?' said Murray's friend, and he read that bit again, 'and it happened again, precisely there, and I couldn't explain it to myself.'[6] Literature, printed so evenly across the page, is in its living reality uneven. Before they do anything else, readers simply need to locate these deep holding-places.

A poem, says Iris Murdoch, 'is in tension between a clarified statement and a confused pointing, and is in danger if it goes too far either way.'[7] Literature offers a place for thinking as something other than either the replicated messiness of original living or that dry, tidied residue of experience called conceptual knowledge. Between the two, a poem in particular provides a holding-ground, a force-field in which thoughts are not just simply stated, flat on the page, but come into being three-dimensionally as part of a human experience of meaning.

In this way literature holds open areas of being. A moment of Shakespearian prose can do it:

> The web of our life is of a mingled yarn, good and ill together: our virtues would be proud, if our faults whipped them not, and our crimes would despair, if they were not cherished by our virtues.
> *All's Well That Ends Well*, IV, iii, 60–63.

Shakespeare's mental act of turn-around, embodied in the rhetorical figure of chiasmus or antimetabole, is like a primal image of the first movements of creativity within human thought, when we no longer think of one thing separately but have to think, almost simultaneously, of two – two opposite thoughts made out of the self-same material. The reader can stay neither in the first half of the sentence ('our virtues would be proud, if our faults whipped them not') nor in the second ('and our crimes would despair, if they were not cherished by our virtues'), but is thrown back instead in between the two as though life were the meaningfully mingled space that emerges between the false linguistic definiteness of pride and despair, of virtue and fault – like a Grecian urn shadowed forth between two facing profiles. In between the two clauses there is an inferred shape or subject which the language exists not to name but to leave for the reader. This ability of language thus to let life *in* can be seen again and again in the prose of Samuel Johnson:

> Evil is uncertain in the same degree as good, and for the reason that we ought not to hope too securely, we ought not to fear with too much dejection.
> *Rambler*, 29.

'For it is necessary to act, but impossible to know the consequences of action' (*Rambler*, 184); 'Thus men may be made inconstant by virtue and by vice, by too much or too little thought (*Rambler*, 63); 'In youth we require something of the tardiness and frigidity of age; and in age, we must labour to recall the fire and impetuousity of youth' (*Rambler*, 111); 'Age looks with anger on the temerity of youth, and youth with contempt on the scrupulosity of age' (*Rasselas*, Ch. xxvi). There is always something missing. But Johnson stubbornly creates a sentence which at least holds together the terms of its own unresolvedness. And unspoken and invisible in the very *middle* of these sentences there is held for ever the resonance of life's perplexity – in the lost area of synthesis or golden mean between age and youth, between acting and knowing, between the realms of too little and too much. In the same way, at a different level, a reader may find between two contrasting or conflicting authors, about *both* of which paradoxically one cares, a means of entrapping something of what is at stake in life for that reader – between Shakespeare and Dante, for example, or Thomas Hardy and D.H. Lawrence, or George Eliot and Nietzsche. Then between the two you have an image of *where* to do some life's work.

At any rate, when you find significant places in a stanza or a sentence, then it is that you want to try to explain them to yourself, to know more of what they keep on meaning every time you return to them. And that's when practical criticism becomes important. Not under that terrible misnomer 'close reading', offered as a sort of myopic rote-technique going through the mechanical repertoire of imagery and alliteration. But practical criticism as a *second* attempt to reperform the poem, this time analytically, with what happened too fast, too all-together in oral performance, now attended to more slowly. Doubtless we shall often need to correct and supplement these readings with historical knowledge, a sense of context, convention and allusion – there is no shortage of stress on historical knowledge these days; but for the student of literature, history exists only to contribute towards reading, and not vice versa. Practical criticism is live, it is not antiquarian. Moreover, to adapt Aristotle's terms, practical criticism is praxis, not technē. Technē, or technique, can be taught: you read the manual, you can mend the machine. But where technique can never adjust, practical skills are more mysterious in the way that gaining experience is mysterious: for practical skills like language acquisition itself can only be learned in practice, not theory. Because theory is all too often a form of technē, of applied simplification. Too often in life we use concepts in a way that is like crudely fumbling with thick fingers for very tiny pins, when what we really need to be carrying out is a delicate act of microsurgery. Practical criticism shows how art operates at that micro level of life which everyday language passes over. Its analyses involve what we actually *do* in reading, not what we say we do.

But if I have been saying nothing new here, then that is precisely my point. Literary critics too often stake their whole *raison d'être* on the need to look for novel interpretations and when they run out, whole new approaches. This desire for a new way is a misunderstanding of what Originality should really mean: which isn't novelty or modishness. Wordsworth says we should never speak of important things as if by rote, however familiar they have grown. They should be perceived again, he says, 'with the freshness and clearness of an original intuition'.[8] Real originality occurs when a thought is not repeated as at secondhand but felt and imagined as if for the first time again. Every thought, said Keats, is the centre of an intellectual world:[9] to reimagine the world that grows out of a thought, as its nucleus, is a great recreative task. It doesn't matter if people have said this or that before. What hasn't been? But if a thought originates with you, it will be as if it was in the world for the first time again. And that a thought will always be held a little differently, because it is you who is holding it and not someone else, is not a ground for scepticism but a sign of an irreducibly individual creativeness. That ever-shifting mixture of sameness and difference is precisely how thoughts keep coming back to life, afresh. Otherwise everything becomes merely a matter of settled secondary knowledge, and a 'text' is merely a thing of the past. But literature, says Newman, again in *The Idea of a University*, is to the race what autobiography is to the individual: it revives memories.[10]

'Real remembering', says Doris Lessing in her own autobiography, 'is – if even for a flash, even a moment – being back in the experience itself. You remember pain with pain, love with love, one's real best self with one's best self.'[11] When the writer in the act of writing or the reader in reading experiences that second pain, it is because the writing or the reading seem like the dynamic memory of some first one, anterior to the text.

Thoughts on a page imply a thinker. In the act of reading readers are naturally led to infer and imagine an intelligent source lodged invisibly but inseparably behind the writing. What makes a text into literature or letters is this trace of something *behind* the text, in an extra dimension beyond the flat use of language for the giving of information. Equivalently, something behind the eyes of the reader stirs and responds.

We have lost faith in the existence of any such anterior reality of being. But the unwritten, silent or inarticulate life, that Wordsworthian 'store' of life-stuff prior to writing, is that out of which writing itself comes into being. It is also that of which writing in turn helps us realize the existence. The most creative language-use depends upon something we cannot yet say, but feel we have somewhere in us. In *Bleak House*, Jo the illiterate sweep is constantly moved on through an inhospitable world whose meanings he cannot read, yet still he dimly thinks, 'I *am* here somehow, too.' There *is* something there. Using shorthand – of which a philosopher would not approve – I say to students, 'You have to have the feeling of the thing before you can do the thinking.' Thinking does not begin the world; thinking needs some inchoate pre-articulate intimation, some Wordsworthian 'thing', first of all to think *off*. Otherwise we are left with that felt vacuum over which modern literary theory and modern being in the West all too often exist, proclaiming there is nothing but 'absence'. But the poet, says Wordsworth in the 'Preface to Lyrical Ballads', 'is affected more than other men by absent things *as if they were present.*' Readers betray that poetic impulse and themselves negatively create absence in texts, when they silently withdraw from a work the readerly imagination which all literature depends upon arousing. 'O reader! had you in your mind/Such stores as silent thought can bring.'

There are writers who offer faith in the reality of that prior inarticulate being that all articulation depends upon. That great Victorian admirer of Wordsworth, John Henry Newman, is one such, when he invites us to think what it would be like to encounter an exceptionally good human being who seems to embody something deep and real inside his very self. A person in whom Being was rightly anterior to conscious verbal knowing is here the moral equivalent of Wordsworth's silent poets, who never put their life-poems into words:

> It is plain, that the gifted individual whom we have imagined, will of all men be least able (as such) to defend his own views, inasmuch as he takes no external survey of himself. Things which are the most familiar to us, and easy in practice, require the most study, and give the most trouble in explaining; as, for instance, the number, combination, and succession of muscular movements by which we balance ourselves in walking, or utter our

separate words; and this quite independently of the existence or non-existence of language suitable for describing them. The longer any one has persevered in the practice of virtue, the less likely he is to recollect how he began it; what were his difficulties on starting, and how surmounted; by what process one truth led to another; the less likely to elicit justly the real reasons latent in his mind for particular observances or opinions. He holds the whole assemblage of moral notions almost as so many collateral and self-evident facts. Hence it is that some of the most deeply-exercised and variously gifted Christians, when they proceed to write or speak upon Religion, either fail altogether, or cannot be understood except on an attentive study; and after all, perhaps, are illogical and unsystematic, assuming what their readers require proved, and seeming to mistake connexion or antecedence for causation, probability for evidence. And over such as these it is, that the minute intellect of inferior men has its moment of triumph, men who excel in a mere short-sighted perspicacity; not understanding that, even in the case of intellectual evidence, it is considered the highest of gifts to possess an intuitive knowledge of the beautiful in art, or the effective in action, without reasoning or investigating; that this, in fact, is *genius*.[12]

You could thoroughly be a thing, you could intuitively do something, but you might well on that very account be unable to explain it. To Newman, this is often what real human beings are like, so inside themselves as to be helpless to take an 'external survey'. Their thinking goes on implicitly, informally, practically, inside their persons and their actions. Newman is marvellous about such people: it does not mean that just because they cannot entirely say what they are or justify what they have got, then what they are or have got does not exist. They simply suffer from that frequent incapacity of human beings to get outside or on top of themselves and make what is in them explicit at the level of verbal explanation. For this is individual experience shaken down into an incarnate reality more complex, more full of itself, than any knowing which it itself can bring to explaining or recalling what it is about. Says Newman, 'All men have a reason, but not all men can give a reason.'[13]

Newman is preaching to students here. And perhaps teachers should value most those students who have, to start with, something about them, in themselves, but are at first unconfident and inarticulate in the second realm of education. Those students have the priorities right in the sense that Ruskin meant, when he said in 'The Nature of Gothic' that it was the fault of modern professionalism 'to prefer the perfectness of the lower nature to the imperfection of the higher'. To enable them to rise to such imperfection, we have to find where people truly start from, not allow them to begin half-way up, inauthentically, through the masking powers of a secondary verbal intelligence.

But we live in an age where education is increasingly being committed to becoming explicit – explicit about aims and outcomes, agendas, processes and skills. It is assumed that the more you can explain to students in advance what they are expected to do, the more they will understand the expectation and the more they will be able to fulfil it. That is technē, not praxis. But literature is a practice that comes out of a deeper sense of language than the giving of information. And it is mad if the *study* of literature establishes its thinking in ways which threaten to become inimical to the sort of thinking literature itself offers.

The inability of Newman's primary people fully to explain themselves is thus not simply an unfortunate personal failing on their part. Implicit being is always ontologically *prior* to such explicit knowing as can be derived from it. And what is implicit in persons is never completely explained or exhausted by what can be explicitly made of it. The secondary externalizing people, in 'the minute intellect of inferior men', can explain more and be clearer and so catch out the primary inner stumblers, like Tolstoy's Levin – yet only because they have less behind them to *be* explained. But Newman's primary people have the root of the matter in them: they represent what is irreducibly prior to all attempts at explication – that implicit and anterior silence of being, that deep memory of life, which literature exists simultaneously both to preserve in itself and to save from extinction. Literature is the only form of explication which can remain in touch with that unspoken ground, can carry that silence behind its words as memory waiting for a reader's imagination to trigger its resonance. It is the only form of explication which can retain implicitly within it, as part of it, what it cannot quite say. For the great literary achievement is to create precisely through words something which becomes more than just words and emphatically *is*.

III

But literature cannot always be left at that.

Consider a naive, young Marcel Proust finishing a novel in which he has been totally and passionately absorbed – reading, like Dickens's David Copperfield, as if for life. 'The last page was read, the book was finished . . . Then, what?'

He gets up in order to relieve his left-over feelings: this emotion, which he has got from books, what is it *for*? What is he to do with it afterwards, outside? Is it all only artificial stimulation? He walks around his bedroom as if trying to release the physicality that reading has inhibited in him, not knowing, literally, what to *do* with himself:

> This book, was it nothing but that? . . . A book having no connec-
> tion with life, [whose] fate in this world was not at all, as we had
> believed, to contain the universe and destiny, but to occupy a
> very narrow place in the library.[14]

What is the true size and real use of a book? What is its relation to the life outside that is itself the book's very subject-matter? Working at increased levels of complication of meaning, literary people often feel, aesthetically, that they must leave such primitive, childish and simple demands behind as merely reductive – demands such as the need for action or for usefulness. But repeatedly at every stage of our evolution that crude but unappeasable old demand for some descendant of action is still felt, even in transmuted form, within the higher levels of sheer mentality. We poison ourselves, says Spinoza, when we have thoughts passively but cannot creatively *do* anything with them. The thoughts or the memories seem rather to be having us rather than we them. When we suffer our experience as a weight and cannot convert it into the energy released by becoming active and creative – then this is what Saul Bellow means by the new sufferings caused by apparent freedom: the sense of redundant energy and purposeless limbo.

If literature always points beyond itself, we cannot simply leave literature alone. Often we feel the need for some further translation of it into explicit consciousness. For response is always implicit *and* explicit, and we do best when we turn backwards and forwards between one and the other, because we are creatures of being *and* of knowing, *and* in that order. For the order in which we do things is what is vital. Only if we get the order right will the explicit not replace the implicit but approximatively stand for it at a different mental level, like a striking memory of what lies pre-articulately behind it. In the same way Wordsworth in the great 'Preface' described our thoughts as the 'representatives' of all our past feelings.

This brings me back, therefore, to the great project of translation and synthesis that Herzog sought, rightly or wrongly, in his task of emotional education.

I think rightly. And what I offer in the rest of this essay is the sketch of a literary project in search of human unity, even though modern sceptics say there is no such thing. For I believe that the pursuit of unity lies behind our impulse to translate across levels and between realms, however liable we are to abuse the impulse and fabricate convenient connections. Global-minded intellectuals think they can move far too easily from one realm to another (turning everything into a matter of politics, say), or from one culture to another (admiring diversity from some touristic position of relativism outside it all). But tasks are always most authentic when there is something *involuntary* involved in them – when we are *not* just looking for what we want, or when what we want comes as a *surprise*, as though we did not always know ourselves but could forget our deeper needs. Literature, written and read, is the form of thinking that most allows an underlying involuntariness to find a space for emergence.

Thus, what the task of translation is like at its most arduously serious may be best described by George Eliot's common-law husband George Henry Lewes in his *Life and Works of Goethe*. It occurs when, in his reading, the poet Goethe is amazed to find some answering equivalent to himself in a dry philosopher who seems to come, as it were, from the opposite or other side of being – the philosopher, Spinoza:

> The closest unions rest on contrasts. The all-equalising calmness of Spinoza was in striking contrast with my all-disturbing activity; his mathematical method was the direct opposite of my poetic style of thought and feeling, and that very precision which was thought ill adapted to moral subjects made me his enthusiastic disciple, his most decided worshipper. Mind and heart, understanding and sense, sought each other with eager affinity, binding together the most different natures.[15]

When Goethe speaks romantically of mind and heart seeking each other, it is as though he means that the philosopher has heart within mind, whereas the poet has mind within heart, and their ways are genuine mirror-images of each other from opposite sides. It is like the figure of chiasmus. To feel without thinking or to think without feeling is not enough: the two seek each other both between and inside individual human beings.

So in *Middlemarch* George Eliot, herself a translator of Spinoza, seeks in Dorothea a human being whose instinctive emotions can be educatively redirected by thought, but whose thoughts can then, as second nature, be worked back down again into sincere feelings rather than just notional duties:

> We are all of us born in moral stupidity, taking the world as an udder to feed our supreme selves: Dorothea had early begun to emerge from that stupidity, but yet it had been easier to her to imagine how she would devote herself to Mr Casaubon, and become wise and strong in his strength and wisdom, than to conceive with that distinctness which is no longer reflection but feeling – an idea wrought back to the directness of sense, like the solidity of objects – that he had an equivalent centre of self, whence the lights and shadows must always fall with a certain difference.
>
> *Middlemarch*, Chapter 21

'Wrought back' there is marvellous. That is what thinking is for.

Goethe was amazed to find himself moved by Spinoza. Someone else might be equivalently startled to find that Newman's apparently dry abstract words could stir on the other side of themselves, in a reader, latent feelings and personal memories, like poetry. It is extraordinarily common, when reading, to think: How can such public or impersonal words recall in me such private and personal feelings? Or, when writing: Who will ever know the personal resonance that surrounds this formal line, this sentence?

It makes a difference what side you start from. It feels minutely but crucially different if it seems that reason is producing feelings rather than feeling producing reasons, though the two faculties are there at their closest. If for Goethe to start as a poet is precisely *not* to start as a philosopher, then the philosopher is still that equivalent other life (the poet's life turned inside-out or back-to-front), which this poetic life has had to surrender or recreate differently in order to be itself. In the vast laboratory of human nature, different compounds are formed out of the same human elements which then sometimes seek each other in tacit recognition of an underlying affinity. Thus the ability of the poet to see himself in the philosopher, or the philosopher to see himself in the poet, heals some apparent breach in Romantic nature, as though there is a thought for every feeling, a feeling for every thought, and the most representatively complete humans are they who, as with the Renaissance ideal of the universal man, can turn from one to another and back again, whichever side they start from.

This is the anterior arena, the melting-pot or the holding-ground that the great literary experiments take place within, like images of original creation itself. For, in mnemotypes of life's creation and evolution, what literature seizes upon can be at the heart of all other disciplines, before they have developed into separate studies. In Shakespeare, says Hazlitt, we are in at the very start of the process of creative transformation, where one thing can become another:

> There is a continual composition and decomposition of [the characters'] elements, a fermentation of every particle in the whole mass, by its alternate affinity or antipathy to other principles which are brought into contact with it. Till the experiment is tried, we do not know the result, the turn which the character will take in its new circumstances.
>
> *Lectures on the English Poets*, 'On Shakspeare and Milton'.

In Wordsworth's poetry, Sir Humphry Davy, the scientist who saw *Lyrical Ballads* through the press, recognized what he himself realized through science – the possibility of infinite combinations of life's finite materials:

> The future is composed of images of the past, connected in new arrangements by analogy, and modified by the circumstances and feelings of the moment; our hopes are founded upon our experience.
>
> 'A Discourse Introductory to a Course of Lectures on
> Chemistry', 1802.

In George Eliot's vision of the world, said James Sully, the characters are not shown as finished and determined but as still interactively 'in the making':

I have observed that the distinction between the characters and the plot of a novel is only a rough distinction. This remark applies with special force to George Eliot's stories. These appear in a remarkable degree, when regarded from one point of view, as the outcome of her characters, from another point of view, as the formation of these characters.

'George Eliot's Art', *Mind*, Vol. 6, 1881, pp.384–5.

In the experimental chemistry of the world's composition, the human agent is never an entirely free or separate thing – and that itself is an index of what creativity is like. Novelists and poets get their language and their characters immersed in a testing medium in which they can only act in suffering, suffer in acting, changed even by their own efforts to make changes. When writing can get you into just such an arena of dense and investigative possibility, imaginatively equivalent to the tests and turning-points of meaning that can go on within a concentrated situation in life, then it is as if the writer has keyed into something like the story of human creation itself.

I want to hold onto that microcosmic image of creative life that writers revive or rescue for us. The current fashion is to read literature as if to expose the fictionality of real life itself, in all its illusory values and unthinking presuppositions. I say the reverse. That we need to try to transfer the powers that go on implicitly within writing back again into the life outside it.

For consider an analogy and its uses.

In *Middlemarch*, there is a young doctor, Lydgate, who seeks to pursue a dual ambition and be both a general practitioner and a specialized researcher, working in both pure and humanly applied fields at once. It is an image of a whole life, translating between practical and theoretic, physical and mental, general and particular. Lydgate might have become the sort of man who would seek to investigate the relation between the production of adrenaline at one level and the experience of free-will at another. Or the sort of doctor that John Berger describes in *A Fortunate Man* as wanting to do two things instead of one: cure his patients as physical creatures, but also at the self-same time, like a novelist translated into real life, think about them as human beings.

In other words, albeit still 'in the making', Lydgate stands for someone wanting to *do* something and do it in such way that makes for a personal career, an experimental journey that does not start from theory but from practice serving as the material for theoretic thoughts, themselves ploughed back into those fresh orientations of practice which test them.

I believe George Eliot thinks: Why couldn't literary people be an equivalent to that? If literary realism stands for anything to George Eliot, it stands for the analogous two-in-one hope that life might help writing, that writing might help life. Every reader knows she was thinking of herself too when she wrote of Lydgate:

> He wanted to pierce the obscurity of those minute processes which prepare human misery and joy, those invisible thorough-fares which are the first lurking-places of anguish, mania, and crime, that delicate poise and transition which determine the growth of happy or unhappy consciousness.
>
> *Middlemarch*, Chapter 16.

Surely there is some memory here of Keats's great letter of 3 May 1818 on human life as a large mansion of many apartments, in particular relation to Wordsworth – the slow and gradual movements of life through openings and thoroughfares, the dark passages and hiding-places through which Wordsworth works his way finally in *The Prelude*.[16] In *Middlemarch*, as with Wordsworth in *The Prelude*, the author functions as his or her own reader, moving in translation between microscopically gradual processes at one end and the consciousness that finally results from them at the other. It is like an image of human evolution itself. And when George Eliot moves between micro and macro levels of meaning, rising from minute or split-second linguistic formulations to a final explicit consciousness of their larger human meaning, she offers readers an almost biological model. Through art there emerges into being the most delicate precision that there is in thinking about human life. But finally, like George Eliot, we too as readers still have to deliver something at the macro level that witnesses and assays some explicit and conscious sense of what has been happening at the level of minute linguistic formation.

We need finally to get something *out* of a poem, just as George Eliot exists to get something out of what she sees happening in her own novel: precipitating some large, albeit provisional, human thought out of a literary resonance which brushes just below the level of concept. And then we need to try out that thought, practically testing it in the analogous realms of meditation or writing or even conduct.

'Simon Lee', for instance, may look like a very simple poem. But the baffled, rueful note on which the poem ends seems to leave it on the very brink of formulating some explicit law. 'Alas! the gratitude of men/Has oftener left me mourning.' In the poem's after-echo, we are bequeathed the silent need for further knowledge: Why was the poet so upset? What is the relation between the sorrow the old man felt tacitly behind his gratitude and the sorrow the young man then expressly felt in front of it? Hasn't it something to do with Wordsworth's mysterious law in the great *Preface* that everything in mental activity hangs upon the perception of similitude in dissimilitude and vice versa?

Why shouldn't literary criticism become a more informal, more personal version of theology and philosophy, using literature – without crude reduction, without mere utilitarianism – as a holding-ground for human thinking? as a form of secular meditation? Literature, as a form of deep thinking, is closer to philosophy than it is to history. But unlike philosophy, literature goes to the preconceptual sources of thought, to the human living places and deep anterior contexts which have in them the origination of thinking, before thought becomes formally and separately explicit. But then, I repeat, at the final stage of literary thinking we should want to get something out of a poem at the macro level, and make ourselves not just passive second-hand commentators, or actors who become for a while what they read, but separate thinking people who dare take things out of books 'not for art's sake,' as Lawrence put it, 'but for my sake.'[17]

IV

This then is a personal sketch towards a theory of creative practice. The three functions of a theory of practice are these, in this order. First, to perform a work by reading it, to get its feel; then to reperform it, at the micro level through practical criticism; and finally, to seek to translate it onto the macro level of translated application. But that this should be the basic order in which we do it, from below upwards, is vital. Why? Because our evolutionary story is one of creatures in the first place, who partially may become creators in the second. Once we basically understand that priority, we can move more freely between these levels, raising and lowering and reintegrating ourselves, mixing it all up, as we go along.

As at once creatures and creators, we deal in matters where strengths and weaknesses are necessarily inseparable. Thus, for example, a book, said the young Proust, can seem so huge and mighty in the midst of reading it and then so small and ordinary when placed back with all the others on the library selves. But that asymmetry is part of what I must call the chiastic relation of life inside Literature and of literature inside Life, of readers giving themselves to poems and then taking poems into themselves, of the world in a book and a book in the world – one thing turning in and out of another, trying itself out in differing ways and compounds. For indeed, that to-and-fro 'ennobling interchange' (in Wordsworth's phrase) is why literature and literary studies cannot be a closed subject. Something here seems true of individual life too: that what feels so important from the very midst, can seem so very little from a perspective outside or afterwards, and we keep having to shift from the one perspective to the other, inside and outside ourselves, rebalancing as we go.

Of all the balances we have to make, none is more vital in a life than maintaining the two-way interaction or translation back and forth between what I call the micro and macro levels – between the dynamic subterranean processes of the under-mind and the achievement of conscious meaning in the upper-mind. If that communication gets blocked, people go wrong and, being at best half themselves, are never whole.

To make clear the necessity of trying to maintain that mental interrelationship, I offer in conclusion a warning example of how indeed it may go wrong, as it mainly does for most of us – an example taken from the career of William Hazlitt, in the 16 years that lay between his youthful 'Essay on the Principles of Human Action' written in 1805 at the age of 27, and his 1821 essay 'On Living to One's-Self' composed when he was 43.

To show briefly what is at stake, I offer only a paraphrase of Hazlitt's 'Essay on the Principles of Human Action', for though it is a work that offers sudden striking formulations of powerfully dynamic ideas, it lacks the sort of organization that allows succinct quotation. Hazlitt himself knew, as he testifies in 'My First Acquaintance With Poets', that the essay was obscure: he could not explain it properly to Coleridge, and Wordsworth disliked it. This failure led Hazlitt only to another failed reformulation on paper of views he could barely express in person, till he 'shed tears of helpless despondency'.[18]

The 'Essay' works underground, below the level of normal consciousness: it is what I shall call a 'micro' theory of the human
mind. For it argues that we are wrong to think of ourselves as
naturally self-interested egos who always act in conscious pur-
suance of some future advantage to ourselves: that would be a
macro theory as of large self-consciously separate units. We are not
like that to begin with. Originally, in a more melted situation, what
we have is not a carefully anticipating self but a primitive capacity
for immediate future action which in the very microsecond of
acting is fuelled not by far-seeing calculations of self-interest but by
an anterior energy which is more speedy and innocent than is an
established conscious self.

A blind instinctive feeling for life arises in search of whatever is
good, wherever it comes from and independently of whomsoever
it later turns out to benefit. The objects of that feeling exist for it
long before any consciousness of a larger, slower subject-being who
is 'doing' the feeling. Rather, the feeling, of itself, by desire or
aversion naturally activates a spontaneous imagination of the future. And feeling and imagination together discharge their energies
into an attempted immediacy of action where action always means
the effort to bring that desired future into being as instantaneously
as possible. There is, in a sense, hardly *time* for action – hardly any
consciously present time that is, since in this primitive timescale the
human aim, so far from being self-interested, is on the contrary
always directed ahead of itself. There is no time for that later
human development of calculation; for what are experienced are,
as it were, preconscious thoughts seeking realization in an action
rather than in the formation of a conscious self to think them. They
are thoughts emerging dynamically prior to the existence of an
autobiographical thinker of them. For the drive to act, through the
forces of feeling and imagination heaving forward, has a built-in
desire to bring the future into instant being, with barely a microsecond's pause. And the future self is precisely what does not yet
exist. It is always in the future or in the present's reaching for the
future; it is continually being created in the very event of action.
This is Hazlitt's version of the Shakespearian chemical experiment.

It is only later, after the associations of ideas about our selves
have built up, that a sense of a future self does become steadily
present to us, says Hazlitt, and that self is really an idea of a past
self transferred forward. We create a secondary conscious idea of
ourselves, back-to-front, from our memory *and*, mindful of protect-

ing our past self, project forward its interests, making our future no more than the future continuation of the past. The freedom of sudden imagination-in-action becomes trapped and incorporated inside the container of memory's idea of an intentionalist self. And even so this second-stage, second-order self forgets the dynamic of human nature by which he previously lived.

Sixteen years later it is as though Hazlitt, in ageing, is himself stuck with just such a later or macro self. He seems to recall 1805:

> For many years of my life I did nothing but think. I had nothing else to do but solve some knotty point, or dip in some abstruse author, or look at the sky, or wander by the pebbled sea-shore –
>
> 'To see the children sporting on the shore,
> And hear the mighty waves rolling evermore.'
>
> I cared for nothing, I wanted nothing. I took my time to consider whatever occurred to me, and was in no hurry to give a sophistical answer to a question – there was no printer's devil waiting for me. I used to write a page or two perhaps in half a year . . . .
> 'On Living to One's-Self', *Selected Essays*, p. 27.

When in his youthful days Hazlitt was quite on his own, he did not think of himself, but looked out of himself even as Wordsworth described. It was as if in his youthful thinking he had a universal mind and not merely a personal one: a mind freely in the universe of things, seeming to represent in its solitude no more and no less than the human mind itself and not just Hazlitt's. Yet gradually he found himself reduced to another grosser yet narrower mode:

> Woe be to him when he first begins to think what others say of him . . . when he undertakes to play a part on the stage, and to persuade the world to think more about him than they do about themselves.
> 'On Living to One's-Self', pp. 26–7.

He began to become socially conscious of himself, to be a mind aware of itself as confined within the limitations of its own body and personality, and operating inside the competitive pressures of the world's sense of time. It was like swallowing your self, thinking in your mind how you affected the others in the world, how there was your sense of what they thought of you, and how as a result there was now your own so-called personality where before you had not even known you had one.

Above all, Hazlitt had developed his own aggressive and defensive interests as a self, competitive interests that narrowed the very definition of self even as it sought to extend its power. This older professionalized Hazlitt may write his higher journalism with a lucidity missing from his youthful 'Essay', but it is a lucidity which is itself in flight from any earlier sense of the ineffable. 'Am I better than I was then?' asks Hazlitt, 'Oh no! One truth discovered, one pang of regret at not being able to express it, is better than all the fluency and flippancy in the world.'[19] Something primary has gone: for it is only, says John Henry Newman, the consolidators, 'the second-rate men' who, though useful in their place, 'prove, reconcile, finish, and explain'.[20]

Of course the idyllic picture of the young Hazlitt, as a first-rate man without strings or ties, may be in part the nostalgically precious creation of the older, more harassed man reacting with hindsight against the demands of the world. But I believe that the older, socially normalized Hazlitt exemplifies what happens when the macro self loses contact with its earlier micro processes. What develops is an autobiographical self, a shrunken but more solid macro-thing, pushed along in time, economically responsible, its freedom of being and mind reduced by a sense of adulthood which precisely fails to live up to the continuity that Wordsworth himself had established between younger and older selves in poetry such as 'The Immortality Ode'. Then we see how our macro selves get formed and ossified, as human, all too human, if there is no access left for a reimmersion in the micro processes of sudden thought, instinctive action or scrupulously intricate writing. Those passionate micro-processes look to reform the consciousness they lead to; they are what we are up to underneath; and their signals, if left and unattended to, become of necessity weaker or less constructive.

If Wordsworth's *Prelude* is about anything, it is about avoiding that fate betokened by Hazlitt. It is about turning the microscopic movements and moments captured in poetry into the level of a macro understanding of the self – which, still within that poetry, can then make sense of itself as both composed of *and* translating those micro moments. That is to say, in *The Prelude* a host of shadowy things

> through the turnings intricate of verse,
> Present themselves as objects recognised,
> In flashes
>
> *The Prelude* (1805), V, 627–9.

– and those momentarily presented flashes, within the mind's dark invisible workmanship, together have made up that settled and continuing existence 'that is mine when I/Am worthy of myself (i, 360–1). 'Among least things' Wordsworth found 'an under-sense of greatest' (*The Prelude*, VII, 710–11) in the interchange between macro thoughts in mind and micro movements in words. This is the continual recomposition that Sir Humphry Davy helps us see in Wordsworth's work – a mental syntax like that offered in the account of the old man travelling in 'Animal Tranquillity and Decay':

> A man who does not move with pain, but moves
> With thought. He is insensibly subdued
> To settled quiet: he is one by whom
> All effort seems forgotten; one to whom
> Long patience hath such mild composure given,
> That patience now doth seem a thing of which
> He hath no need.

Those last four lines turn round upon themselves, changing as through time itself the very level of patience's operation, and enacting a syntactic equivalent to micro-movements within the brain, before finally delivering the meaning's outcome. It is the kindred journey of his own mind that Wordsworth tries to trace in *The Prelude*.

It is desperately hard to maintain a purposeful rhythm in a life, to keep alive a sense of a continuing journey. We can lose ourselves easily, like writers who give up in the midst of manuscripts they think no one will ever read. In a world often without structures and vocations, it is writing that helps create a continuing possibility of forward moves and sustains the checking between macro and micro levels. People who read should write about what they think, in whatever form they can – unless (or even if) they can put their reading into action in other ways. Universities offer courses, as frameworks, which should serve to make that writing more possible, more sanctioned. Often, it is best when adults come back into part-time courses, while still living the rest of their lives, though it is also good to catch people young, when the rest of their lives are more to do with the future, which the teacher does not see except imaginatively. But the proper status of literary work, even when done as it should be with all one's might, is still part-time: for that pays proper respect to the rest of the time, out of which the literary work itself comes.

Notes

1. Bruno Bettelheim, *Recollections and Reflections* (London: Thames & Hudson, 1990), pp. 28, 31.
2. Saul Bellow, *More Die of Heartbreak* (London: Secker & Warburg, 1987), pp. 99–101.
3. Saul Bellow, *Herzog* (Harmondsworth: Penguin, 1965), pp. 214, 280, 100.
4. John Henry Newman, *The Idea of a University*, first published 1852, 1858 (London: Longmans, 1912), pp. 275–6 (University Subjects II, para.3).
5. F.R. Leavis, *Valuation in Criticism* (Cambridge: CUP, 1986), p. 260. I am indebted to Douglas Oliver's *Poetry and Narrative in Performance*.
6. Les Murray, *The Paperbark Tree* (London: Minerva, 1993), p. 259.
7. Iris Murdoch, *Metaphysics as a Guide to Morals* (London: Chatto, 1992), p. 88.
8. Wordsworth, *Prose Works*, W.J.B. Owen and Jane Worthington Smyser (eds), 3 vols (Oxford: OUP, 1974), ii, pp. 78–9.
9. Letter to Benjamin Bailey, 13 March 1818.
10. John Henry Newman, *The Idea of a University*, p. 227 (Discourse ix, para. 6).
11. Doris Lessing, *Under My Skin* (London: HarperCollins, 1994), p. 218.
12. John Henry Newman, *University Sermons* 1826–43 (London: SPCK, 1970), pp. 83–4 (Sermon v: Personal Influence, the Means of Propagating the Truth).
13. *University Sermons*, p. 259 (Sermon xiii: 'Implicit and Explicit Reason)'.
14. *On Reading Ruskin*, translated by J. Autret, W. Burford and P.J. Wolfe (New Haven, Conn. and London: Yale University Press, 1987, pp. 109–10.
15. G.H. Lewes, *The Life and Works of Goethe*, first published 1855 (London: J.M. Dent, n.d.), p. 176.
16. *The Prelude* (1805), XI, 336; XIII, 65.
17. Letter to Ernest Collings, 24 December 1912.
18. Hazlitt, *Selected Essays*, ed. Geoffrey Keynes (London: Nonesuch, 1970), p. 511.
19. 'My First Acquaintance with Poets', *Selected Essays*, p. 511.
20. *Essay in Aid of a Grammar of Assent*, first published 1870 (Westminster, Md.: Christian Classics, 1973), p. 380.

9

Thirty-Three Variations on a Theme of Graham Greene

GABRIEL JOSIPOVICI

Of course I should be interested to hear that a new novel by Mr E.M. Forster was going to appear this Spring, but I could never compare that mild expectation of civilised pleasure with the missed heartbeat, the appalled glee I felt when I found on a library shelf a novel by Rider Haggard, Percy Westerman, Captain Brereton or Stanley Weyman which I had not read before.

Graham Greene: 'The Lost Childhood'.

1. My earliest memory of the pleasure of books: I lie in the sun at the poolside in the small town in Egypt where I grew up. It is midday. I am suddenly overwhelmed with pleasure at the thought of the long afternoon siesta when I will be able to carry on reading Enid Blyton's *The Castle of Adventure*.

2. The pleasure of reading by oneself is quite different from that of having one's parents read to one. The latter does not feel like pleasure at all, more like an essential part of life, whose abrogation would devastate one almost as much as the disappearance of one's parents themselves. The thought of an afternoon reading *The Castle of Adventure*, on the other hand, is bound up, like the thought of sex, with one's growing awareness of oneself as both private, bounded by the contours of one's body, and immersed in a world of others.

3. What does not get into even the best critical essay: A friend writes to me from Paris about the pleasures of reading the novels of Thomas Bernhard: 'I find myself waking up at three in the morning with a broad grin all over my face.' Yet *that* is what the best criticism is always trying to convey.

4. 'A good read.' Firm in their belief (which is completely justified) that this is the ultimate criterion, newspaper reviewers forget that one person's good read is another person's big yawn. I, for example, go on finding Kafka and Beckett good reads but find I am bored stiff by Ian Fleming (or A.S. Byatt's *Possession*).

5. Does this mean that there is no such thing as objective quality, only personal taste? One does not need to be a philosopher to realize that there are two truths jostling each other here: (1) Some books are better than others; (2) no objective criteria will ever be devised to establish that hierarchy.

6. But if there are no objective criteria how can we say with certainty that some books *are* better than others, that Kafka *is* better than Ian Fleming? Northrop Frye's answer seems eminently sensible: Don't worry your head about such questions in the abstract; you will soon find that you finish some books and not others, that you return to some books and not to others.

7. Borges was once asked: How have you managed to read so much, Mr Borges? I haven't read so much, he replied, only since I never read anything I don't enjoy I have remembered all I have read.

8. Of course there are books which we read compulsively but which, by the time we have reached the end, leave us dissatisfied. And there are others, which we may have struggled through with effort, which nevertheless leave us at the end with the sense that we would like to reread them. Most detective stories fall into the first category; *Ulysses*, for me, into the second.

9. There are books too which we read with pleasure and excitement at some point in our lives but which we find unreadable later on. This does not necessarily mean that we have grown more discerning, only that for a while we entered into their orbit and have now passed out of it. Auden mentions the poems of Rilke in this connection; I think of Lowry's *Under the Volcano*.

10. There are also of course some books we could not get on with at all when we first read them but which seem utterly delightful when we return to them much later on. Jane Austen's novels are a case in point for me.

11. Different again is the case of books which have a particularly powerful charge and which one can only reread at certain moments in one's life. Dostoevsky's novels are a prime example of this for me.

12. That is the trouble with traditional aesthetics: it fails to take into account the fact that books (and pieces of music and works of art) may mean a great deal to us because of our personal circumstances but, when these circumstances disappear, or change, they cease to have that meaning.

That is the trouble too with the academic study of literature. A noted teacher and critic once told me how he came to academic life. As a sailor on board a submarine during the war he found *Tristram Shandy* in the ship's library and thought he would sample it. He then found himself reading it avidly for the next three months, never knowing whether he would be alive to go on reading the next day. The book spoke so profoundly to him that he vowed that if he did get out of the war alive he would dedicate his life to passing on this new-found passion to others. But when he began to teach, and assigned *Tristram Shandy* to his students, he found them in large part bored and uncomprehending. But that, he realized with sorrow, was only to be expected: it was, after all, only the next week's assignment.

13. There are, of course, works which did not mean very much to us when we were made to read them at school or university, but whose quality gradually dawns on us, in large part just because we were made to read and reread them. Shakespeare is the central example of this for me. For a long time, like Wittgenstein, I could not reconcile my own experience of the plays with the universal consensus. Perhaps, I thought, one had to be English to appreciate Shakespeare. Or perhaps I was just not temperamentally suited to him. But constant subjection to the plays has brought about a total change in my attitude. Now I look back at my younger self and wonder how it was I was so blind in this instance when, by and large, my judgement was so acute in most other instances – or at least has remained so constant.

14. Clearly this never happened to Wittgenstein, though his struggles to understand why he could not respond to Shakespeare can help us to understand Shakespeare far better than the untroubled enthusiasm of most Shakespearean critics. 'I do not think that Shakespeare would have been able to reflect on the "lot of the poet",' he writes in the volume put together by his editors under the title *Culture and Value*. And again: 'Nor could he regard himself as a prophet or as a teacher of mankind. People', he goes on, 'stare at him in wonderment, almost as at a spectacular natural

phenomenon. They do not have the feeling that this brings them into contact with a great *human being*. Rather with a phenomenon.' This shows that one's response to culture can often be at odds with the insights of one's best work. For what Wittgenstein is articulating here is very much the aesthetic of any nineteenth-century Viennese bourgeois, a kind of watered-down Romanticism, where the model of the great artist is Goethe or Beethoven. Shakespeare's greatness lies precisely in the fact that he never does reflect in *propria persona* on 'the lot of the poet' or regard himself as a prophet or teacher. Rather, like Bach and Mozart, he works on the material to hand with performance rather than 'the masterpiece' in mind and as a result reveals possibilities latent both in the genres and the language he found around him which no one else had been or has since been able to articulate. But this, one would have thought, was precisely what should have excited the interest of the author of the *Philosophical Investigations*. Unfortunately, when it came to reading others rather than doing philosophy, Wittgenstein fell back on the mental clichés of his time and place.

15. What happened with me with Shakespeare has so far failed to happen with Tolstoy. I love some of the shorter pieces, notably *The Death of Ivan Ilyich*, but the great novels get, if anything, worse with each attempted rereading. There are wonderful moments, of course, but both what he is aiming for and his method of procedure do not interest me and fail to move me. For the moment at least the world and I will have to differ.

16. But what does it matter? There are so many authors I want to reread that I am happy to leave open the question of whether I am right or wrong in my view of Tolstoy. The bullying tactics of F.R. Leavis, laying down the law as to what is good and what is bad, leave him looking foolish and help no one.

17. Lucien Freud once remarked: When I lose faith in my work a visit to the National Gallery restores me.

Such comments are light-years away from the Bloomian notion that artists are always struggling to destroy their strong precursors. In my experience artists are always quite happy to ignore those precursors who have nothing to offer them while never ceasing to voice their gratitude to those they feel have given them the confidence to go their own way. Dante's tribute to Virgil in the first canto of the *Commedia* is closer to the mark than Harold Bloom's heavy-handed Freudian theories: 'O glory and light of other poets, may the long study and the great love that have made me search your volume avail me! You are my master and my author. You alone are he from whom I took the fair style that has done me honour.'

18. Bloom's remarks, though, do apply to critics, who are, by and large, ambitious for themselves in ways artists, no matter how conceited, never are. Perhaps this is because criticism, lacking any element of craft, is much more closely tied to the naked ego. The old Oxford ethos of the tutorial as a conversation about the qualities of canonical works, though it has come in for a great deal of scorn in recent years, is actually much closer in its premises to an artist, like Lucien Freud, than it is to Bloom, and all the better for that.

19. This does not mean, of course, that artists too are not often envious or jealous. He is a rare and saintly figure who can ignore the attention he feels inferior artists are getting, especially if he himself is being ignored. Picasso, who kept asking his friends: Am I not the best? Am I not the best? is much more typical of the artist than Kafka or Beckett. But even here it is the work the artist is concerned for, not himself. And even Picasso kept back *Les Demoiselles d'Avignon* for years, though he must have recognized its significance.

20. It is because artists know how difficult is the making of art that they have such respect for their precursors. That is why painters are the best commentators on art and writers the best readers. The intensity of Keats's reading of Shakespeare or Picasso's response to Ingres has to do with the fact that these artists *matter* to them in a way in which they can never matter to the authors of academic monographs. It makes one want to ask: Who would you rather have been taught Shakespeare by, Keats or Professor X? And if we can't have Keats then surely what we want is the nearest thing to him in the academic community. That person, in my experience, was Hugo Dyson at Oxford in the late fifties. As he stomped up and down between the lectern and the front row of his audience Dyson visibly struggled to convey the power, tenderness, audacity and depth of Shakespeare's plays; and the sense of their effect on him, more than any specific thing he said, was largely responsible for my feeling that this was indeed writing like no other and that for purely selfish reasons I should persevere with it. But Dyson wrote no books and in today's climate would probably not even have got

an academic post. Perhaps we should ask ourselves who loses in such a climate.

21. Critics tend to undervalue but also to overvalue the books they write about. Artists, who use their predecessors if and when they need them, come closer to reality, which is that reading, though of profound importance to human life, is not the most important thing. When you have finished my book, Proust says, you will have discovered how to go your own way. That does not only mean your own way as a writer but as a human being. Artists know that works of art are not monuments but doors.

22. That is why I have no sympathy with the bibliophilia of someone like Walter Benjamin. Of course a beautiful book is a pleasure to handle and makes reading easier. But whether I read a book in a first or twentieth edition makes no difference. In the end, it seems to me, books are meant to be devoured and passed on, not bought and placed on a bookshelf, only to be taken down to show to other bibliophiles.

23. Hölderlin has a little poem in which he berates the Germans for their idealism, for their willingness to take books for reality:

> Never laugh at the child who with his whip and spurs
>   On his horse made of wood deems himself bold and great,
>   For, you Germans, you too are
>   Poor in deeds and with fancies filled.
>
> O, like lightning from clouds, from day-dreams does
>   Action issue? Will books suddenly come to life?
>   O beloved ones, then take me,
>   Make me pay for my blasphemy!

(Trans. Michael Hamburger)

24. Wallace Stevens would frequently fast from books, feeling that reading was becoming an addiction from which he needed to wean himself.

25. It is easy to understand Greene's dictum as a licence for philistinism. Impossible though to misunderstand Kafka's comments on reading in a letter written to his friend Oskar Pollack when he was nineteen:

I think we ought to read only the kind of books that wound and stab us. If the book we're reading doesn't wake us up with a blow on the head, what are we reading it for? So that it will make us happy, you write? Good Lord, we would be happy precisely if we had no books, and the kind of books that make us happy are the kind we could write ourselves, if we had to. But we need books that affect us like a disaster, that grieve us deeply, like the death of someone we loved more than ourselves, like being banished to forests far from everyone, like a suicide. A book must be the axe for the frozen sea inside us. That is my belief.

26. The only books worth reading, Kafka says, are those which come at us from way beyond our horizon, they must be as far beyond our capacity to imagine them as any disaster. Yet, like any disaster which unexpectedly befalls us, shatters our carefully built world, they will then force us to face up to things which we had previously, prudently repressed. The books we ourselves write cannot, naturally, be like that. Yet Kafka spent his life trying to write precisely such books, and with some success. In this he is typical of the greatest artists.

27. When Greene contrasts the 'missed heartbeat', the 'appalled glee' with which he greeted a new book by Rider Haggard with the 'civilised pleasure' of reading Forster, he makes Rider Haggard sound like pornography. No such confusion can pertain to Kafka's remark that 'a book must be the axe for the frozen sea inside us.'

28. It is fairly easy, in the abstract, to distinguish pornography from the kind of literature Kafka is talking about. But is it so easy to distinguish the kinds of excitement generated by the actual reading of the two types of book? Is it too moralistic, too pat, to say that pornography, like any kind of addiction, closes one to the world, whereas what Kafka is talking about opens one to it? That is the kind of thing reader-response theory, allied to the sort of psychological reading Peter Brooks has undertaken for the classic novel, should perhaps be exploring. Is our response to *Great Expectations*, for example, closer to our response to pornography than is our response to *The Iliad*? And does the fact that the former is in prose and the latter in verse have anything to do with it?

29. Both Greene and Kafka make a sharp distinction between an excited, passionate reading, and 'civilised reading'. Barthes too

makes this kind of distinction, though in connection not with reading but with looking at photographs when, in his fine last book, he talks of the difference between *punctum*, that which touches you violently and unexpectedly, and *studium*, that which merely interests you. Yet is there not something too divisive about such distinctions. May not *studium* turn into *punctum*? And what of all those books we read not for study or to improve ourselves, but for sheer pleasure, yet which do not exactly fill us with appalled glee or affect us like a disaster – in my case the novels of Raymond Chandler, Evelyn Waugh and the best of P.G. Wodehouse and George V. Higgins?

30. And what of the classics? If reading George Eliot or Spenser is, for me, only *studium*, and Donne and T.S. Eliot always *punctum*, there are countless authors who seem to fall between these two categories. Is Lucien Freud's remark about the benefits of the National Gallery the one to remember here?

31. There are times, though, when walking around the National Gallery or any large bookshop reminds me of Kierkegaard's remarks about Don Giovanni and his compulsive philandering as an aspect of boredom. Here is all the culture in the world, from the Italian primitives to the Impressionists, from Buddhist scriptures to *Oblomov*: I am seized by the desire to see it all, read it all – but soon the excitement gives way to headache and all I want to do is get out into the open air as quickly as possible.

32. Looking at pictures and reading books needs time. It needs peace and quiet. We must feel out what we really need. Only then will works of art be able to affect us, even if not – or only rarely – in the decisive fashion asked for by Kafka. But the miraculous thing is that the best works of art, if we give them half a chance, teach us how to listen and look and read, themselves slow us down, open us up, lead us away from our egos and our anxieties towards a truer self.

33. Of course there are those who deny the whole notion of 'a truer self'. No one can teach the simple pleasures of reading either. There are those who will simply be unable to understand what Greene, let alone Kafka, is talking about. That, surely, is their loss.

Part Four
The Novel

10

Theorrhoea Contra Realism

RAYMOND TALLIS

INTRODUCTION: THE DISPARAGING OF REALISM

Over the last few decades, the realistic novel has been derided by literary theorists associated with the structuralist and post-structuralist schools of thought – the so-called post-Saussurean critics. Their criticisms have not been adequately answered because the underlying theoretical arguments – supposedly derived from Saussure – have not been examined with sufficient care. There has consequently been a tendency to assume that there is a powerful case against realism which can only be either accepted or uneasily ignored.

We are told that realism is dead while the non- or anti-realistic novel is alive and kicking. Of course, realistic novels continue to be written and read. But this evidence of life is illusory. According to Robert Scholes those who still write in the realist tradition are like 'headless chickens unaware of the decapitating axe'.[1] Michael Boyd asserts that, although 'hacks will no doubt continue to write soporific illusions just as some readers will continue to require such products for their easy consumption . . . the modern novel defines itself in terms of its rejection of the conventions of formal realism.'[2]

We are, it seems, to look elsewhere for fictional instruments to sharpen our perception of the world, to liberate us from the automaticity that pilots us through our days and to help us explore the realities in which we are situated and by which some of us are oppressed. The realistic novel is dead, and such posthumous life as realism enjoys is to be found in the work of middlebrow and blockbusting authors who squat paperbacked ingloriously on railway stations, waiting to be consumed by the mindless looking for an equally sedating but slightly more interesting alternative to sleep.

The acknowledged fathers of the contemporary literary novel – Beckett, Pynchon, Roussel, Barth, Borges, Marquez, Barthelme, Calvino, Sollers, to name a few chosen at random – create or created dream-worlds, anti-worlds, word-worlds and non-worlds, as do many lesser figures of equally serious purpose. The house of fiction is overrun by fabulists, by writers with their hands deep in what Philip Larkin once scornfully referred to as the myth-kitty. Science fiction is now mainstream and many of its practitioners, not greatly troubled to understand science, seem equally unperturbed by Wilde's dictum that 'It is only the unimaginative who ever invent.'

Even those writers who locate their fictions on earth and still have a use for characters drawn from daily life and for plots remotely related to ordinary experience are pleased to allow anti-realistic elements into their works. Indeed, a modest degree of apparently deliberate implausibility seems to metal the fast lane to academic critical favour. Many 'serious' novelists, in whose work formal experimentation is not especially evident, now include goblins, unfortunates who are twice-born or undergo innumerable incarnations, creatures with magic powers and other such implausibilia in their cast of characters, in an endeavour, perhaps, to look fashionably South American. Pseudo-science, magic, playful erudition, parody and above all whimsy unite practitioners as different as Salmon Rushdie and Kurt Vonnegut. Whimsy has emerged as the most potent temptation of the late twentieth-century novel as moralism and sentimentality was that of the nineteenth; the author-as-Puck has replaced Little Orphan Annie and it is not self-evident that Puck-marked modernism and postmodernism are much of an advance over the mushier reaches of Victorian fiction.

Mimesis – successful or otherwise – is no longer even an issue. For many advanced critics, plausibility is a literary vice, not the minimal art and virtue of fiction. As Nuttall put it in his *A New Mimesis*,[3] 'one of the immemorial ways of praising a writer, that is by saying that he or she is true to life, has become obscurely tabu, as if it involved some misconception of the nature of literature and the world.' To break with plausibility is to refuse to subscribe to the *illusionism* that is the distinctive vice of the realistic novel. A story that suspends disbelief or is open to interpretation in a quasi-realistic sense has failed to be sufficiently advanced. In order to guard against this, truly modern fiction will signpost its own artifactual – and advanced – state – its status as a piece of *writing* – by referring to itself, contradicting itself, breaking out into a delirium of puns or fading into a blank page where the reader can reflect on the nature of the narrative act.

Do I exaggerate? I do not. There is a famous and much-commented on opening paragraph in Alain Robbe-Grillet's *In the Labyrinth*. The first sentence announces that it is raining and the second that the sun is shining. This has been interpreted by critics to be an attack on the mimetic contract implicit in realistic fiction. The initial assumption that the novel refers to an external reality is ruthlessly brushed aside and we are, according to one critic, 'forced to realise that the only reality in question is that of writing itself which uses the concept of the world in order to display its own laws.'[4] On this basis, it would seem that to tear the mimetic contract to shreds, to subject the referential function of language to a radical critique and, in passing, to undermine the foundations of mindless bourgeois normality, all that is necessary is to enact the Magrittean cliché by writing down:

THIS IS NOT A WRITTEN SENTENCE

As Wilde might have said, one would have to have a brain of stone to burst out laughing at the death of Little Reference. But the wild claims made on behalf of many anti-realist writers who – to use Terry Eagleton's absurd phrase – 'explode our assurance' – are symptomatic of the critic's belief in the perniciousness of realism and its ripeness for destruction. To write, as one of Elizabeth Bowen's characters once said, is always to rave a little. And to write as a critic is not uncommonly to rave a lot.

Antipathy to realism is probably ultimately a matter of taste, but it has mobilized some apparently powerful arguments in its support, and it is these that I wish to examine. I must make clear, however, that my aim is not to attack anti-realistic fiction. My defence of realism is not intended as a formal proof of the worthlessness of fantasy or of fiction that consists of word games. It merely happens that I have a strong personal preference for realistic fiction – for fiction that is not obviously fantastical or self-referential – and I resent the implication of much literary theory that this taste is symptomatic of an infantile disorder. Or, worse, of Podsnappery. Mr Podsnap's world, it will be recalled, was not a very large world, morally or geographically. He resisted whatever was different, dismissing it as 'Not English!'. And he expected art to live up to his own high standards:

Elsewise, the world got up at eight, shaved close at a quarter past, breakfasted at nine, went to the city at ten, came home at half past

five, and dined at seven. Mr. Podsnap's notions of the Arts in
their integrity might have been stated thus. Literature: large
print, respectively descriptive of getting up at eight, shaving
close at a quarter past, breakfasting at nine, going to the City at
ten, coming home at half-past five, and dining at seven.

Well that is *not* what a preference for realism is about. Speaking
for myself, nothing human is alien to me; only aliens from outer
space are, especially aliens who can't make up their minds whether
or not they are crossword puzzles. By all means read or even write
science fiction or word-game novels yourself; but do not expect me
to take an interest in people who have 17 legs rather than two or to
enjoy the erudite whimsy of the postmodernist textualizers merely
on theoretical grounds.

AUTOBIOGRAPHICAL EXCURSUS

When I first encountered post-Saussurean theory – the main target
of this essay – I took it on its own estimate as, at least in 'insular'
England, a voice in the wilderness, a pariah living on the margin,
excluded from the high tables by provincial, timid, conservative
and unreflective hostility. I soon saw that this was not the case. The
actual dominant position of 'marginal' and 'marginalized' theory
was confirmed by a substantial correspondence with readers of two
books I published towards the end of the 1980s – *In Defence of
Realism*[5] and *Not Saussure*.[6] I received letters from young academics
utterly oppressed by a mode of thought with which they were out
of sympathy, but which had to be swallowed and regurgitated, for
that way lay advancement in their chosen discipline. Several post-
graduates wrote that they could not get anyone to supervise a
thesis that was overtly hostile to, or that chose not to engage with,
post-Saussurean thought. The spread of post-Saussurean theory
within departments of English literature is extraordinary: there is
now hardly a major university in the United Kingdom without its
representative theorrhoeist.

Since I am a physician and medical scientist and teacher, and not
a professional critic, about 90 per cent of the time I find it hard to
feel that it matters if some literary critics fulfil their dream of
travelling on the international gravy jet on the strength of ideas
about literature that are daft and/or wrong. This poses no threat to

my family, my patients, the education of my students, my practice of medicine or to the scientific disciplines upon which it is based. My patients in Salford were not awaiting the outcome of the debate between Derrida and Searle with baited breath. And the legislators and administrators and politicians who determine the resources available for health care and how those resources should be spent are unlikely to have heard of Paul de Man.

About 10 per cent of the time, however, I feel differently. It can't be a matter of indifference if large numbers of students – who represent a privileged minority and a significant slice of the future intelligentsia – are taught an all-encompassing view of the world-as-self-deconstructing-text, a view of 'reality' that is so difficult to grasp that, for the most part, they have only the choice of un-critically accepting or uncritically rejecting it. For this reason, I do not regret using up some of my spare time researching and refuting structuralism and post-structuralism. Paul de Man may not directly have a malign influence on my Salford patients, but theory-stupefied ex-students, actively untrained in rational and truly critical thought, might do, if they were to get into positions of influence.

I also resent the attitude of superiority towards the work of art that characterizes the writing of many advanced critics. The intel-lectual 'overstanding' that permits critics to 'place' novels and poems by seeing them as mere manifestations of a wider historical or social text invisible to the writer is complemented by a moral superiority that makes reading the classics in universities and even in schools simply a matter of catching authors out. Consider Terry Eagleton's exhortations in an article addressed to sixth formers: we must, he says:

> take from [this elitist culture] what we can, read it against the grain, expose the labour and oppression which went into its making, and thus turn it against the kind of society which gave birth to it. If we can find ways of reading and interpreting which allow us to do this, then the study of English literature might be just defensible, even important.[7]

Moral superiority is justified when one appreciates, with Professor Eagleton's help, what a shabby lot the 'great' writers were:

> Most of the agreed major writers of the literature, for example, have been thoroughly imbued with the prejudices of their age,

elitist, sexist, frequently reactionary in outlook, illiberal in opinion. Of the agreed major authors of twentieth-century English
literature, two (Pound and Yeats) fellow-travelled with fascism,
while others (Eliot, Lawrence) displayed extreme right-wing,
pseudo-fascistic sentiments. Wordsworth wrote in praise of capital punishment, Edmund Spenser advocated the oppression of
the Irish people, Joseph Conrad detested popular democracy,
George Eliot feared the radical working class, Alexander Pope
sneered at women and Shakespeare is unlikely to have been
over-enthusiastic about Jews.

(Ibid.)

The thought of young readers being in a permanent state of
intellectual and moral superiority to literature is not very inspiring.
It is one thing to approach the canonical works with a reflective
and sometimes dissenting intelligence; quite another to approach
them with a sense of superiority that comes from being in possession of an all-purpose tool to place, unmask and demystify them.
As an education for our future administrators, legislators, administrators, politicians and opinion-formers, this leaves much to be
desired.

Beyond this cause for public concern there is another reason
for continuing to challenge post-Saussurean thought: it has expro-
priated many of the most interesting and profound philosophical
questions. There is hardly a fundamental problem that it has not
pre-empted with its know-it-all-know-nothing arrogant scepticism, its confident uncertainties about the real world. The problem
of universals, the nature of the self, the relationship between language and extra-linguistic reality – all these questions and many
more have been wrapped in its meta-textual fog. These philosophical questions require urgently rescuing.

And so, too, does realistic fiction. For the critique of realism
lies close to the epicentre of the confusion that reigns in advanced critical thought The most interesting and annoying arguments against realistic fiction originate from post-Saussurean
theorists. They are not, however, the only ones. For the sake of
completeness – and to forestall the objection that I have overlooked
the best arguments – I shall list and briefly discuss some other
popular reasons for claiming that realism is outmoded, though my
main concern is with the post-Saussurean assault on referential
realism.

REALISM IS METHODOLOGICALLY PASSÉ

The weakest argument against realism is that it is stylistically conservative and that to write realistically must be to subscribe, implicitly, to an outmoded view of the world. The force of this argument depends entirely upon the mistaken assumption that contemporary realists are obliged to write like certain earlier realists, and to adopt the well-tried methods of Flaubert or Dreiser or even, God help us, Wilbur Smith. This argument can be dealt with very easily: realism, as an *aim* – to represent reality or to situate a novel in a world that operates under the constraints of somebody's world – and these constraints will be different in Manchester and Rwanda – does not entail commitment to the practices of previous realistic novelists. Even less does it entail subscription to their political, moral or metaphysical beliefs. In practice, a realistic novelist is obliged to be a tireless innovator if he or she is to let the world into the printed page. Realists will not be stylistic conservatives or, necessarily, conservatives of any other kind.

REALITY IS NO LONGER REALISTIC

The case against realism has also been developed from the assumption that there is something rather special about contemporary reality that makes it unsuitable for realistic treatment. This is expressed most directly in Norman Mailer's story *The Man Who Studied Yoga*:

> Marvin asks Sam if he has given up his novel, and Sam says 'Temporarily'. He cannot find a form, he explains. He does not want to write a realistic novel because reality is no longer realistic.

This passage, which has been widely quoted, is, ironically, taken from one of Norman Mailer's least incompetent and more realistic presentations of a complex bit of reality.

Different writers give different reasons for asserting that twentieth-century reality is qualitatively different from all that has preceded it, so that its essence, to quote Gerard Graff, is 'unreality'. Certain themes, however, are sounded again and again: first, modern reality is more horrible than anything that has gone before;

secondly, it is predigested, in a manner that has no historical precedent, by the organs of the mass media; and thirdly human artefacts intervene between man and nature to an extent not previously seen, so that the individual's environment is a rapidly changing man-made one rather than a stable natural one.

It is a peculiar but not uncommon kind of snobbery to believe that one lives in the worst of all times – the most abominable, the least comprehensible, the most rootless. Such a belief is the diagnostic sign of an underdeveloped historical sense. Anyone with the scantiest knowledge of what happened before today will know that the history of the world is largely a history of pain, injustice and chaos. Local reality has always resisted complete understanding, and the whole of 'reality' has never been within the grasp of an individual mind. Human life has always been torn with extremes that have often outreached the consciousness of the man with a pen in his hand. It is, therefore, no more a sign of moral or intellectual insensitivity to try to write a realistic novel in 1996 than it was in 1857.

It has also been argued that we live in a world that is more fragmented than before. Gerard Graff, for example, speaks of the way in which:

> modern technology, war, politics, commerce, social engineering and journalism . . . by promoting continuous discontinuity and upheaval have assaulted our assurance of reality.[8]

Everyone will be familiar with such sentiments. They do not stand up to the briefest reflection on the nature of ordinary life. Human consciousness has always been riven by discontinuities. To dwell merely on the physiological facts, the world has always been served up to living creatures through the lens of a body that has fluctuating neurophysiological properties. Ordinary life is marked by intermissions of consciousness: sleep, dreams, delirium, epilepsy and coma are scarcely twentieth-century innovations. The invention of the jet plane or the microprocessor has not cut deeper into the continuity and uniformity of an agreed-upon reality than do coma or even the ordinary sleep that the reader may be on the verge of even now. Here is not the place to discuss where the myths of the organically unified societies of the past have come from but perhaps I may be permitted the suggestion that they are usually based upon the habit of confusing the unwritten history of experience with the history of written ideas. Moreover, as Merquior has suggested, there may be vested interests in sustaining the confusion:

> That a deep cultural crisis is endemic to historical modernity seems to have been much more eagerly assumed than properly demonstrated, no doubt because, more often than not, those who do generally do the assuming – humanist intellectuals – have every interest in being perceived as soul doctors to a sick civilisation.[9]

All of this is really a long aside, but it is enough, I hope, to undermine the too easy assumption that reality was more realistic then than it is now. Most of those who try to prove that contemporary reality is so different that it is no longer amenable to realistic treatment typically do so by giving realistically described accounts of bits of contemporary reality, and so fall victim to pragmatic self-refutation.

REALISM IS POLITICALLY NAIVE – OR WORSE

There are political arguments against realistic fiction. The most interesting ones are presented with particular lucidity in Catherine Belsey's impressively articulate and almost persuasive *Critical Practice*,[10] published in the 1980s. At their heart is the claim that reality is an ideological artefact and that realism overlooks or seeks to conceal or deny this. In recent decades, this has has been the crux of neo-Marxist hostility to realism; ultimately, it derives from the paranoiac Althusserian notion of literature as being merely one among many of the Ideological State Apparatuses designed to maintain sufficient status quo to ensure the reproduction of the conditions of production. Realism, by pretending to present reality objectively, objectifies or naturalizes what is in fact historically and socially derived. There is not space to do justice to the rather complex arguments here.[11] Suffice it to say that Pierre Macherey – a Marxist critic and therefore on the side of the ideological angels – has shown very clearly how the most innocent attempt to represent reality is likely to lead to an *exposure* of the contradictions inherent in it rather than to collusion with the status quo. He makes this point forcefully in *Towards a Theory of Literary Production*:

A work is established against an ideology as much as it is from an ideology. Implicitly the work contributes to the exposure of ideology, or at least to a definition of it; thus the absurdity of all attempts to 'demystify' literary works, which are defined precisely by their enterprise of demystification.[12]

The works he is is referring to include the novels of L. Tolstoy – scarcely a forerunner of contemporary anti-realism. Macherey mounts a powerful case for realistic fiction as a way of making ideology visible, the realistic epiphany as a means of *exposing* what otherwise would remain silent or invisible and so pass unchallenged. For, he says, 'no ideology is sufficiently consistent to survive the test of figuration.'[13]

The ideological argument also falls victim to self-contradiction, for much of its anger against society is based upon realistic appraisal of what goes on in the world at large. 'Serbs are raping Muslim women while the world stands idly by' is, all too sadly, a realistic statement. Moreover, in Althusser's scheme of things, ideology and false consciousness are almost coterminous with intelligible experience. There is no room outside of ideology for the opposing view to establish itself. So much for the ideological argument.

THERE ARE NO SUCH THINGS AS TRUE STORIES

The impossibility of realistic fiction has been argued on the grounds that stories are differently structured from life. The basis of this critique of the pretensions of realism is captured in the famous passage from Sartre's (brilliantly realistic) *Nausea*:

When you are living nothing happens ... There are never any beginnings ... There isn't any end either ... But when you tell about life, everything changes; only it's a change nobody notices; the proof of that is that people talk about true stories. As if there could possibly be such things as true stories; events take place one way and we recount them the opposite way.[14]

The trouble with this as an argument against realistic fiction is that it is also an argument against realistic statements, in particular those large-scale realistic statements that engaged intellectuals such as Sartre believed in and acted upon, for example 'The French are committing atrocities in Algeria'. It is noteworthy how often epistemological and other modes of scepticism tend to be forgotten when someone is angry or outraged.

THE POST-SAUSSUREAN CRITIQUE OF REALISM

By far the most interesting arguments against the possibility or validity of realistic fiction originate from critics who have been influenced by Saussure's famous lectures on theoretical linguistics, collected posthumously by his pupils. These are the theorists who have contributed most to the the avalanche of theorrhoea – a term I owe to the late J.G. Merquior – that engulfs literary studies. And before plunging into post-Saussurean theory it will be appropriate to make one or two general observations about so-called 'theory'.

Richard Rorty has written of 'a kind of writing ... which is neither the evaluation of the relative merits of intellectual productions, nor intellectual history, nor moral philosophy, nor social prophecy, but all of these mingled together in a new genre.'[15] It is this that is called 'theory'. In certain quarters this is seen as the natural successor to literary theory which in turn has displaced literary criticism as the main business of English studies. 'Theory' is not to everyone's taste; for some, it seems to be composed of theories meta-theorized to the point where you cannot remember where they came from and can no longer see or care whether they are true. Theorists mock readers who, after a few pages of 'theory', thirst for first-order discourse, for facts and reports on experiences, for perceptions and ideas. They are amused by the naivety of those who do not wish merely to situate ideas but also to work with them, to try to understand them, to test them, to develop and extend them. For 'theory' is all about knowing all about theories without engaging with them on their own terms; it is about being able to 'place', for example, the General Theory of Relativity without having to know how to derive its fundamental equations. It is, in short, intellectually derelict, taking to the extreme the vice of substituting allusion for argument in those places where clearly defined premises and conclusions are required.

It is an infectious vice, even or especially when one is arguing about post-Saussurean theory. And one of the features that has most disfigured recent literary criticism has been the dialogue of the deaf and the name-calling that has passed between the

aficionados of theory and their opponents. Critics seem to divide into
those who accept post-Saussurean theories with little understanding
of the incompetent philosophy and worse linguistics that underpin
them; those who dismiss them as merely fashionable but pernicious
and try to refute the ideas without engaging with them; and, finally,
those who ignore the ideas with varying degrees of unease. Now that
the post-Saussurean movement is on the wane – though not as fast as
may have been expected – the position of the third group may seem to
have been proved the wisest. Why bother tilting at windbags? However,
the decline of post-Saussurean theory has resulted from extrinsic, not
to say extra-textual, causes: the death of some of the major players; the
posthumous disgrace of Paul de Man; the accommodation of the
academic nervous system to stimuli no longer novel; and so on. For
this reason, it is all the more important to see what the theorists were
about and why they were wrong, to drive the stake through the
corpse's heart in order to guard against resurrection.

At the heart of the matter are Saussure's revolutionary ideas
about language and the use that has been made of them by literary
theorists and others. So before going any further, it is necessary to
say something about these ideas, which are developed in the lectures published posthumously by his pupils.[16]

These are the relevant Saussurean principles:

1. The linguistic sign is arbitrary.
2. The linguistic sign is a signifier combined with a signified.
3. Neither the signifier nor the signified enjoys an independent
   existence outside of the *system* of language.
4. The linguistic system is a set of differences, and its component
   signifiers and signifieds, being purely differential, are essentially negative.

The arbitrariness of the linguistic sign is hardly controversial.
Indeed, it is a very old notion that Saussure did not claim to originate. It does not imply (as Saussure was at pains to point out) that the
choice of which words to mean what things was left entirely to the
discretion of the speaker. No, the linguistic sign was arbitrary in the
sense of 'having no natural connexion with the signifier'. Words do
not have meanings in virtue of the fact that their token instances
resemble the objects they are used to refer to. 'Cat' does not look,
sound, smell, etc. like any cat and it wouldn't do its job better if it
did; indeed, non-arbitrariness would be an embarrassment rather
than an advantage.

But Saussure's assertion of the arbitrariness of the linguistic sign cuts deeper into the relationship between language and extra-linguistic reality. The linguistic sign, he asserts, is a 'double entity', one formed by the association not of a name and a thing but of a *signifier* or 'sound-image' and a *signified* or 'concept'. Neither the signifier nor the signified enjoys an independent existence outside of the *system* of language; concept and sound-image exist as determinate, identifiable entities only within the system and, in this sense, are intra-linguistic. The units, defined by such differences, can be grasped only through the network of other units. This crucial point warrants further elaboration.

Consider first the signifier. According to Saussure, this is a set of contrasting features realized in sound opposed to other contrasting features realized in other sounds: it is a bundle of phonic *differences*. This conception of the signifier led the way to the great advances in phonology that was the main and still largely undisputed achievement of structural linguistics. Jakobson and others were decisively influenced by the Saussurean intuition that the protean sound patterns of natural languages were underpinned by a universal structure, composed of a limited number of elements and a finite range of permissible combinations. The realization that actual words (spoken or written tokens) served only as the physical realization of abstract, contrasting sound-features opened the way to numerous advances in our understanding of phonological relationships between languages and of how the brain extracts verbal tokens from the acoustic material served up to its ear.

The signified, too, is not a naturally occurring entity but a 'concept' – and one whose boundaries are determined only within the linguistic system by its opposition to other concepts. It is not, however, intra-psychic – a mental entity like a mental image: like the signifier, it is not a *thing* but a *value*, and it has value only within the *system* where it coexists with other opposing or different values. The denial of the prelinguistic reality of the signified is the most revolutionary aspect of Saussure's theory – and the one that has generated the most lavish and exciting misinterpretations. The signified is not a 'thing' 'out there'; nor is it a prelinguistic psychological entity. The signified is purely relational:

> The conceptual side of value is made up solely of relations and differences with respect to the other terms of language . . . differences carry signification . . . a segment of language can never

in the final analysis be based on anything except its non-coin-cidence with the rest. *Arbitrary* and *differential* are two correlative qualities.[17]

Verbal meaning is thus specified not in virtue of an external relation between a sound and an object but of an internal relation between oppositions at the phonetic level and oppositions at the semantic level.

So far so good. Few people would dispute that language is more of a system than a word heap and that its component signs are arbitrary in Saussure's sense. And it is perfectly obvious that the semantic catchment area of individual terms rarely corresponds either to patches of space-time or to 'natural kinds' (or 'types of patches of space-time'). Most people would be prepared to accept that linguistic value, as Saussure meant it, is negative or differential and that it is the differences between linguistic units rather than their positive contents that carry verbal meanings. But what has all this got to do with the validity or possibility of realistic fiction?

THE POST-SAUSSUREAN DENIAL OF REFERENCE

To get from Saussurean linguistics to the post-Saussurean case against realism, we need to believe that Saussure demonstrated that *reference*, in the sense required for realistic fiction, is not possible. Now many critics think this to be the case. Robert Scholes, way back in the era before structuralism was replaced by post-structuralism, for example assserted quite baldly that structuralist criticism:

> has taken the very idea of 'aboutness' away from us. It has taught us that language is tautological, if it is not nonsense, and to the extent that it is about anything it is about itself.[18]

I think we would all agree that, if this really were the case, then there wouldn't be much of a future for the realistic novel. The question to which we must address ourselves, therefore, is whether Saussure's ideas do in fact undermine the commonsense view that language may be used to refer to an extra-linguistic reality – to a reality outside of language; whether, in short, we have to subscribe to Derrida's notorious claim that there is nothing outside of the text.

Let us examine the nature of reference as it would seem to common sense. It may be illustrated diagrammatically:

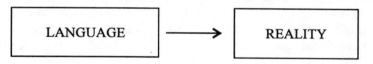

This model implies that language and reality are two separate realms but that the one – LANGUAGE – can somehow reach out to the other – REALITY. Post-Saussurean theorists believe either that:

1. Written or spoken reality is intra-linguistic:

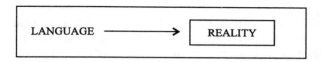

or that:

2. There is an extra-linguistic reality but language is closed off from it:

These two views converge in the claim that reality is accessible to language only in so far as reality is intra-linguistic. If it is further claimed that all structured awareness of the world is mediated through language, then we arrive at the position that reality is available to *us* – to consciousness – only in so far as it is intra-linguistic – a position which may be seen as a linguistic version of idealism.

Weaving in and out of these more explicitly philosophical theses about the relation between language and reality are certain ideas more specifically concerned with the relation between *literature* and reality which have been grouped under the rubric of 'intertextuality'. 'Intertextuality', like 'ideology', is a magic word whose scope can be modified dramatically to meet the polemic needs of the moment. But the central notion is that textual forces are more important than extra-textual ones in determining the form and content of a work of literature, that generic conventions are more influential in this regard than, say, the feelings and experiences or even the biography of an individual writer, or the properties of the reality he or she is apparently writing about. This is another apparent argument against the claim of realism to be about the external – in this case extra-literary – world.

The more radical accounts of intertextuality see this as an inescapable feature not only of highly stylized literary texts but of all discourse or, indeed, of *any* – howsoever fragmentary – articulation of reality. This opens directly on to the claim that the referent of all texts is itself a textual fragment and the further suggestion that society or the world is a boundless text. Edward Said spoke of 'wall-to-wall text' and Julia Kristeva suggested that even the notion of intersubjectivity may be replaced by that of intertextuality. Since both reader and writer are texts, the consumption of literature – and indeed living itself – become matters of textual intercourse.

The specific thesis about literature, then, merges with the more general, and more radical, claims either that reality is intra-linguistic or that language is closed off from extra-linguistic reality. This has been famously advanced by Derrida in the *Grammatology*:

> Reading cannot legitimately transcend the text towards something other than it, towards a referent (a reality that is metaphysical, historical, psychobiographical etc.) or towards a signified outside a text whose content . . . could have taken place outside of language . . . outside of writing-in-general. *There is nothing outside of the text* [there is no outside-text; il n'y a pas de hors texte].[19]

Let us now look at these two ideas: that reality is intra-linguistic, and that language is a closed system. These are the two pumps from which theorrhoea pours.

IS REALITY INTRA-LINGUISTIC?

Let us first of all examine the idea *that reality is to a greater or lesser degree intra-linguistic*, that prior to language the world is formless and possibly senseless, that the idea of a non-linguistic experience, of an experience without an interpretative articulation, is impossible. This has a long history that antedates post-Saussurean literary theory and, indeed, Saussure himself. But it was Saussure's claim that the the signified was intra-linguistic, and that prior to language the mass of thought was shapeless, that led the first generation of structural linguists in the 1930s to search for evidence of this in the apparent relativity of fact to linguistic divisions.

No one, I think, would wish to challenge the obvious truth that language is implicated in the construction of reality. What is at issue, however, is the *extent* to which reality is intra-linguistic and language the agent or medium by virtue of which reality is structured or constituted; more particularly, the radically nominalist assumption that the traffic is all one way: that language structures reality but reality does not influence the structure, the system of differences, that is the form and content of language.

Now there is a sense in which it is correct to say that reality consists of what gets talked about: to be is to be the subject of an assertion. This is certainly true of social reality; and the transformation of an infant into a fully developed human being consists at least in part of an induction into an almost infinite set of discourses. Becoming a person, entering language and acquiring a world are intimately connected processes. A historical era descends through time and enters its newest inhabitants largely through words. Much of our world belongs to the realm of knowledge, and this is verbally organized and access to it is verbally mediated. The reality that anyone inhabits is a vast inverted pyramid of discourse poised on a tiny apex of experience.

What of this apex? Is *this* free of language? Apparently not. Language is not only a means of transmitting general knowledge but also of categorizing immediate experience. We make sense of sense experience by generalizing it and at least in part subsuming it under linguistic categories. Though *sensations* may be of particulars, *perception* involves classifying experiences under universal categories, the majority of which will be derived from or enshrined, or stabilized, in language. In so far as it is perceived rather than being merely sensed, an object is at least nascently verbalized. Language, then, not only structures higher-order, propositional knowledge of the world but also permeates even our experience of particulars.

So much is incontrovertible. But does this force the conclusion that reality is intra-linguistic to such a degree that 'realistic' novels, novels that seem to be 'about' an extra-linguistic reality, are a kind of fraud? Or that architectural plans are sets of discourse? Or that the law isn't about the rights and wrongs of individuals but about the properties of certain texts? Are we obliged to believe that the manner in which reality is differentiated is an internal affair of language? Does it follow from the intra-linguistic nature of the signified that reality cannot be at once articulated and extra-linguistic? Do we have to accept Lacan's claim that 'it is the world of words that creates the world of things'?

The example most often invoked in support of the structuralist contention that factual reality reflects language rather than vice versa is the vocabulary of colour terms. The spectrum of colours is a continuum but this continuum is invariably spoken of and, it is concluded, often experienced as if it consisted of distinct and discontinuous segments – the named colours. The division of the spectrum into colours varies from language to language: English, for example, has a range of 11 primary colour terms whereas the Philippine language of Hanunoo makes do with four. This has been taken to imply that the perception and discrimination of even such basic sensory experiences as those of colour are determined by one's native language and it has been invoked in support of the more general hypothesis that reality is experienced in accordance with the manner in which it is linguistically structured.

Over 20 years ago, comparative linguistic studies by Berlin and Kay cast doubt on this relativism by suggesting that there is a universal set of 11 colour categories from which individual languages take different subsets. Actually, this evidence, though it may undermine the Sapir-Whorf hypothesis, is an unnecessary weapon in the attack on structuralism since the linguistic relativity argument collapses under its own contradictions. The suspiciously well-worn example of colour terms, far from being a decisive case for structuralism, is a conspicuous own goal. How so?

If it *is* a universal property of the human mind or brain to segment reality in accordance with linguistic categories, how could it be possible that (to use Jonathan Culler's words in his argument for the structuralist view[20]) 'everyone knows that the spectrum of colours is a continuum'? What do they know it *with*? Not the brain, nor the mind, clearly, for they are supposed to be under the thrall of language. Can it be with ESP? And how, furthermore, are they able to *say* (as Culler does in discussing this example) that it is a *spectrum*? It seems as if the linguistic straitjacket can be taken off at will so that we can inspect it and talk about it and can compare reality as it really is (the continuum of colours) with reality as it is said to be or is conventionally perceived (the segmented spectrum). If we do dissect nature along the lines laid down by our native languages, it would appear that we are not always obliged to do so. Direct experience would seem to be able to circumvent – and so reform – language.

One of the key arguments for extreme linguistic relativism would seem, therefore, to be self-defeating: obtaining the evidence the argument requires depends upon our performing what *ex hypothesi* should be impossible, namely seeing the difference between what is (linguistically) said to be the case and what is actually the case. The observation that different races of people dissect the same bit of nature differently according to their different native languages presupposes that that same bit can be repeatedly identified independently of language. As Leech has pointed out:

> Even though there is no corresponding concept in one's own language for a concept in another language, one can nevertheless provide a description (if necessary a very detailed description) of its referents.[21]

We often *say* what it is that 'they' or 'we' do not have a word for.

The truth is that the manner in which the world is linguistically differentiated depends upon the needs of the community of language speakers. The fact that the Eskimo – to take another suspiciously well-worn example (which has, anyway, recently been disputed[22]) – have terms to distinguish ten or more different types of snow whereas Kalahari bushmen do not is a tribute not to the degree to which language shapes our perceptual grids but to the influence of extra-linguistic experience and need over the development of language – to the fact that snow is a bigger issue inside the Arctic Circle than it is in sub-Saharan Africa. In determining the way in which we speak about reality – and hence describe it – the interaction between linguistic and extra-linguistic factors is two-way. It is not only language that calls the shots.

IS LANGUAGE A CLOSED SYSTEM?

One persistent post-Saussurean belief is that Saussure's demonstration that language is structured, that it is a system, implies that language is closed off from anything outside of itself. The fallacious belief that all systems or all structures are in some sense closed has been expounded with exceptional clarity by Terence Hawkes in his popularizing *Structuralism and Semiotics*.[23] Language, he says, is a structure in the Piagetian sense and the transformations of such a structure:

> act to maintain and underwrite the intrinsic laws which bring them about, and to 'seal off' the system from reference to other systems.
>
> (Ibid., p. 16–17)

In consequence, a language is closed off from reality:

> A language does not construct its formations of words by reference to patterns of 'reality', but on the basis of its own self-sufficient rules. The word 'dog' exists and functions within the structure of the English language without reference to any four-legged barking creature's real existence. The word's behaviour derives from its inherent status as a noun rather than its referent's status as an animal. Structures are characteristically 'closed' in this way.
>
> (Ibid., p. 17)

Hawkes' use of the word 'behaviour' is revealingly ambiguous. Of course, the word 'dog' does not behave like a real dog. It doesn't, for example, make a mess on the pavement. But this merely rules out of court a crude mimetic theory of language: the idea that words stand proxy for objects – and on a one-to-one basis. Such a theory has not been seriously held outside of Swift's Laputa and the Academy of Lagado. Out-ruling this theory, however, has a kind of carry-over effect; it seems to suggest that the word's behaviour in another sense – the occurrence of its tokens and the verbal company they keep – is also unrelated to what is happening in the outside world, in particular to the behaviour of dogs.

'A language does not construct its formations of words by reference to patterns of "reality", but on the basis of its own self-sufficient rules', says Hawkes. Let us consider three formations of words:

The dog is barking.

The dog is quacking.

The dog is deconstructing medieval texts.

The first formation is very common, the second very rare and the third has probably never occurred before. How very like the corresponding situations in life! Is this purely coincidental? Or could it be that formations of words are constructed (not by language but by language users – an important point to which I shall return) by reference to patterns of reality?

Behind the claim that discourse is closed is a confusion between the system or structure and the specific utterances or writings produced by individuals utilizing that structure – between two things, *langue* and *parole*, that it was part of Saussure's achievement to separate. *La langue* is the system of language, the language as a system of forms, while *parole* is actual speech or writing, the speech acts and writing acts that the language makes possible. And this muddle is reflected in the fact that it is unclear whether Hawkes is using the word 'word' to refer to the token or the type: tokens instantiate verbal types on actual occasions of speech or writing. Obviously, no *structure* or *system* could determine or influence the use I make of it on a particular occasion and no *type* could legislate over its own occurrences as tokens. Of course, the *system* is non-referential, in the same way as the structure of the cerebral cortex is not itself a sensory field.

Consider this claim by Catherine Belsey:

> If discourses articulate concepts through a system of signs which signify by means of their relationship to each other rather than to entities in the world, and if literature is a signifying practice, all it can reflect is the order inscribed in particular discourses, not the nature of the world.[24]

What she says, essentially, is that if language operates in accordance with certain rules and using entities that are intra-linguistic, then all that language can express is those rules and the only reality it can refer to is intra-linguistic. The force of this argument depends entirely upon *the false assumption that that which is expressed is identical with that in virtue of which expression takes place.* Or the meaning of what is meant is that in virtue of which meaning gets specified. This is rather like saying that if I were to point to a dog, that which I point to is not really a dog but a pointee, whose properties reflect the rules governing pointing.

We may accept the validity of the Danish linguist Trier's assertion that the meaning of lexical elements is *specified* by their relatedness to and difference from other elements; but this does not license the conclusion that their meaning in use is constituted by this. As (true) Saussurean linguists have pointed out, while the words in the lexical field derive their *value* only from their opposition to one another, their *meaning* is fixed only in relation to a particular act of signification. Value and meaning are not the same; the former belongs entirely to the system, whereas the latter does not. The purely notional signifiers and signifieds are such values; they are not meanings. The intra-linguistic nature of the signifier and the signified does not entail that *meanings* (and even less referents) are intra-linguistic.

The confusion between value and meaning, and the corresponding confusion between the signifier and the sign in use, lead directly to the suggestion that meaning is purely differential or structural, or that meanings are sets of differences; that meaning is a matter of binarily opposed *forms* and not of *contents*; that the whole of the meaning of 'light' lies in its opposition to 'dark' and vice versa.

In practice, the meaning even of such obviously opposed terms as 'light' and 'dark' – easy cases, one would have thought, for structuralists – is only in part determined by their mutual opposition. They may divide the semantic patch between them through having a common border and give each other semantic shape through their mutual pressure. But this does not imply that their meanings *are* those borders, *are* that pressure. It is values, not meanings, that are pure edges or borders, without content. For the opposition between light and dark is based on previously intuited meanings in turn rooted in actual extra-linguistic experience. If 'light' and 'dark' did not already have such meanings, then there would be no grounds for seeing them as being an opposed pair any more than, say, 'light' and 'custard' or 'prime numbers' and 'Roland Barthes'.

It is a structuralist commonplace that the system allocates meanings to words because 'there is no meaning without structure'. But it is obvious that precisely the opposite is at least as true: that there would be no perceptible structure to the system of language without intuitions of meaning. That this has not been appreciated is due to the fact that the methodological principle of structuralism, the basis of its 'discovery procedures', became thought of as an intrinsic feature of the object under study.

FROM THE STRUCTURALIST TO THE POST-STRUCTURALIST CRITIQUE OF REFERENCE

The post-Saussurean critics, however, go further than suggesting that meaning is the same as value by implying that not only the meaning but, indeed, the referent of a particular utterance or group of utterances is the same as *the signified*. How else would it follow from the intra-linguistic nature of the signified that the referent, too, is intra-linguistic and language is closed off from extra-linguistic reality? To get from Saussure to the post-structuralist attack on referential realism, we have to assent to the following extraordinary propositions:

1. Value (e.g. of the signifier) = Meaning (of the sign in use).
2. Meaning (of the sign in use) = The Reference (of the sign or phrase).

It would not be appropriate here to dwell on the difference between meaning and reference; this has been the subject of an enormous literature since Frege's famous paper in the 1890s on *Sense and Reference* – a literature that has escaped the attention of the linguistically and philosophically uninformed post-Saussureans. Suffice it to say that meaning is general and reference may be particular and that the transition from one to the other frequently and crucially involves the mobilization of deictic coordinates – rooting what we say in the here-and-now defined by the speaker's physical context – which, in ordinary discourse, is indubitably extra-linguistic.[25] There is no way, therefore, other than by extreme carelessness, combined with a remarkable ignorance of what has been written about meaning and reference over the last one hundred years, that one could assimilate reference to meaning, even less reference to (intra-linguistic) value.

In the light of what has been said so far, it might be thought impossible even to imagine how more completely Saussure could be traduced. Nevertheless it is possible. And this is where we come to Jacques Derrida's revision of Saussure and the endless chain of signifiers. Derrida has suggested that language is so enfeebled that not merely is it incapable of reaching a genuine red-blooded extra-linguistic referent but that it cannot even reach its own signifieds.

In order to see how he achieves this position, it is necessary to go to his famous essay *Différance* where he tells us that:

as the condition for signification, this principle of difference affects the whole sign, that is both the signified and the signifying aspects.[26]

And he proceeds to conclude from this that the sign as a whole, the sign in use, is also a matter of pure difference:

> the play of differences . . . prevents there from being any moment or in any way a simple element that is present in and of itself.
>
> (Ibid., p. 139)

This helps him to the conclusion that meaning – as it is carried by a particular discourse – is also a matter of difference and that it is an *effect* of language rather than pre-existing, and being expressed in, it. His final position is that the referent is purely negative or differential; from which it follows both that it is intra-linguistic and that it is absent or at least non-present. Since one cannot differentiate between types of nothing – nothing is nothing and that's the end of it – the difference between the signifier and the signified collapses. This is expressed by Jonathan Culler as follows:

> It follows from the purely differential non-substantial nature of the sign that the difference between the signifier and the signified cannot be one of substance and that what we may at one point identify as a signified is also a signifier.[27]

In Derrida's topsy-turvy world, this is taken to mean that language is a matter purely of signifiers that do not touch extra-linguistic reality – discourse is an 'endless chain' of signifiers.

This is, of course, nonsense: what is true of the signifier and the signified is not true of the actual sign as used on actual occasions, the verbal token, as Saussure pointed out:

> Although both the signifier and the signified are purely differential and negative when considered separately, their combination is a positive fact; it is even the sole type of positive fact that language has.[28]

This caveat, however, is ignored, or, rather, overridden. Saussure, we are told, simply could not face the implications of his revolutionary insights.

This, at least, is implied in the *Grammatology*. In this abominably written book – bad even by Derrida's standards – he appeals to the writings of the philosopher C.S. Peirce to support his view that discourse consists of an endless chain of signifiers. It is not necessary to go into Peirce's complex and subtle triadic theory of signs or to try to elucidate his concept of an interpretant. For the present purposes, we need only take from Peirce what Derrida has taken. Derrida observes that Peirce has shown that, since signs are interpreted and interpretation generates other signs, one sign leads to another, seemingly *ad infinitum*. Moreover, signs tend to originate out of signs. As Peirce says:

> If a man makes a new symbol, it is by thoughts involving concepts. So it is only out of symbols that a new symbol can grow. *Omne symbolum de symbolo.* [29]

The chain of signs is thus endless and beginningless.

Should this cause us any concern? Since the chain of signs could be broken only by the emergence of an uninterpretable sign – in short a meaningless object or event – the endlessness of the chain must surely be a reflection of the intelligibility and coherence of the world. It should therefore cause no concern. But Derrida interprets Peirce's sign theory to imply that the chain of *signifiers* – note *linguistic signifiers* not *natural signs* – is endless, and so evidence for his own quite different view that the signifier never reaches a signified.

To confuse the sign as a whole with the signifier is of course unforgivable, especially in a writer who bases his entire *œuvre* on the implications of Saussure's ideas. But there is nothing unusual about this: this kind of carelessness is epidemic, perhaps obligatory, amongst theorrhoeists. Even so, Derrida's argument seems too vulnerable – too obviously flawed – to have carried conviction even among those unaccustomed to sustained or consistent thought. In order that the post-Saussurean conflation of sign, signifier and signified should have become a cornerstone of modern literary theory, a further confusing element is needed. This is provided by the introduction of the term 'transcendental signified' in a crucial but very obscure passage in the *Grammatology*.

Since one sign leads to another *ad infinitum*:

> From the moment there is meaning, there are nothing but signs. *We think only in signs.* Which amounts to ruining the notion of the

sign at the very moment when, as in Nietzsche, its exigency is recognised in the absoluteness of its right.[30]

One is left only with 'play' – the free play of the signifier –

the absence of the transcendental signified as the limitlessness of play, that is to say as the destruction of onto-theology and the metaphysics of presence.

This argument permits Derrida and his millions of epigones to conclude that the chain of signs never terminates at anything that is simply present; it always points to the next sign. In consequence, it is reduced to signs of itself – to traces, to signifiers. This has an astonishing metaphysical consequence: we never arrive at presence unmediated by signs – immediate presence, presence itself. Immediacy, presence are impossible, elusive dreams dreamt up in the tradition of what he calls 'Western metaphysics'. Thus Derrida.[31]

It is, of course, untrue that the emergence of 'meaning' in natural signs results in the evaporation of presence to traces of traces. The paw marks are a sign to me of a lion. But, over and above their character as signs of a *general* meaning, they have *particular* existence, presence, as depressions in the dust. Yes, they are that which means 'lion', they carry the meaning 'lion' on this occasion; but that is not all that they are. They continue to exist when they are not meaning and they have features that are quite independent of their meaning, or that are not involved in the specification of the meaning 'lion'. Their location two inches rather than two feet from a particular bush, their being dampened by rain, their being seven in number rather than six, etc. are not features relevant to the discrimination of their general meaning. So, existing and signifying, being present and signifying something that is absent, are not alternative states. *On the contrary, being a sign is predicated upon being an existent that is present.* And this is true, whether the sound is a verbal or a natural sound or sight.

We are no more entitled to infer from the fact that one sign may lead to another *ad infinitum* that the signified is never reached than to conclude from the fact that since every effect is itself a cause and the causal chain is interminable that there are no effects – that the chain of causes never 'arrives at' effects. Of course, there is no 'transcendental effect' which would bring the causal chain to an end; but this does not mean that there are no effects at all. *Omne causa de causis* – all causes themselves arise from causes – does not imply that there are no 'effects/things/events'.

It is interesting to see how the Derridan argument traduces Saussure in this further way: glossing over the difference between linguistic and natural signs and imagining that the latter, too, were the result of a combination of a signifier and a signified. This is an inevitable consequence of failing to see the force of Saussure's distinction between natural and arbitrary signs or to appreciate the true nature of the signifier and the signified.

The fact that the signifier does not reach a 'transcendental signified' should be cause for concern only if the signifier were the sign itself and the 'transcendental signified' were a referent. And manifestly neither of these things is the case. However, the 'transcendental signified' is a useful smokescreen phrase, behind which a good deal of what I have elsewhere called *leger de Man* can take place. It is used, variously, to mean: the signified; the meaning of a sign; the referent of a chain of signs in use; or the ultimate termination of the chain of signs – in plenitude or closure of meaning, in absolute presence or in God. Because it means all of these things, those like me who are stupid enough to believe in the reality of the signified and do not believe that language is an endless chain of signifiers apparently also believe in the transcendental signified; and this means that we believe that the chain of signs somewhere comes to an end, that a final meaning can be reached and that there is a place where signs give way to absolute presence – to God, Who is both absolute presence and final meaning; that we subscribe to what Derrida calls onto-theo-teleology. Since most contemporary readers are liable to be atheists and since, too, Husserlian 'absolute presence' is so elusive, merging the notion of the signified with that of the *transcendental* signified is certain to discredit the former and give plausibility to the idea that discourse is an endless chain of signified-less signifiers. The concept of the 'transcendental signified', in other words, enables Derrida to move almost imperceptibly from the arguable position that no sign opens directly on to a plenitude of meaning/presence, i.e. is underwritten by God, to the claim that there is no signified at all, or none anyway that the linguistic signifier can reach out to.

CONCLUSION

The conclusion that all signs, not merely linguistic ones, lack signifieds is the inescapable reduction to absurdity – or the self-refutation – of Derrida's 'post-Saussurean' position rather than its 'daring' conclusion. And the time has come to draw my own, less daring, conclusion – that language *can* refer to an extra-linguistic reality. There is nothing in Saussure's writings to support the post-Saussurean belief that the reference required to establish realistic fiction is illusory and that that fiction is therefore a cheap fiddle. Derrida's mishandling of the basic terms in structuralist linguistics underlines the perceptiveness of Saussure's observation in the *Course*:

> No-one disputes the arbitrary nature of the linguistic sign, but it is often easier to discover a truth than to assign to it its proper place.[32]

Post Saussure does not imply propter Saussure.

More generally, none of the arguments advanced against realism that I have examined withstands close inspection. In particular, the beliefs of the post-Saussureans about the nature of language, based on an elementary misunderstanding of Saussure and a careless misuse of the terms he introduced into linguistic theory, could not, if they were true, be either expressed or communicated; nor would they have any specific implications for realistic fiction. Once the post-Saussurean critique – and other groundless bases for arguing against realism – are set aside, the many fascinating questions raised by the hopes and achievements of realistic fiction may be fruitfully addressed. Realism, after all, is the great unfinished adventure of the novel and one of the most powerful instruments available to us for furthering human consciousness and self-consciousness.

Notes

The defective foundations of structuralism and post-structuralism, in particular their assault on extra-linguistic reference and the notion of truth have been argued in more detail elsewhere, especially in *Not Saussure*

(1995). *In Defence of Realism* (1995) focuses more specifically on the theoretical arguments that have been mobilized against realistic fiction and the inconsistencies in the application of these arguments by critics who purport to subscribe to them.

1. Robert Scholes, *The Fabulators* (New York: Oxford University Press, 1967), p. 6.
2. Michael Boyd, *The Reflexive Novel: Fiction as Critique* (Toronto; Lewisburg: Bucknell University Press, 1983), p. 9.
3. A.D. Nuttall, *A New Mimesis* (London: Methuen, 1983), pp. vii–viii.
4. Jonathan Culler, *Structuralist Poetics* (London: Routledge & Kegan Paul, 1975), p. 193.
5. Raymond Tallis, *In Defence of Realism* (London: Edward Arnold, 1998; reissued, London: Ferrington, 1995).
6. Raymond Tallis, *Not Saussure* 2nd edn (London: Macmillan, 1995).
7. Terry Eagleton, 'English in Crisis', *The English Review*, vol.1, issue 1 (September 1990), pp. 25–6.
8. Gerald Graff, *Literature Against Itself: Literary Ideas in Modern Society* (Chicago: University of Chicago Press, 1979), p. 10.
9. J.G. Merquior, *From Prague to Paris: A Critique of Structuralist and Post-Structuralist Thought* (London: Verso, 1986), p. 260.
10. Catherine Belsey, *Critical Practice* (London: Methuen, 1980).
11. The arguments are set out in detail in *In Defence of Realism*, Part II: 'Althusser and "Ideological" Arguments Against Realism' – (London: Edward Arnold, 1988; second edition, London: Ferrington, 1995), pp. 43–90.
12. Pierre Macherey, *A Theory of Literary Production*, translated by Geoffrey Wall (London: Routledge & Kegan Paul, 1978), p. 133.
13. Ibid., p. 195.
14. Jean-Paul Sartre, *Nausea*, translated by Robert Baldick (London: Penguin, 1965), pp. 61–2. The arguments alluded to here are addressed in greater detail in *In Defence of Realism*, op. cit., Chapter 2 'As if There Could Possibly be Such Things as True Stories'.
15. Richard Rorty, 'Professionalised Philosophy and Transcendental Culture', *Georgia Review*, Vol. 30, 1976, 763–4.
16. Ferdinand de Saussure, *Course in General Linguistics*, translated by Wade Baskin (London: Fontana; Glasgow: Collins, 1974).
17. Ibid., pp. 117–18.
18. Robert Scholes, 'The Fictional Criticism of the Future', *TriQuarterly*, Vol. 34, Fall, 1975. Paul de Man famously claimed that 'it is not *a priori* certain that literature is a reliable source of information about anything but its own language' ('The Resistance to Theory' in *The Resistance to Theory* (Minneapolis: University of Minnesota Press, 1986), p. 11).
19. Jacques Derrida, *Of Grammatology*, translated by Gayatri Chakravorty Spivak (Baltimore, Md.: Johns Hopkins University Press, 1976), p. 158.
20. Culler, op. cit., p. 14.
21. Geoffrey Leech, *Semantics* (Harmondsworth: Penguin Books, 1974), p. 29.

22.   See Steven Pinker, *The Language Instinct: The New Science of Language and the Mind* (Harmondsworth: Penguin, 1994).
23.   Terence Hawkes, *Structuralism and Semiotics* (London: Methuen, 1977), pp. 16–17.
24.   Belsey, op. cit., p.46.
25.   I have here skated over what is an absolutely fundamental point. For a more adequate treatment, see my essay 'Philosophies of Consciousness and Philosophies of the Concept, Or, Is There Any Point in Studying the Headache I Have Now?' in *Enemies of Consciousness: A Critique of Anti-Humanism* (London: Macmillan, forthcoming).
26.   Jacques Derrida, 'Différance'. The translation I have used is from *Speech and Phenomena and Other Essays on Husserl's Theory of Signs*, translated by David B. Allison (Evanston, Ill.: Northwestern University Press, 1973), p. 139.
27.   Jonathan Culler, *On Deconstruction: Theory and Criticism after Structuralism* (London: Routledge & Kegan Paul, 1983), p. 188.
28.   Saussure, op. cit., pp. 120–1.
29.   Quoted in Derrida, *Of Grammatology*, op. cit., p. 48.
30.   Ibid., pp. 49–50.
31.   Another passage from *Of Grammatology* expresses the key element in Derridan thought, in the Derridan muddle:

> meaning thinkable in principle within the full presence of an intuitive consciousness. This reference to the meaning of a signified thinkable and possible outside of all signifiers remains dependent upon the onto-theo-teleology I have just evoked. It is thus the idea of the sign that must be deconstructed through a meditation upon writing which would merge, as it must, with the undoing of onto-theology . . . One is necessarily led to this from the moment that the trace affects the totality of the sign in both its faces. That the signified is originarily and essentially (and not only for a finite and created spirit) trace, that it is *always already in the position of the signifier*, is the apparently innocuous proposition within which the metaphysics of the logos, of presence and consciousness, must reflect upon writing as its death and its resource. (op. cit., p. 73)

32.   Saussure, op. cit., p. 68.

11

Readings of Realism

MICHAEL IRWIN

This essay will question one or two fashionable misconceptions about realism and illustrate the proposition – which should be a truism – that high realist art is an intricate medium that not only repays but requires diligent reading. The illustrations have accordingly been selected for unostentatious complexity rather than immediate impact.

I

The student who says in a seminar that Lawrence is splendidly true to life will be answered with smiles of conscious superiority as if he had committed some mild bêtise. The assumption behind the smiles is, quite simply, that modern literary theory has exploded the idea that literature is in any way authentically true to life.

This observation, made in A.D. Nuttall's *A New Mimesis*,[1] still holds true a dozen years later. That it does so despite the cogent countercase advanced by Nuttall himself, or by Raymond Tallis in his *Defence of Realism*,[2] is symptomatic of the extent to which university English students and even teachers can be confused by certain half-received half-truths of literary theory.

The confusion is seriously damaging. Realist fiction has been by far the most accessible and popular genre of literature. The English Department that undervalues it is slighting or patronizing the responses of generations of readers, and in so doing puts a tourniquet round its own throat. Will enthusiastic readers, the obvious potential students of English, continue to apply to university if that enthusiasm is to be dampened or dispersed?

An early, and elegant, contemporary opponent of realism was Gabriel Josipovici. The arguments he sets out in *The World and the Book*[3] aren't, of course, exclusively his own, but he puts with

205

convenient terseness a case which seems to have gained wide currency. He condemns what he sees as the involuntary solipsism of the nineteenth-century realists, their failure to understand that neither they nor anyone else could perceive an objective external world, that we are all confined within the limits of our own subjectivity. The modernists, he claims, were by contrast obsessed with this dilemma, seeking to dramatize it in their work, and indeed in their very mode of writing, thus opening out a new philosophic and artistic dimension.

A preliminary point to be made about this analysis is that the radical distinction it proposes looks less radical on closer scrutiny. If we are all, inescapably, in the same solipsistic cage our realization of that fact arguably has little practical consequence. For example, such awareness might well be, and in nineteenth-century fiction might well have been, subsumed by convention. The tacit understanding would be roughly as follows: 'Ultimately the "realities" we speak of are pseudo-realities, but for the purposes of this fiction let us set aside that consideration and assume that we can deal in objective truths.' A convention of this kind would be readily understood and readily accepted, since it is the very convention on which our day-to-day lives are founded. We *behave* as though we are dealing with 'realities'.

One might set that argument aside, and still feel that the modernists' self-consciousness doesn't necessarily represent much of a gain. It could even be contended that an unconscious solipsist – which is what Josipovici takes 'the traditional novelist' to have been – is likely to offer, by virtue of that very unconsciousness, starker literary demonstrations of our enclosed state. Involuntarily such fictions would dramatize the author's limitations of vision, and by inference those of mankind at large. What does the modernist gain by the calculated attempt to rattle the bars of the cage? It is to Josipovici's credit that he is very distinct here. His book concludes with a chapter in which he bravely tries to answer his own question, why it is that a modern literature which 'depicts an extreme solipsism', which treats of 'death and loss and degradation and the self enclosed in its private world', should nevertheless (in his view) produce 'a powerful sense of joy and release'. The answer is that such work:

> ... allows us to experience the limits of our world and so to sense what lies beyond, the absolutely other, distinct from me

and my desires. And this momentary and silent experience, as Proust knew, is worth all the deep thoughts and beautiful phrases that have ever been penned.

It's possible, I think, to take Josipovici's point and still conclude that his teleological claim offers a dubious bargain which sells some of his favourite writers short. On this view there's a lot of *A la Recherche* (for example) to get through before the promised 'momentary' experience can be attained: a groat's worth of insight bought with a million of perusal.

More fundamentally, it needn't merely be flippant, after a solemn nod in acknowledgement of the portentous unfamiliarity of 'the absolutely other', to remark 'What's the weather forecast?' or 'Pass the jam'. Between occasional moments of transcendence what interests most of us is, in fact, 'me and my desires' or other people and their desires. An approach to literature that seems to exclude or discount such primary human responses is surely radically defective, if not effete.

It's only fair to say that Josipovici's concern is less to attack realism *per se* than to celebrate modes of writing that in his view go beyond it. Many of those who have been more directly dismissive of the genre have floundered between misunderstanding and misrepresentation. Raymond Tallis has crisply exposed the fallacy of the claim, repeatedly advanced as a truism, that 'Realists try to copy reality':

> The source of this misconception lies in the loose use of words, so that the aim of referring to, reporting on, doing justice to, celebrating, analysing, and being constrained by, reality shifts to that of replicating, mirroring, reproducing or copying it. Certain intermediate terms – 'mimesis', for example – thicken the confusion. At the heart of the muddle is a tendency to assimilate the iconic truth of a representational mode of signification to the referential truth of an expressive mode of signification – so that accurate or successful descriptions are thought of as if they were pictures.[4]

Any fool – and the great nineteenth-century novelists were very far from being fools – can see that it would be impossible to 'copy' reality in a work of fiction and in any case pointless to do so. A novel does not deal in 'realities'. It may feature, for example, a description of a young woman in a blue dress, but there is no

woman, there is no dress. Both have been invented. Moreover this
indistinct, incomplete mental construct will be at least as recalcitrant to 'description' as a real woman would be. We cannot exchange clear mental pictures by means of words. All that the author
can hope to do is to prompt the reader to imagine a figure sufficiently similar to the woman imaginatively envisaged.

Such truths would seem self-evident if it were not for the frequency with which they seem to have eluded those theorizing
about the workings of fiction. Virginia Woolf provides relevant
examples of the confusions I have in mind in her essay 'Mr Bennett
and Mrs Brown'[5] – especially apt examples in that the essay has
acquired a certain authority, having often been quoted approvingly
by subsequent critics as though it made sense.

Her general concern was to distinguish the approach to character-
creation of certain younger novelists, such as herself, from that of a
previous generation, as represented by Arnold Bennett among
others. To show what she understands by 'character' she tells the
'true' story of a recent train journey in which she happened to have
been seated near an elderly woman who attracted her attention.
This woman, whom she labels 'Mrs Brown':

> . . . was one of those clean, threadbare old ladies whose extreme
> tidiness – everything buttoned, fastened, tied together, mended
> and brushed up – suggests more extreme poverty than rags
> and dirt. There was something pinched about her – a look of
> suffering, of apprehension, and, in addition, she was extremely
> small. Her feet, in their clean little boots, scarcely touched the
> floor.

Woolf pays careful attention to this woman and the man she is
travelling with – 'a man of business I imagined, very likely a
respectable corn-chandler from the North'. Mrs Brown creates
such an 'overwhelming and peculiar impression' that Woolf feels
impelled to deduce or imagine more about her: 'The important
thing was to realize her character, to steep oneself in her atmosphere.' She argues that different kinds of novelist – for
example an Englishman, a Frenchman and a Russian – would
read, and present, Mrs Brown differently. Each would have a
partial view. She hypothesizes the possible responses to her
Mrs Brown of Wells and Galsworthy, but particularly those of
Bennett:

Mr Bennett, alone of the Edwardians, would keep his eyes in the carriage. He, indeed, would observe every detail with immense care. He would notice the advertisements; the pictures of Swanage and Portsmouth; the way in which the cushion bulged between the buttons; how Mrs Brown wore a brooch which had cost three-and-ten-three at Whitworth's bazaar; and had mended both gloves – indeed the thumb of the left-hand glove had been replaced.

Woolf goes on to quote at some length from *Hilda Lessways* to enforce her point. Bennett deals in surfaces, in things, in streets and houses. The underlying human truths have escaped him: 'With all his powers of observation . . . Mr Bennett has never once looked at Mrs Brown in her corner.'

There is enough acerbity in the essay to suggest that Woolf was attempting a magisterial put-down of realism in general and Arnold Bennett in particular. Many subsequent commentators have seemed ready to take the will for the deed. But Woolf's argument is ill-based and self-contradictory. The parable she presents suggests that novelists characteristically draw from the life, attempt to describe and enlarge on something or someone specific that they have encountered. This is surely untrue. But even if, for the sake of argument, the claim is accepted, her criticism of Bennett's approach remains curiously muddled. Her conclusion that he 'has never once looked at Mrs Brown in her corner' is reached within a few pages of her suggestion that he would notice 'every detail' – for example her brooch and her gloves. Nor can she reasonably claim that he is in some sense noticing the wrong things and missing the essentials, since she herself has set out to gain her audience's attention by paying attention to just such particulars. As she eventually concedes, concerning her own problems with Mrs Brown: 'All I could do was to report as accurately as I could what was said, to describe in detail what was worn . . . ' Nor was this an unreasonable proceeding, given that it had been those very phenomena which attracted Mrs Brown to her attention in the first place. Her extracts from *Hilda Lessways* are beside the point, merely implying that Bennett is likely to include documentary material irrelevant to characterization: this is very different from suggesting that he fails to 'see' Hilda. A charge Woolf might have made, but doesn't, is that Bennett's account of Mrs Brown would prove – in the terms of the essay – too full, too exhaustive, that greater truth could be achieved

through greater selectivity. But such a criticism, so far from signifying an essential difference of approach, would rather insinuate
that her 'realism' was superior to his.

It might be argued that I am being obtusely literal in my reading
of the essay. Woolf is using Mrs Brown simply to make the *general*
point that 'all novels . . . deal with character'. After all, she is to
claim later that 'Mrs Brown is eternal, Mrs Brown is human nature,
Mrs Brown changes only on the surface'. But this is a hopeless
defence. Mrs Brown was by no means presented by Woolf herself
as representing 'human nature': she was very much an individual,
a powerful and imposing presence. That was the point. Moreover it
was precisely 'surface' details which displayed that presence
and which Woolf used to solicit our interest. Without those details
the Mrs Brown of the essay would have no existence. Because
she looked and sounded 'interesting' Woolf paid attention to her,
was induced to draw inferences and to hypothesize in an attempt
to get at the 'real' Mrs Brown. It's worth noting, in passing, that
many of these inferences themselves involve surface detail: Woolf
pictures, for example, 'queer ornaments, sea-urchins, models of
ships in glass cases'; she doesn't make straight for the (imagined)
inner life.

The chief oddity of the essay is that it implicitly contradicts one of
the main points that Woolf appears to want to make. Physical
details, it would seem, may, after all, constitute an important record – they are significant, they can be read, they prompt deduction
and speculation.

II

If Woolf *had* been looking for an example of an indiscriminate
'realist' it must be admitted that Bennett was a reasonable choice.
But it wouldn't be easy to find a comparable case among the major
nineteenth-century writers of fiction. Josipovici is oddly cagey
about naming names when denigrating 'the traditional novelist',
but George Eliot seems to have been one of those he had in mind.
Yet Eliot, so far from being an unreflecting realist, frequently admits to working to conventions, and repeatedly shows her awareness of the limitations of picturing in words. In *Middlemarch* she
asks 'How can one describe a man? I can give you an inventory . . .'
In *Daniel Deronda* she remarks: 'Attempts at description are stupid:

who can all at once describe a human being?' This is no unthinking literalist.

It's more surprising that Thomas Hardy should make similar points in the very first chapter of his first published novel, *Desperate Remedies*. In the course of introducing his heroine, Cytherea, he has already given an account of her clothes: 'an elegant dark jacket, lavender dress, hat with grey strings and trimmings, and gloves of a colour to harmonise . . .' He has pictured her hair, her eyes, her habits of movement at some little length. Arnold Bennett would presumably have approved. There has been a full page of such description before the author comments: 'But to attempt to gain a view of her – or indeed of any fascinating woman – from a measured category, is as difficult as to appreciate the effect of a landscape by exploring it at night with a lantern – or a full chord of music by piping the notes in succession.'

It becomes clear, as the narrative proceeds, that this is not an incidental observation. Hardy repeatedly shows a conceptual interest in problems of description. Implicitly he poses questions as to how we see, and how we imaginatively construct images that we have not seen. *Desperate Remedies* is full of sound pictures, which are precipitated into visual terms by the character who has been listening. The most lavish exercise of this kind is the scene in which Cytherea, in bed with Miss Aldclyffe, hears a series of strange nocturnal sounds and finds herself impelled to visualize: 'To imagine the inside of the engine-house, whence these noises proceeded, was now a necessity.' In such cases Hardy conjures up mental pictures not only for the character concerned but for the reader also, and in so doing shows his understanding both of the force of the visualizing impulse and of its volatility.

There is a curious little set-piece on the theme of description in the second chapter of the novel, when Cytherea is trying to find out more about Edward Springrove, a colleague of her brother's, whom she has yet to meet. When she asks 'What is he like, Owen?' she receives the unsatisfactory reply: 'I can't exactly tell you his appearance: 'tis always such a difficult thing to do.' Having elicited the further information that Springrove is 'of the middle height', she tries a new tack:

' . . . I saw a man in the street today whom I fancied was he – and yet I don't see how it could be . . . He had light brown hair, a snub

nose, very round face, and a peculiar habit of reducing his eyes
to straight lines when he looked narrowly at anything.'
  'Oh no. That was not he, Cytherea.'
  'Not a bit like him in all probability.'
  'Not a bit. He has dark hair, almost a Grecian nose, regular
teeth and an intellectual face . . . '

Further pressed, Owen throws in the information that Springrove
'is rather untidy in his waistcoat, and neck-ties, and hair.' Cytherea
feels able to observe: 'Ah, there now, Owen, you *have* described
him!'
  Hardy may have persuaded the more thoughtful reader that the
case isn't as simple as that. The 'description' Cytherea has
prompted is clearly a lot better than nothing. It greatly narrows the
range of visual possibilities: Springrove is like *this* rather than like
that. But she and the reader are left to draw their own mental sketch
within the loose categorization provided. Nor is it by any means
certain, as Hardy goes on to show, that one's visual experience of a
new acquaintance will be of the straightforward social kind that
Owen's mode of description implies. Cytherea eventually encounters Springrove abruptly, and by chance, when she is expect-
ing to see Owen:

  . . . she acquired perceptions of the new-comer in the following
  order: unknown trousers; unknown waistcoat; unknown face.
  The man was not her brother, but a total stranger.

It is some little time before she is able to look at him coolly and take
in his height, his soft-arched eyebrows, the single line on his fore-
head, the dark grey suit, the 'disarranged' neck-cloth with 'a de-
posit of white dust' in its creases.
  After these four different views of Springrove Hardy offers two of
Miss Aldclyffe. When Cytherea goes to meet her prospective em-
ployer she finds herself in a gloomy room which is irradiated only
by 'a very thin line of ruddy light, showing that the sun beamed
strongly into [the] room adjoining'. Apprehensive about the interview to come 'Cytherea fixed her eyes idly upon the streak, and
began picturing a wonderful paradise on the other side as the
source of such a beam . . . ' She hears Miss Aldclyffe's carriage
arrive, she hears her footstep and her voice. Only then does the
door open: 'The stranger appeared to the maiden's eyes – fresh

from the blue gloom, and assisted by an imagination fresh from nature – like a tall black figure standing in the midst of fire.' The two women walk to meet one another in the 'orange light', which modifies the appearance of both as each appraises the other. Again Hardy proceeds, after this first sighting, to provide a more conventional facial portrait of the older woman – 'Roman nose', 'round prominent chin' and so on.

Here is a young author, in his first published work – and that a sensation novel – playing conceptual games, in a lighthearted way, with the sort of descriptive passage that can easily be formulaic. He demonstrates that physical description is by no means pointless. Human beings instinctively draw mental pictures, and enjoy being given the verbal promptings which will help them to do so. On the other hand the value of such promptings is limited and relative. Our sense of what we see can be coloured by temperament, expectation, self-interest, mood, circumstance. Hardy shows how this can be true for various of the characters in his fiction, and implies that it must be true for his readers also. So far from being reductively 'objective' his descriptions have subjectivity programmed into them. It is this very awareness of the instability of his medium that gives him, in this area of description, an art to develop and games to play.

III

Defoe was notoriously persuasive when dealing with things – tools, cheeses, bullets, gold pieces, articles of clothing – objects interchangeable between the real world and the fictional one. He also shows a great gift for describing processes, as, for example, in *A Journal of the Plague Year*, where coins are extracted from a possibly infected purse with the aid of gunpowder, a bucket of water and a pair of tongs, or as when the young Colonel Jack tries to hide his money in a hollow tree. Such passages are read attentively because we can cross-check the details against the observable possibilities of everyday existence, asking ourselves whether this was the right way to accomplish a given task, or whether we could have carried it out ourselves.

Less obviously, perhaps, Defoe shows a considerable talent for dialogue. Here is an extract from a conversation that takes place early in *Robinson Crusoe*, after the first day of Crusoe's first voyage has culminated in a frightening storm. In the morning he is approached by a shipmate:

> 'Well, Bob,' says he, clapping me on the shoulder, 'how do
> you do after it? I warrant you were frighted, wa'n't you,
> last night, when it blew but a cap full of wind?' 'A cap full,
> d'you call it?' said I, ' 'twas a terrible storm.' 'A storm, you fool,
> you,' replies he,'do you call that a storm? Why, it was nothing at
> all ... '

Plainly Defoe has an ear for the idioms and cadences of vernacular speech. The reader listens to the narrator as to someone telling an anecdote in a pub. As with the descriptions of process, the appeal is to common experience. This is respectable realist art, though it makes no great imaginative demands on the reader.

Defoe is less comfortable when left and right hands must play simultaneously – that is to say when he needs his dialogue to be embellished by description or ancillary information. In *A Journal of the Plague Year* a group of Londoners trying to escape into the country are stopped by suspicious villagers and questioned by a Constable:

> 'What do you want?' says John.
> 'Why, what do you intend to do?' says the constable.
> 'To do,' says John; 'what would you have us to do?'
> *Constable.* Why don't you be gone? What do you stay there for?
> *John.* Why do you stop us on the king's highway, and pretend
> to refuse us leave to go on our way?[6]

The dialogue continues in this way, set out as in a play, for several pages. In effect it is reduced to a formal exchange of information, almost as though Defoe were writing a handbook for the use of possible future escapees. There is no space for any such visual detail as 'clapping me on the shoulder'. But it appears that the medium isn't doing everything that the author requires: he feels obliged to add a commentary by means of footnotes. For example, the first line quoted above carries the note: 'It seems John was in the tent, but hearing them call, he steps out, and taking the gun upon his shoulder, talked to them as if he had been the sentinel placed there upon the guard by some officer that was his superior.' Action and dialogue have been awkwardly separated out.

In *Roxana* an interview between the heroine's daughter and the Quaker begins in indirect speech but then sidesteps into the theatrical mode:

> ... after some time, my Girl began, and said, I suppose you know me, Madam.
> Yes, says the QUAKER, I know thee; and so the Dialogue went on.
> Girl. Then you know my Business too.
> Quaker. No verily, I do not know any Business thou can'st have here with me.
> Girl. Indeed my Business is not chiefly with you.
> Qu. Why then do'st thou come after me thus far?
> Girl. You know who I seek.[7]

Again the conversation isn't assimilated. At its close Defoe announces '*I return to the Discourse*', and the normal narrative mode resumes. Again he seems to find the dialogue format confining, this time adding bracketed stage directions: '*(And with that she cry'd.)*'; '*(Offers to go.)*'

In these passages Defoe is struggling – at a fairly primitive level – with a problem that was to concern all the major eighteenth-century novelists, a version of the general problem posed by the conflict between the simultaneity of experience and the linearity of print. When characters in a fiction are speaking, what are they doing, what are they thinking? How is the reader to be enabled to hear and see at the same time? One of the great achievements of the emerging genre was to find ways of solving that problem – ways of dramatizing our common experience of a variety of impressions being taken in simultaneously. Richardson's experiments in this area are various, understandably patchy, but inventive and often brilliant. Here is a relatively simple example, from an early interview between the beleaguered Clarissa and her unhappy mother:

> Sit down, Clary Harlowe; I shall talk to you by and by: and continued looking into a drawer among laces and linens in a way neither busy nor unbusy.
> I believe it was a quarter of an hour before she spoke to me (my heart throbbing with the suspense all the time); and then she asked me coldly, what directions I had given for the day?
> I showed her the bill of fare for this day and tomorrow, if, I said,

it pleased her to approve of it. She made a small alteration in it; but with an air so cold and so solemn, as added to my emotions.
Mr. Harlowe talks of dining out today, I think, at my brother Antony's.
Mr. Harlowe! – not my father! Have I not then a father! thought I?
Sit down when I bid you.
I sat down.
You look very sullen, Clary.
I hope not, madam.
If children would always be children – parents – and there she stopped.
She then went to her toilet, and looked in the glass and gave half a sigh – the other half, as if she would not have sighed could she have helped, she gently hemmed away.
I don't love to see the girl look so sullen.
Indeed, madam, I am not sullen. And I arose and, turning from her, drew out my handkerchief, for the tears ran down my cheeks.
I thought, by the glass before me, I saw the mother in her softened eye cast towards me: but her words confirmed not the hoped-for tenderness.[8]

It is easy to underrate the originality of a passage such as this precisely because the mode seems so natural, so modern. I want to use it to show some of the almost incidental strengths of realism and consider the demands that they make on the reader.

Both Clarissa and her mother are in a highly charged state, grief-stricken and tense. Each is fearful on the one hand of a devastating quarrel, on the other of weak capitulation. Their very pain makes it difficult for them to speak out, or to speak at all. How, then, is the strength of their feelings to be conveyed? In this case we see through the eyes of Clarissa. Anxiously she interprets every small sign implied in movement or tone. She observes not only the fact that her mother looks through the linen-drawer but also her way of doing it; even the manner with which Mrs Harlowe makes a slight alteration to the bill of fare 'adds to her emotions'. When there is a reference to 'Mr Harlowe' – as opposed to 'your father' – Clarissa mentally sets an exclamation mark after the name. She notes not only that her mother sighs, but exactly how how she sighs, or half sighs. Even when she turns away from her she watches her face in the dressing-table mirror. Her responses – which we, along with

Anna Howe, are invited to share – are hyper-attentive. And this very sensitivity of reaction is a tacit measure of her own vulnerability to hurt.

This is a modest illustration of one of the great achievements of realism. Tragedy proclaims its intensities; everyday life does not. We feel incomparably more than we articulate. In a conversation with a hurt friend or a jealous lover three-quarters of what passes will go beyond words, a matter of inference, of minute signals instantly understood. The realist draws on this capacity for intimate attention: as compared to that of the tragedian such work will be circumscribed in action and the rhetorical volume will be turned right down, but as a corollary the eye and ear of writer and audience must become correspondingly more acute. Our response to work of this kind must be all of a piece with our response to real life situations of comparable intensity. In both cases what is demanded is close reading.

In the passage under discussion Clarissa strains to take in not only what is said but what is insinuated by tone or gesture. The very medium dramatizes her involvement. So far from the dialogue being separated out, as in Defoe, it is folded in with the action, even to the extent of deforming the grammar: 'I showed her the bill of fare . . . if, I said, it pleased her to approve of it.' The odd, jerky paragraphing implies pauses or silences. An unfinished sentence, an unfinished sigh, hints at thoughts that cannot be expressed. Action, or even inaction, becomes an index of feeling, susceptible of more than one reading. Does Mrs Harlowe remain silent so long in order to increase Clarissa's nervousness, or because she cannot bring herself to say what the family requires her to say?

Within the economy of *Clarissa* family scenes such as this train the reader to develop the responses that will be needed to make full sense of the numerous later encounters between Clarissa and Lovelace. Richardson is developing a method of notation for highly charged domestic encounters. It begins to matter whether a given character bows, sits, stands, turns away. A shift of posture can mark a shift in the balance of power in a given relationship. Clarissa and Lovelace strive to interpret one another: the thoughtful reader strives to interpret both. Powerful causes are deduced from minute effects.

In modified form this method of Richardson's was to become a central feature of realist fiction. Elizabeth Inchbald makes startlingly sophisticated use of it in *A Simple Story* (1791). Her technique is so dependent on dispersed hints that it can be illustrated only by a fairly lengthy quotation. At this juncture in the novel the passionate Miss Milner, who has fallen in love with her guardian, Lord Elmwood, believes he may be about to propose to Miss Fenton. Her distress has affected her health. Unknown to her he has just found out from her friend, Miss Woodley, about the state of Miss Milner's affections, and his own feelings have been stirred.

Miss Milner, not having spirits to go abroad, passed the evening at home – she read part of a new opera, played upon her guitar, mused, sighed, occasionally talked with Miss Woodley, and so passed the tedious hours till near ten, when Mrs. Horton asked Mr. Sandford to play a game at piquet, and on his excusing himself, Miss Milner offered in his stead, and was gladly accepted. – They had just begun to play when Lord Elmwood came into the room – Miss Milner's countenance immediately brightened and although she was in a negligent morning dress, and looked paler than usual, she did not look less beautiful – Miss Woodley was leaning on the back of her chair to observe the same, and Mr. Sandford sat reading one of the Greek Fathers at the other side of the fire place. Lord Elmwood as he advanced to the table bowed, not having seen the ladies since morning, or Miss Milner that day; they returned his salute, and he was going up to Miss Milner, (seemingly to enquire of her health,) when Mr. Sandford, laying down his book, said,
    'My lord, where have you been all day?'
    'I have been very busy,' replied his lordship, and walking from the card-table went up to him.
    Miss Milner began to make mistakes, and play one card for another.
    'You have been at Mr. Fenton's this evening, I suppose?' said Sandford.
    'No, not at all to-day,' replied his lordship.
    'How came that about, my lord?' cried Sandford.
    Miss Milner played the ace of diamonds, instead of the king of hearts.
    'I shall call to-morrow,' answered his lordship, and going with a very ceremonious air up to Miss Milner, said, 'He hoped she was perfectly recovered.'
    Mrs. Horton begged her 'To mind what she was about.'
    She replied, 'I am much better, sir.'[9]

The scene is rare in eighteenth-century fiction in showing how a well-to-do family might spend a quiet evening at home. But the subdued pastimes, a little reading, a little music, a game of cards, later a cold supper, add up to something more than an inert background to the episode: they establish a register of conduct and demeanour. Four of the five people eventually present are in a state of strong emotion. Mr Sandford is hostile to Miss Milner and anxious for Lord Elmwood to marry Miss Fenton; Miss Woodley is embarrassedly aware of having betrayed her friend's secret; Miss Milner herself dreads the possibility that her guardian may have just proposed to Miss Fenton, or may be about to do so; Lord Elmwood is trying to come to terms with his newly discovered love for his ward. Yet in this restrained social atmosphere none of these feelings may be alluded to by those concerned; nor does the author choose to intervene with her own account of them. Like Richardson she encourages the reader to notice small clues. The description of the desultory activities which occupy 'the tedious hours' becomes an evocation of tension. When Lord Elmwood finally arrives Miss Milner's anxiety is shown solely by the mistakes she makes in playing cards. He and she, for all the strength of their love, are limited to an exchange of social noises. Lord Elmwood and Miss Woodley, we later learn, studiously avoid one another's eyes, while the watchful Sandford 'still made his observations'. Only Mrs Horton is unconscious of the hidden stresses of the evening.

Unlike the *Clarissa* scene this one is narrated objectively: the reader has a fuller all-round understanding of the situation than do any of the participants. Our eye is shifted from one to another. Inchbald's self-imposed task is to convey the underlying energies of the scene while remaining strictly faithful to the social realities of courtesy and control. Jane Spencer's excellent Introduction to the World's Classics edition of the novel quotes a wonderfully apt tribute to Inchbald's art in a letter from Maria Edgeworth:

> I am of the opinion that it is by leaving more than most writers to the imagination, that you succeed so eminently in affecting it. By the force that is necessary to repress feeling, we judge of the intensity of the feeling; and you always contrive to give us by intelligible but simple signs the measure of this force.

The tacit further compliment is that Inchbald sufficiently motivates her readers to read these 'intelligible but simple signs' and shows them how to do so. She teaches a new kind of awareness.

Inchbald wasn't alone, of course, in this project. As even this brief essay has implied, she was heir to a tradition. Fanny Burney, a little earlier, and Jane Austen, a little later, employed a roughly similar methodology and notation. In all three cases what was involved went beyond a literary method. Readers were taught to hear and see more not only in books but in life. It isn't a coincidence that about this time embarrassment becomes a fictional theme. The heightened perceptiveness of the genre makes it capable of registering snubs, snobberies, vulgarities, petty bullyings in play below the horizon-line of 'official' morality. An art that derived so directly from social observation automatically taught lessons about social conduct. If you could recognize the improprieties of the Branghtons or the Bennets then you might notice – and amend – some of your own.

IV

This essay has dealt only with odd corners of realism, one or two areas of description and modes of technique. It hasn't touched on such large themes as work, money, crime, weather, landscape . . . But even this narrow inquiry should have enforced the point that the invention, selection and distribution of descriptive detail in a realist text constitute a dense, demanding art. When the trick works there is the uplifting sense for the reader – as no doubt originally for the writer – of a passage or episode dilating into multi-dimensional richness. A wide variety of information, and of kinds of information, is concatenated together, challenging our alertness and understanding very much as they are challenged by the complexities of a difficult situation in real life.

I'd like to be able to move beyond the 'odd corners' and close by presenting a rounded analysis of some reasonably typical specimen of realist art. But the taut interrelatedness of high realism scarcely allows for detailed exposition within the scope of an essay of this kind. I hope, therefore, that some relevant points may be sufficiently hinted by means of an atypical specimen, in which certain characteristic realist effects happen to be writ conveniently large. The passage that follows is from Hardy's *The Well-Beloved* (Part Second,

Chapter three). Jocelyn Pierston, a successful sculptor, has returned from London to the Isle of Slingers, missing an Academy night to revisit 'that God-forsaken rock'. What has drawn him back to his former home is the funeral of Avice Caro, a local girl, his lover 20 years before. Arriving late he sees the ceremony from afar:

> Against the stretch of water, where a school of mackerel twinkled in the afternoon light, was defined, in addition to the distant lighthouse, a church with its tower, standing about a quarter of a mile off, near the edge of the cliff. The churchyard gravestones could be seen in profile against the same vast spread of watery babble and unrest.
>
> Among the graves moved the form of a man clothed in a white sheet, which the wind blew and flapped coldly every now and then. Near him moved six men bearing a long box, and two or three persons in black followed. The coffin, with its twelve legs, crawled across the isle, while around and beneath it the flashing lights from the sea and the school of mackerel were reflected; a fishing-boat, far out in the Channel, being momentarily discernible under the coffin also.

Read in isolation the passage, so odd in perspective, so visually eclectic, might seem positively surreal. In context it is less so. Various features of the scene are familiar to the reader from earlier references: *The Well-Beloved* (which features a map of the 'Isle') is powerfully localized and atmospheric. Moreover the novel has been sharply stylized throughout as an idiosyncratic attempt to anatomize the workings of love. Like a Shakespearian comedy it explores the nature of romantic fascination or infatuation by means of exaggerations, simplifications, speedings-up. Pierston is a man who falls in and out of love with a frequency and suddenness bewildering even to himself. The death of Avice occasions one of these sudden lurches of feeling. For the first time he falls back into love, and with a dead woman.

Surveying the ceremony with his hat off 'he was present, though he was a quarter of a mile off'. If he had been at the graveside his feelings might well have been conventionally limited, or even numbed: he would have been watching, at close quarters, only the interment of an anonymous coffin. From his wide-angle vantage-point the scene is transformed, expanded but crammed, 'sublimed . . . by early association', teeming with the various energies of sea and wind, folding in ancient buildings, a fishing boat and the twinkling mackerel that its crew could be striving to catch. Even the coffin comes alive, moving on its human legs like some huge insect. A funeral could hardly be more vibrant and inclusive.

Though unseen in this tableau Avice is present in all its details. The episode makes two major points – makes them both poetically and diagrammatically. Pierston loved Avice largely because she had come to epitomize for him the strange locality in which both he and she had grown up: 'in her nature, as in his, was some mysterious ingredient sucked from the isle'. Moreover this love, so far from dying with Avice, has now flared into an intenser life than ever. The scale and force of the funeral scene are proportioned to the scale and force of Pierston's reactions. What he sees is an impressionistic account of what he feels, and if that account conveys not only passion and grandeur, but also an element of the incongruous and even the absurd it is all the truer to Pierston's ironic self-awareness and Hardy's own wry view of sexual love.

The passage can be 'read' quickly because it sketches in bold strokes a hyperbolic species of love, lavishly, even morbidly romantic. Subtler, homelier, more stable feelings are regularly conveyed in realist fiction by this technique of displacement, but the notation has necessarily to be more complex, more minute. As the detail to be interpreted may be dispersed and cross-related over many pages, so the gap between the reader's instinctive apprehension and the normal procedures of critical exposition can become unmanageably wide. To explicate the brimming circumstantiality of a single episode in, say, *Anna Karenina* would be an involved and protracted task.

As a stop-gap, however, one or two primary generalizations may be risked. At the heart of realist art is the conviction that human beings think and feel associatively, and that the humblest of physical phenomena may therefore be charged with unlikely but communicable significances. The risks of the mode are great. At one extreme a particular association may be potentially trite, as when lovers exchange vows by moonlight; at the other it may prove emptily private, devoid of resonance for the reader. But when a great realist writer is on form the trick is achieved, the medium becomes luminous, even the smallest descriptive detail is felt to matter. And in so far as a cloud or an insect or a glove or a sandwich can be given artistic meaning in fiction the real-life counterpart is potentially transformed. Our humblest diurnal thought processes take on a new status. Self-impressed, like Monsieur Jourdain, we feel that we move among meanings and help to create them. For the university teacher of literature such claims carry major corollaries. Unless for the most elementary purposes of definition, generalized statements about realism are futile – false to the particularities intrinsic to the mode. Because the techniques they deploy are characteristically unobtrusive, major realist texts, and even good minor ones, must be read alertly and analytically if they are to be seriously read at all. So full a response requires a good deal of time – both reading time and teaching time. If a university syllabus allows adequate opportunity this investment of reading time will usually be volunteered: students *enjoy* lingering over a literary form that bears directly on common experience and offers both to invoke and to challenge the values by which they live.

The literature department that fails to create space for such study has probably ceased to be, in any serious sense, a *literature* department – though it may be a perfectly reasonable department of something else and should revise its title accordingly. The discussion here reaches a frontier of academic taste, beyond which argument must eventually give way ·to agreements to differ. Nonetheless it seems appropriate to end on something very like a moralistic note. The realist novel has been a democratic, a generous, enterprise in implicitly undertaking the great task of constructing art from the materials of ordinary life. To underrate that enterprise is obtuse and thin-blooded. To slight it is mean-spirited.

Notes

1.   A.D. Nuttall, *A New Mimesis: Shakespeare and the Representation of Reality*, London: Methuen, 1983.
2.   Raymond Tallis, *In Defence of Realism*, London: Edward Arnold, 1988.
3.   Gabriel Josipovici, *The World and the Book*, London: Macmillan, 1971.
4.   Tallis, op. cit., p. 195.
5.   The version of the essay quoted here is the revised, expanded text as featured in *A Woman's Essays* (Selected Essays: Volume One), ed. Rachel Bowlby, London: Penguin Books, 1992.
6.   Penguin edition (ed. Anthony Burgess and Christopher Bristow), p. 151.
7.   Oxford: Oxford Paperbacks (ed. Jane Jack), p. 319.
8.   Everyman edition, 1962, Vol. I, p. 89.
9.   Oxford: World's Classics edition (ed. J.M.S. Tompkins), pp. 132–3.

12

Watching a Writer Write:
Manuscript Revisions in Mrs Gaskell's *Wives and Daughters* and Why They Matter

JOSIE BILLINGTON

In what follows I shall be paying close attention to the choices made by a novelist in the process of writing. My intention is not, however, merely to offer an exercise in applying practical criticism to primary sources. My purpose is rather the reverse – to demonstrate how primary sources of this kind offer a defence of practical criticism. For what we shall see in the manuscript extracts I have selected below is a writer making minutely careful choices, attending to fine shades of meaning and to subtle implications sheerly as a matter of course. Reading closely, these extracts compellingly suggest, is what *writers* habitually do. Writing is itself, this material argues, a form of practical criticism. Thus what we call 'close reading', I shall seek to illustrate, is not a mere technique invented by 'new' (and now outmoded) critics. Rather, it is a mode of attention equivalent to the writer's own – a vigilance both demanded and merited by the scrupulous care which writers themselves customarily bring to their work.

In going back to the manuscript of Mrs Gaskell's *Wives and Daughters*, then, I am not looking to it as an editor might – by way of appeal to the manuscript as an authority for the published text. As Angus Easson points out 'the manuscript can only be regarded as a stage in the novel's composition.'[1] Yet it is precisely because it is the first stage of composition that the manuscript is of interest to me here. For my object is to show the way in which a writer's characteristic habits of mind, seen arising in the origins of composition, can teach us how to read her prose – the writing itself thus helping, implicitly, to set the rules for reading it.

Now in the John Rylands Library, Manchester University, the manuscript is Mrs Gaskell's original draft and the copy used for printing the serial edition in the *Cornhill Magazine* (it is marked-up by the printer throughout). It shows relatively little reworking. In fact the writing almost literally does not stop. The manuscript has neither chapter headings, nor, more significantly, chapter divisions – save on two or three occasions. The form of the manuscript of *Wives and Daughters* must be accounted for partly by the sheer pressure of time Mrs Gaskell was under – the result at once of an inordinately busy life and of the need to meet serial deadlines. But the fact that the manuscript just keeps going suggests, too, a dislike of interruption, as though the underlying movement and tempo of the novel is of primary importance to her. It suggests, also, a habit of mind and composition which simply goes on, in time with its own first thoughts. This, if nothing else, makes Mrs Gaskell's minute and momentary second thoughts – such revisions as there are – of particular interest.

But there is another special reason for going back to the manuscript of a work which has seemed to offer itself more as an easy read than as a candidate for exegesis and whose subtle achievements have consequently been overlooked. '*Wives and Daughters,*' as Laurence Lerner says, 'is surely the most neglected novel of its century – the one where the gap is greatest between its intrinsic excellence and the neglect it has fallen into.'[2] The manuscript of *Wives and Daughters* helps to explain that neglect even in exposing its injustice. For it shows a writer habitually attending to matters so small, subtle and apparently insignificant as almost to be beneath a reader's notice. It is the great virtue of this manuscript, in fact, to reveal to us that Mrs Gaskell's was a form of vision so bravely subtle as to have positively risked the danger of being underrated.

One further (and final) preliminary. In the examples which follow, it is impossible to distinguish with absolute certainty between immediate second thoughts and corrections which are the result of later revision. The handwriting and slightly greater clarity of the early part of the manuscript (from which these extracts are largely taken) gives the impression that Mrs Gaskell was somewhat less hurried and able to write at a more leisurely pace in the early stages of the novel, and biographical evidence seems to bear this out – though she was under pressure throughout. Therefore, it is just possible that the corrections are indeed the result of Mrs Gaskell's having had time to go back and reflect on her work. But there is no

change of pen or of pressure to indicate a later revision. And I shall
be arguing that internal clues strongly suggest the greater
probability: that the corrections are almost invariably the result of
immediate reflection. In teasing out the significance of these
small revisions, I shall of necessity be demanding quite a lot of hard
work from my own reader. For the space of these few, brief
examples, that is to say, I shall require the same close attention to
tiny matters of textual detail as Mrs Gaskell is manifestly paying all
the time.

To begin, then, with a fairly straightforward example and to
provide a little background and context for all of these extracts.
Early in the novel, Molly's father, Dr Gibson decides to remarry in
order to provide his daughter, now a vulnerable teenager, with a
mother. The wife whom he chooses, Mrs Kirkpatrick (a widow), is
a woman severely limited in intellect and sensibility, who though
not actively unkind, has had little time for or interest in her own
daughter. Molly's one consolation in the face of such domestic
change is the arrival of this new step-sister, the beautiful and win-
ning Cynthia, whom Molly admires and loves. In this first example,
however, Molly is feeling slighted and excluded by the greater
attention which Roger (Molly's friend and mentor) is paying to
Cynthia. The first version is from the published version, the second
is from the manuscript;[3] I number the lines of the manuscript for
the reader's convenience:

> The short conversation had been very pleasant, and his manner
> had just the brotherly kindness of old times; but it was not quite
> the manner he had to Cynthia; and Molly half thought she would
> have preferred the latter.
>
> *Wives and Daughters* (Oxford), p. 252.

1.   The short conversation
2.   <It>had been very pleasant, and his manner
3.   had just the brotherly kindness of old
4.   times; but it was not quite the manner he
5.   half
6.   had to Cynthia; and Molly   thought she would
7.   have preferred the latter.   (MS, p. 371)

The insertion at line 5 – of 'half' – looks merely casual, hardly an
important revision at all. Moreover, not only does the revision

seem rather perfunctory and off-hand, its *effect* is actually to leave the thing itself rather open and vague, even woolly we might think. It is the kind of imprecision which a tidier mind might have written *out* of a sentence rather than written into it.

And yet it is just this kind of seemingly lax revision which helps us more clearly to recognize Mrs Gaskell's mode of writing. For to see that little word – 'half' – *as* an insertion is now to notice the fine tuning and fine shading of relativism which Mrs Gaskell also makes in this sentence at *first* thought: 'His manner had *just* the brotherly kindness of old times'. It is that little word 'just' which is so painful to Molly. Her gain – Roger's *brotherly* kindness – is also now her loss: for – 'it was *not quite* the manner he had to Cynthia'. 'Just' begets 'not quite' begets 'half'. Mrs Gaskell's second thoughts, then, are sometimes things that come second, but sometimes they are incorporated into her first thoughts. And even the revisions which might more properly be called *second* thoughts are often less corrections as such than a paradoxically deliberate and careful blurring of her first thoughts – as we may see too in the next example.

When Cynthia arrives home from her school in France – soon after her mother's remarriage, but earlier than her jealous mother has expected – Mrs Gibson 'profess[es] herself shocked' at Cynthia's not having taken the time to stock herself with new gowns and 'useful French patterns':

> Molly was hurt for Cynthia at all these speeches; she thought that they implied that the pleasure which her mother felt in seeing her a fortnight sooner after her two years' absence was inferior to that which she should have received from a bundle of silver-paper patterns. But Cynthia took no apparent notice of the frequent recurrence of these small complaints. Indeed, she received much of what her mother said with a kind of complete indifference, that made Mrs Gibson hold her rather in awe; and she was much more communicative to Molly than to her own child.
>
> (*WD*, p. 226)

1.   Molly was hurt for Cynthia at <all>
2.   she thought that they
3.   th[is]ese speeches | ;/ <which> implied
4.   that the pleasure which her mother felt in
5.   seeing her a fortnight sooner after her two

6. years' absence was inferior to that which
7. she should have received from a bundle of
8. silver-paper patterns. But Cynthia took no
9. apparent notice of the<se> frequent
10. recurrence of these small complaints.
11. Indeed, she received much of what her
12.   a kind of
13. mother said with   complete indifference,
14. that made Mrs Gibson hold her rather in
15. awe; and she was much more communicative to
16. Molly than to her own child.[4]

(MS, p. 334)

The evidence to suggest that 'a kind of' (the insertion at line 12) is
an immediate revision rather than a later one really lies in the sort
of self-checking additions which we see Mrs Gaskell naturally making *at the time*, in the sentence at lines 8–10. The inclusion of 'no
apparent notice', and of '*frequent* recurrence' in relation to '*small*
complaints', are the modifications of a mind constantly readjusting
itself, as though Mrs Gaskell were instinctively rewriting even as
she writes. It is as if the manuscript corrections are only a more
visible sign of a revisionary *habit* of mind. And this is more than a
mere relativizing instinct on Mrs Gaskell's part. For the inserted 'a
kind of' is itself enticingly vague, and not so much a relativizing
addition to the noun phrase as an ambivalent *thing* in itself – a
defence for Cynthia or a bafflement to Molly or both. We don't
know for sure. It is as though, in such instances, Mrs Gaskell were
now more nearly getting hold of something which is itself still
elusive. What I called 'blurring' earlier on, then, is really Mrs Gaskell going beyond mere precision into greater precision. She does
the same thing again in the revision at lines 2–3, where 'which
implied' is replaced by '*She [Molly] thought that they implied* that the
pleasure which her mother felt in seeing her . . . was inferior to that
which she should have received from a bundle of silver-paper
patterns.' We almost have to see '<which> implied' underneath
'she *thought* that they implied' in order to recognize how definitive
a change the cancellation of the relative pronoun really is: 'which'
now seems like an easy-going, even lazy authorial word, in com-
parison to 'she thought' which is much more Molly's puzzled effort
than Mrs Gaskell's explanation. Whether Molly is right or wrong is
one issue. But at the same time Mrs Gibson's speeches still might of

themselves imply that the pleasure which she feels in seeing Cynthia *is* inferior to that which she should have received from a bundle of silver-paper patterns; *or* they might indicate mere thoughtlessness on Mrs Gibson's part; *or* they might be a mixture of the two. Again, we can't be sure. The revision with 'a kind of' leaves the thing richly indeterminate. And yet Mrs Gaskell is not playfully making the thing complex and uncertain for its own sake. For what is certain in each of these cases is that something is going on here – it just isn't possible quite to locate what it is. 'A kind of' might mean that Cynthia isn't in fact hurt; or that she doesn't want Molly to know that she's hurt; or that she doesn't herself want to know how much she is pained – and the truth, probably, lies somewhere in between. But Mrs Gaskell is not merely playing with the indeterminacy (Cynthia's indeterminacy, after all, is what makes her so frightening). Rather, it is Mrs Gaskell's close reading of life as she sees it which produces in these revisions a density of possible meanings in place of a single or settled one.

And it is the sheer effortless density of Mrs Gaskell's vision which is so apparent in this manuscript extract. For even at the first stage of composition, Mrs Gaskell is manifestly doing more than one thing at once: rewriting even as she writes, she holds open several possible thoughts within the same thought *and* in several minds at the same time. For she shifts her centre of gravity so easily here from Molly's puzzlement and pain over Cynthia to Cynthia's assiduous self-concealment; and then, within the same sentence – the last of the extract (lines 11–16) – she shifts again effortlessly to the so penetrable mind of Mrs Gibson: 'She [Cynthia] received much of what her mother said with a kind of complete indifference, that made Mrs Gibson hold her rather in awe; and she was much more communicative to Molly than to her own child.' This makes it worse of course: that Mrs Gibson can talk more easily to Molly is what in part creates the 'hurt' that Molly feels 'for Cynthia' and again even adds to Cynthia's 'indifference'. Yet that the seemingly easy connective – 'and' – which introduces that final move is not in fact so simply casual as it might look, is clear from the following example, where, some time after her father's second marriage, and increasingly aware of his irritation with his new wife, Molly finds herself weighed down at heart by the domestic situation at home:

It seemed as if there was not, and never could be in this world, any help for the dumb discordancy between her father and his wife. Day after day, month after month, year after year, would Molly have to sympathise with her father, and pity her step-mother, feeling acutely for both, and certainly more than Mrs Gibson felt for herself.

(*WD*, p. 432)

1. It seemed as if there was not, and never
2. could be in this world, any help for
3.   dumb
4. the   discordancy between her father and
5. his wife. Day after day, month after
6. month, year after year, would Molly have to
7. sympathise with her father, and yet pity
8. her stepmother, feeling acutely for
9.   and
10. both;   certainly more than Mrs Gibson
11. felt for herself.

(MS, p. 607)

It looks in the published version as if Mrs Gaskell were simply going on, in that final clause, with characteristic revisionary ease. But to see the connective 'and' at line 9 as a thoughtful *addition* is to recognize that even in their apparent casualness these easy-going connectives are a kind of semantic *signal* of Mrs Gaskell's habitual shifts of centre and of dimension. Mrs Gaskell is almost cunningly self-disguising here – artfully making the thing look art*less* and, moreover, making it seem as though she were just amiably going along with the relativism rather than (as she actually is) tough-mindedly recognizing and accepting it. Lines 6 to 8 in the original read: 'year after year, would Molly have to sympathise with her father, and <yet> pity her stepmother': the cancellation of 'yet' is as if something is now taken out by Mrs Gaskell for the same reason that 'a kind of' in the earlier extract was put in. 'Yet' puts one sympathy in simple conflict with the other, but the cancellation turns the thing into something far harder and far more confusing for Molly – not one sympathy as against the other but one sympathy on top of and added to the other: 'year after year, would Molly have to sympathise with her father, and pity her stepmother'. Now it is Molly who is in several minds at the same time – feeling those divided and incompatible sympathies both at once. Once again, Mrs Gaskell is going beyond easy or exact categories and defini-

tions to something more subtly and richly inexact, more authentically complex and confused.

My next example, which occurs only a page or so before the above
one, is a related instance of Mrs Gaskell's taking out a word in order
to *add* layers of meaning. The cancellation of 'even' at line 8 of the
manuscript makes what is in fact a huge and surprising shift for
Molly towards sympathy with her stepmother, unsurprisingly normal at the same time:

> She [Mrs Gibson] saw she was often in some kind of disfavour
> with her husband, and it made her uneasy. She resembled Cyn-
> thia in this; she liked to be liked; and she wanted to regain the
> esteem which she did not perceive she had lost for ever. Molly
> sometimes took her stepmother's part in secret; she felt as if she
> herself could never have borne her father's hard speeches so
> patiently . . .
>
> (*WD*, p. 431)

1.   often
2. She saw she was   in some kind of disfavour
3. with her husband, and it made her uneasy.
4.   resembled
5. She <was like> Cynthia in this; she liked
6. to be liked; and she wanted to regain the
7. esteem which she did not perceive she had
8. lost for ever. <Even>Molly sometimes took
9. her stepmother's part in secret; she felt as
10. if she herself could never have borne
11.   hard
12. her father's   speeches so patiently . . .

(MS, p. 606)

The loss of 'even' makes the whole thing more innocent, more
unsignalled. Molly does not think – 'Even I . . .' The word, unspoken, is turned into Molly's incarnate reality. The sympathy
happens involuntarily and unexpectedly, *and* perfectly naturally.
And yet look at what Mrs Gaskell does leave in and leave behind at
lines 5–8: 'she liked to be liked; and she wanted to regain the esteem
which she did not perceive she had lost'. 'Which' is one of those
seemingly careless signals I was talking of earlier. The pronoun
looks so innocuous, looks to be going on to the next narrative thing,

when in fact, at that little word, the sentence slips the narrative and crosses a threshold into a whole new dimension and new level of meaning: 'lost for ever'. But Mrs Gaskell just goes on as if nothing had happened – 'Even Molly sometimes' . . . A tough lady, as I say.

I now want to turn to an example which, clinchingly I think, shows Mrs Gaskell both putting something in and at another level taking something out at the same time. Mr Gibson, having told Molly of his decision to remarry, is now preparing to leave her:

> 'I think it's better for both of us, for me to go away now. We may say things difficult to forget . . . I will come again tomorrow. Good-bye, Molly.'
>
> For many minutes after he had ridden away – long after the sound of his horse's hoofs on the round stones of the paved lane, beyond the home-meadows, had died away – Molly stood there, shading her eyes, and looking at the empty space of air in which his form had last appeared.
>
> (*WD*, p. 115)

1. 'I think it's better for both of us, for
2. me to go away now. We may say things
3. difficult to forget . . . I will come again
4. tomorrow. Good-bye, Molly.'
5. For many minutes after he had ridden away
6. – long after the sound of his horse's hoofs
7. on the round stones of the paved lane,
8. beyond the home-meadows, had died away –
9. Molly stood there, shading her eyes, and
10.   empty
11. looking at the   space of air in which
12. his form had last appeared.

(MS, p. 173)

With the insertion of 'empty' (line 10), Mr Gibson is himself put back into that 'space of air' as though the space were yet holding his form, as loss. Yet it is the kind of loss which might seem as slight, as negligible as the revision which thus delicately enforces it. Molly's father has not gone for good, after all: he will be coming back. This is no more than a hiatus in the middle of continuity. It is not even a real *event*, so much as the residue of an event. And yet as Molly stares into that empty space of air, we realize that all that has not been said, all that has not been dealt with in the situation itself, for fear of creating future memory ('We may say things difficult to forget') is itself hardening, in that place called 'empty', into the stuff that memory will be made of. It is not the event which will become a part of who Molly is, so much as what is left unfinished by its being over. Nothing is made of this – seemingly. But the insertion helps us see that Mrs Gaskell is attending here to a some-thing that might appear to be nothing but is not.

It isn't in the big events, things dramatically signalled as import-ant, that we should look for meaning in a great realist such as Mrs Gaskell. The most real things for Mrs Gaskell are the things that happen around or underneath events, or in their aftermath – the things that happen implicitly, in life's interstices, in the spaces that Mrs Gaskell leaves behind even as she writes onwards. And so we do have to look closely if we are not to *over*look those features of Mrs Gaskell's art which, as a result of their very subtlety, are already substantially hidden – the delicate fine tuning, the myriad tiny shifts and adjustments, the tender pieties which, with the encouragement of the manuscript, we have seen to be going on amidst the apparently seamless fluency of her prose. The seeming unimportance of these things is inseparably connected to how powerful they are. For it is a part of Mrs Gaskell's very craft that she should attend to small things which make a big difference – 'Molly *half*-thought', 'a kind of', 'staring into the *empty* space of air' – with such apparent casualness that a reader may well miss their signific-ance. So we see it in my final passage – which I include (now without reference to the manuscript) in order briefly to demon-strate that the so-called close reading I have applied to the manu-script is only a way of authenticating the kind of reading we need to bring to Mrs Gaskell's prose all the time.

As the new situation with her father and his future wife now becomes a reality, Molly struggles to readjust:

> Thinking more of others' happiness than of her own was very fine; but did it not mean giving up her very individuality, quenching all the warm love, the true desires that made her herself? Yet in this deadness lay her only comfort; or so it seemed. Wandering in such mazes, she hardly knew how the conversation went on; a third was indeed 'trumpery', where there was entire confidence between the two who were company, from which the other was shut out. She was positively unhappy,

and her father did not appear to see it; he was absorbed with his new plans and his new wife that was to be. But he did notice it; and was truly sorry for his little girl; only he thought there was a greater chance for the future harmony of the household, if he did not lead Molly to define her present feelings by putting them into words. It was his general plan to repress emotion by not showing the sympathy he felt. Yet, when he had to leave, he took Molly's hand in his, and held it there, in such a different manner to that in which Mrs Kirkpatrick had done; and his voice softened to his child as he bade her goodbye, and added the words (most unusual to him), 'God bless you, child!'

(*WD*, p. 138)

'But he did notice it' is not isolated dramatically in a new paragraph. Rather, Mr Gibson's silent noticing exists cheek-by-jowl, in the same paragraph, with Molly's silent, lonely pain, imitating the simultaneous closeness and distance that goes on between humans in the same world. For the real matter here – the richly nebulous under-event which this paragraph is gently disclosing, even as it seems simply to be going on in time – is this: that in amidst the silence between them, father and daughter are neither completely together – 'She was positively unhappy, and her father did not appear to see it' – nor yet are they completely separate – 'Yet when he had to leave, he took Molly's hand . . . in such a different manner . . . and his voice softened . . .' A happening only half-shared is what is really happening in this passage. The complexity of its shifts and moves – 'But he did notice . . . only he thought . . . yet when he had to leave . . .' – exists not for its own sake but in order to register what is so irreducibly and finely complicated in relations of love and family.

It is the syntax of a writer quietly immersed in the rich complexity of this situation – inhabiting the undramatic space within it where, in families and in life as this writer envisions it, everything tacitly occurs. And Mrs Gaskell goes tactfully past the apparently little thing which matters most here – 'But he did notice it' – in recognition that to insist upon the importance of such matters would be to lose the subtlety of their reality. Mrs Gaskell's implicitness is not simply a fact of her art: rather her implicitness as a writer proceeds from a mode of attention to human life so loyally exact as to have reproduced the very size of those apparently least things which she knew to matter most.

Notes

1. 'Since Gaskell accepted a process of rewriting at the printing and proofing stage, undertaken both by herself and by editor and printers ... the practice consistently observed in the *Cornhill* offices has tacit authorial approval and should be accepted. Caution is needed therefore in going back to the manuscript as a superior authority.' 'A Note on the Text', *Wives and Daughters* (Oxford, World's Classics, 1987), pp. xxvii–xxix.

2. Introduction to Penguin edition of *Wives and Daughters* (Harmondsworth, Penguin, 1987), p. 7.

3. I give below a key to the symbols I shall be using:

    < > = cancellation;
    [ ] = word/part of word written over preceding cancellation;
    / = inserted (usually punctuation in body of text).

    The leaving of a space in the midst of a line indicates a word/phrase written above, in amendment.

4. 'all' (line 1) though cancelled in the manuscript reappears in the *Cornhill* edition – one of those revisions which we must presume Mrs Gaskell either made herself at the proofing stage or of which she tacitly approved.

13

'Green Glass Beads'

DORIS LESSING

This is an astonishing thing I am doing, trying to find words to persuade people, and particularly young people, of the advantages of reading. Only when I sat down to the task did I begin to see how astonishing. Until recently it would have been taken for granted that everyone with even the beginnings of an education should read. Recently: let's say thirty years. Not merely the middle-class children used to read, but children from poor schools too. Education included reading good books. Television made the change, not radio, which saw itself at its beginnings as an educator, as well as an entertainer.

There used to be something called The Cultivated Person, and reading was the best part of his education. Women have been getting an education now for a century, but before that the cultivated person was usually male. Fortunate women whose parents had private libraries gave themselves an education. Virginia Woolf was one. Otherwise she would have remained an ignoramus. It took me a long time to see that I was in the same tradition: there were bookcases crammed with books in the livingroom, and the fact that this went on in a farmhouse in the middle of Africa hid from me that after all I was not the first person to educate myself with the aid of books.

'Reading maketh a full man' – said the great Bacon in the time of the first Queen Elizabeth. That is how we used to think. A humanist education meant reading. For instance, in the old Russia, if you were intending to be a doctor, you studied literature as a matter of course. Anton Chekov came out of this tradition.

What did this cultivated person read? The classics, first of all, from Greece and Rome. Then, the classics of poetry and prose from their own country, with at least an acquaintance with the classics of other European countries. Above all, in Britain everyone was soaked in the most glorious prose ever written – the Bible, and this was at least part of the reason why we have so many great writers.

As for man, his days are as grass: as a flower of the field, so he flourisheth.
For the wind passeth over it, and it is gone: and the place thereof shall know it no more.

Or again:

When I consider thy heavens, the work of thy fingers, the moon and the stars, which thou hast ordained;
What is man, that thou art mindful of him? and the son of man, that thou visitest him?
For thou hast made him a little lower than the angels, and has crowned him with glory and honour.

Words like these, rhythms like these, were part of everybody's experience.

All that has gone, and we are the poorer for it. A common culture has gone, which did unite the people of this country.

And educated people across Europe could meet and share a common framework of ideas, thoughts and references. The literatures of different countries influenced each other. For instance, Richardson's novel, written in letters – *Clarissa* – influenced all of Europe, and particularly Russia. It was Lovelace, not Clarissa herself who was the new phenomenon, and he gave birth to a whole line of anarchic heroes. Ibsen the Norwegian playwright changed the theatre of all Europe. Bernard Shaw was admired as far away as China.

The difference between then and now is that there used to be a consensus about what was good and what was bad literature. This is no longer true. Partly it is because Europe no longer dominates the world, does not see itself as the exemplar for the whole world, so that other countries and cultures influence us; partly because there are classes and kinds of people writing who were not writing at all until recently. Women's writing as a self-conscious and political force is new. So is writing by black people. A continual reassessment goes on about what is good or not. But there is another reason. When people read, as a matter of course, the great literature of their own and other countries they acquire a standard by which to judge newer books. This is why young people should read great literature. It is not a question of 'copying' or even being influenced by great writers, but being fed by them, absorbing excellence. But now that people read less, they have lower standards, accept worse books, don't know how to judge them. And have no defence against current silliness, such as that there is no difference between, let's say, *War and Peace* by Tolstoy and the latest romantic or even pornographic rubbish.

There is another difference. It is no longer possible to read all the good novels, good books, being written. This is an astonishing thing, for as usual the doomsayers are croaking the novel is dead, literature is dead. But the truth is, good novels are everywhere. As I travel about I always ask my publishers to give me a list of the good writers in that country, and the list is usually a long one. And when I sample these novels I find they are indeed good. I believe this time will be seen as the silver age of the novel. The novel is our way of talking about ourselves, our lives. It is supremely a product of our time. We forget the novel is a recent phenomenon, perhaps four centuries old. Usually, the European novel is reckoned to begin with Cervantes, and *Don Quixote*. Before then, it did not exist. In this country, Britain, the novel began with an explosion of originality and invention. They were quite different from each other. *Tom Jones*, by Fielding, is a wonderful story, but its author was a magistrate, and it has in it little homilies on good behaviour and reflections on the human condition. Just like *War and Peace*, in fact. *Tristram Shandy* is a surreal kind of book, which has been influencing our literature ever since. Salman Rushdie's novels, for instance. *Clarissa* was written in letters. *Moll Flanders* is the story of a prostitute, written in the first person. With such beginnings no one can make rules for the novel, it is flexible, can be anything it likes, and only the author can say what her or his story should be like. This flexibility is why novels adapt so easily to different cultures. They have been written in verse, been long and short, been as fantastic as *Alice in Wonderland*, can be science fiction or border on journalism, as when a writer takes a story from the newspapers and makes a work of the imagination from it: the borderline between novels and journalism is sometimes very shadowy. Recently we have see the novel take off into 'magic realism' as in the writing from South America. *A Hundred Years of Solitude* could not have been written a hundred years ago.

It is from the most direct and intimate experience that I know how important books can be. I left school when I was 14 and that was after the most sketchy schooling. I was hardly educated at all. I can identify only too easily with those innumerable young people – and sometimes older people too – who feel they have missed out on education, and would like to do better.

The bookshelves at home were full of books not only because my parents took books with them to Africa, but because they continually ordered books from London, every kind of book and periodical. In those days it took a long time. First the letter from the farm in Africa took over a month to get to London. There the order had to be processed. Then the parcels of books took a month or so by ship to reach Africa. They went from the port by train to old Salisbury, were put on another train, and were fetched from the station by a servant who bicycled or walked in the seven miles. I shall never forget my excitement as the books were unwrapped. What had arrived this time? A remarkable mix of books, and I seized *Black Beauty*, or *Little Women*, or *Pride and Prejudice*, or *The Mayor of Casterbridge*, or the story of Alexander the Great, and bore them off to my room, where books were piled on chairs, on the empty bed beside mine, around the walls – where they were always in danger of being devoured by fishmoths or white ants. There is another big difference between then and now. Much more was expected of children. Things were not made easy for us. No one ever said to me, Don't try and read that book – let's say *Oliver Twist* – it is too old for you. It was taken for granted that I would skip what I didn't understand, and slowly learn to read difficult words and grasp difficult ideas. The classics – Dickens, Stevenson, Hardy, the Brontës, George Eliot – were not simplified then for children. I think children are patronized now. They are capable of much more. It doesn't matter if you skip through a book for the sake of the story. Later you will come back to the parts you skipped, and find them easy. The fact is, I was your archetypal autodidact. There are disadvantages to this, not least that you are always making discoveries that later you find are commonplaces of knowledge, and a revelation may turn out to be what you would have been taught as a matter of course in your fifth year at school. On the other hand, such discoveries are your own, and become part of you in a way that taught facts can never be.

I was infinitely advantaged, because of the books in our house and because my parents expected me to read. But suppose I had not had this good luck? Then it would have been a question of whether I was lucky with a teacher. Again and again I have heard someone who loves books and reading say: 'I was fortunate, I had this wonderful teacher who turned me on to reading.' These teachers, these lovers of books, to be found tucked away in the schools and universities – how valuable they are, and how unvalued, except by their pupils who may cherish thoughts of them all their lives. Without my parents I would have needed to find a public library, and someone to advise me. There was something else they did for me. They read to me when I was small and they told me stories. This is the greatest gift parents can give their children – reading to them, telling stories. All their lives, the children will remember these times as the vividest of their childhoods. Such children will become readers and love books.

Libraries are not what they were, unfortunately, but still adequate as a beginning. But books, and some of the best of them, can be cheap. Recently we have seen the classics in the bookshops for a pound each. What then is needed is a literary friend or teacher who can advise, make suggestions. Above all you need the strength of mind not to read a book simply because it is a classic and you feel you ought to. There is a right time for everyone to read a certain book. A book that can be dull, uninteresting, when you are 12 can be magical ten years later. And the state of mind you bring to a book can make it seem a different book even within a period of weeks. I recently had this experience. I read a book called *A Lady's Life in the Rocky Mountains* by Isobella Bird, a famous Victorian explorer, and I felt as if I was actually there, riding down a narrow mountain path in a blizzard, with my horse's hooves wrapped in torn-up underclothes to stop them slipping on the ice, exhilarated, frightened – alive – or sleeping out in a shed in the depths of winter with snow drifting over me from the broken roof. A couple of months later I read the book again and found nothing much there. It was not the book that had changed, I had. I had been particularly alive and receptive when I read it first, but the second time I was not. I am sure that many children, given a book too old or too young, have been put off reading.

Asking too little of young people, or children, is not only a matter of giving them easy things to read, but of not giving them enough. Once, if you were taking literature at A level, that meant not just three or four set books and a Shakespeare play, but quite an extensive amount of background reading as well.

Yet there is a new thing happening. For instance, on the Underground it is observable that in any carriage you find yourself there are always three, four or more people reading books, and these are often young. Yet it is said that young people don't read because they have spent their childhoods watching television. I think that what is happening is this: young people reaching their late teens, their early twenties, realize how disadvantaged they are when compared with people who had a background of general reading. I have seen this several times now: young people start reading. Better late than never.

In what way disadvantaged? Someone with a literary background will find, when talking to some younger person, moments of incomprehension, sometimes frankly acknowledged. 'I've never heard of that.' 'Who was that?' 'I don't know that word.' And you realize that this person is, simply, ignorant. I have heard them described as educated barbarians: people who have gone through the school system, doing perhaps very well, but ending up knowing no history, and having read nothing. A general and wide reading of novels, let alone books acknowledged to be educational, gives you a background of information, general knowledge, a sort of parallel or additional education: what Bacon meant when he said, 'Reading maketh a full man.'

This is an aspect of literature not often enough acknowledged. If we leave aside the aspect of novels we call 'aesthetic' – that is, the pleasure of good prose, a well-balanced tale, a sense that this is excellence of values and of judgement – then as well and beyond there is information. Jane Austen said something to this effect in *Northanger Abbey*, replying to those people who said that novel-reading was frivolous:

> There seems almost a general wish of decrying the capacity and undervaluing the labour of the novelist, and of slighting the performances which have only genius, wit, and taste to recommend them. 'I am no novel reader – I seldom look into novels – Do not imagine that *I* often read novels – It is very well for a novel.' – Such is the common cant. – 'And what are you reading, Miss —?' 'Oh, it is only a novel,' replies the young lady; while she lays down her book with affected indifference, or momentary shame. 'It is only Cecilia, or Camilla, or Belinda;' or, in short, only some work in which the greatest powers of the mind are displayed, in which the most thorough knowledge of human nature, the happiest delineation of its varieties, the liveliest effusions of wit and humour are conveyed to the world in the best chosen language.

Thus Jane Austen. And here is D.H. Lawrence: 'The novel is a perfect medium for revealing to us the changing rainbow of our living relationships.' And: 'Obviously, to read a really new novel will *always* hurt, to some extent. There will always be resistance. The same with new pictures, new music. You may judge of their reality by the fact that they do arouse a certain resistance, and compel, at length, a certain acquiescence.'

The novel in its few short centuries has created a landscape of the world for us, and without it we would be ignorant people indeed. We know how people in different cultures and at different times thought and felt. The best example is old Russia, prerevolutionary, and those magnificent writers who have never been matched anywhere else since, Gogol and Tolstoy, Dostoevsky and Turgenev, Chekov and Bulgakov – what a galaxy, for that was the golden age of the novel. And they informed the world how things went on then, before the Revolution, and it is to these writers that the historians go when they look for the flesh to cover their bones of fact and statistics. How do we know about the English eighteenth century? Through the novelists, Fielding and Richardson, Austen. And the nineteenth century? Dickens and Trollope, the Brontës, George Eliot, George Meredith, Hardy. America during the great Slump in the 30s and 40s? The writers, like Steinbeck. How women are thinking and feeling? The writers, in the explosion of women's writing, in the last thirty or so years. Black people? The writing that is coming out of Africa now, and America, some of it magnificent. Again and again, some area of our experience we know about only through television programmes and newspapers is taken up by a novelist, and is crystallized for us, made clear, made general, explained. While we read, admiring the skill, the frankness and the story telling, we are being informed too.

It is amazing to me that we take this virtue of the novel for granted, have never given it the applause it deserves. The novel, literature, in every country is a mine of information, a treasurehouse of knowledge about how people think, act, feel, dress, walk, behave – about every detail of lives that otherwise we would know nothing about.

Try and imagine what our view of our world would be like without the novel? I'm not talking about obvious and immediate reactions to a novel charting new territory (like the effect Mrs Beecher Stowe's *Uncle Tom's Cabin* had on the slave trade in America, for instance. Or *Cry the Beloved Country* by Alan Paton on public opinion here about conditions in Southern Africa, or Dickens's novels about conditions among the poor in Britain – and I could go on) – but of the mass of detail, of the warp and weft, the texture of lives. I have a friend who is a businessman, who travels a lot for his work. He says that before he goes on a business trip to a country he has not visited before, he buys the novels of that country, because that is where he learns how people think and feel and react, and none of this is to be found in business reports.

Suppose we had novels for the Middle Ages, as we do for later times? What wouldn't we give for them; let us imagine a novel written by a merchant's wife at the time of the wool trade, a love story, perhaps, but in the telling would go too what people put on their tables, how they cooked, what they wore, how they thought – it would be as if a light had been switched on in a dark room.

What a pleasure it would be . . . but at the end of this piece I am using a word that perhaps should have come first. When young people are taught about books in schools and universities the word pleasure is not, I think, much used. And the pursuit of literature can become a heavy and serious business. But what I look back on, a lifetime of reading, always finding new books, new kinds of books, new authors is – simply – pleasure. What a wonderful journey it has been, that began when I was five or six, and suddenly discovered that I could read, because I put together the letters 'c -i -g -a -r -e -t -t -e' off a cigarette packet and shouted, 'I can read!'

What intoxications there were, and even now, remembering, I can feel the shivers of delight I felt then turning a page to discover, for instance:

> The splendour falls on castle walls
> And snowy summits old in story . . .

or:

> In Xanadu did Kubla Khan
> A stately pleasure-dome decree:
> Where Alph, the sacred river, ran
> Through caverns measureless to man
> Down to a sunless sea.

or Harold Monro's 'Overheard on a Saltmarsh':

> Nymph, nymph, what are your beads?
> Green glass, goblin. Why do you stare at them?

Give them me.
                              No.
Give them me. Give them me.
                              No.
Then I will howl all night in the reeds
Lie in the mud and howl for them.

Goblin, why do you love them so?

They are better than stars or water,
Better than voices of winds that sing,
Better than any man's fair daughter,
Your green glass beads on a silver ring.

Hush I stole them out of the moon.

Give me your beads, I desire them.
                              No.
I will howl in a deep lagoon
For your green glass beads, I love them so.
Give them me. Give them.
                              No.

I suppose what I find hard to bear is the thought that young
people are deprived of, or deprive themselves – of such magic, such
delight.